RONNIE BARKER

The Authorized Biography

Bob McCabe

Published by BBC Books, BBC Worldwide Ltd, 80 Wood Lane, London, w12 0TT

First published in hardback in 2004 © Essential Works Ltd 2004.
This paperback edition first published in 2005.

Reprinted 2005 (twice)

The moral rights of the author have been asserted.
Parts of this book have previously been published under the title *Ronnie Barker –
All I Ever Wrote – The Complete Works*, 1999.

Produced for BBC Books by Essential Works
168a Camden street, London, NW1 9PT

ISBN: 0 563 52246 1

Commissioning Editor: Ben Dunn
Project editor for the BBC: Sarah Emsley
Production Controller: Peter Hunt

The author and publishers have made every reasonable effort to contact all
copyright holders. Any errors that may have occurred are inadvertent and anyone
who for any reason has not been contacted is invited to write to the publishers so
that a full acknowledgement may be made in subsequent editions of this work.

All photographs courtesy Ronnie Barker or © BBC except :
Section 2 : page 6 (above) Pictorial Press;
page 6 (centre and below) and 7 (below) Dave Bennett / Alpha;
page 7 (above) and 8 courtesy HBO Films.

Set in Scala
Colour separations by Radstock Reproductions, Midsomer Norton
Printed in Great Britain by Clays Ltd, St Ives plc

Contents

Acknowledgements

I am deeply grateful to Ronnie and Joy Barker, for their graciousness and hospitality. I am also indebted to Ronnie Corbett and David Jason for their time and consideration.

Thanks also to the beautiful Barry Cryer, the divine Josephine Tewson, the goddess-esque June Whitfield and the be-knighted Peter Hall. Sydney Lotterby was also a huge help, as was Humphrey Barclay.

On a sliding scale (just kidding!) – I am deeply indebted to a number of editors, primarily Rod Green, Mal Peachey and John Conway – staunch men the lot of them.

Finally, for love and reminding me how easy it is to get it wrong – Lucy, Jessie and Jack – you have my heart (now give it back!).

Bob McCabe

Foreword

To any keen watcher of television over the last thirty years or so, the name Ronnie Barker has always meant a guarantee of entertainment in its highest possible form. His name has meant that a programme in which he is to appear will ensure an evening to remember for perhaps the entire nation. He has shared his natural and perfect gift of comedy with us all. There is no-one in show business who can come anywhere near his multiplicity of talent and I doubt that anyone will.

I have been fortunate indeed to have shared so many happy and funny hours with Ronnie, not only on a working basis, but also at his home, with him and his lovely wife, Joy (who also has a wonderful sense of humour and a very sharp wit), and the rest of the warm and friendly Barker family.

On the following pages of this book one will learn a little more about this very clever man's early career and rise to fame. Anything that gives us an insight into his great talent is worth a read.

It's impossible to sum up in a few words the full extent of Ronnie's comic gift, but to give just a hint of the R. B. I've known and loved, I can relate the following tale: one day during rehearsals for *Open All Hours*, he and I invented some very silly and funny piece of business which made both of us laugh long and loud. As we began to subside, Ronnie turned to me and remarked, quite seriously, 'Aren't we lucky. Here we are both getting paid just to make ourselves laugh!' I would like to add, 'Yes, but you've also made the nation laugh, too.'

David Jason, OBE

CHAPTER 1

Hark at Barker

FROM THE *CAMBRIDGE DICTIONARY* –
barker (noun) old-fashioned – a person who advertises an activity at a
public event by calling out to people who are walking past.

NOT FROM THE *CAMBRIDGE DICTIONARY* –
Ronnie Barker (nouns – two of 'em) – perhaps a little old-fashioned,
has done some advertising and called out to
lots of people at public events.

Barkers were so called because they were loud, barking out in fairgrounds or outside concert halls to pull in the punters. But they had to be more than merely loud. If you were merely loud, you would be no more than an annoyance to those passers-by you were trying to entice into your premises. Barkers had to be slick; they had to charm their customers. It wasn't enough just to yell, 'Roll up! Roll up! Come inside and see the show!' – a good barker had to be much cleverer than that. A good barker could engage his audience with his banter; he could make them laugh; he could keep his patter going until the punters had parted with their entrance fee. A good barker was an entertainer.

No-one could say that Ronnie Barker has not lived up to his name. His verbal dexterity has always set his performances apart, especially in the monologues he wrote for *The Two Ronnies* television shows. Take, for example, this extract from the solo sketch 'An Ear In Your Word':

> A very good one to you all and evening. My name is Willie Cope. I am the President of the Getting Your Words In The Wrong Order Society and I've been asked by the BCB to come a night too long to aim the society's explains, and picture you firmly in the put. Firstly, I would like to say here and now – but I can't. I always say to seem now and here which nose be absolutely get-where. And most of our troubles have this member. It is very difficult to undersay what people are standing, especially if, as I did then, people only get half their back words-wards. As you can imagine, funny and gentlemen, you get some ladies combinations.

Perhaps, then, Ronnie was born to be an entertainer – a Barker born to be a barker. He certainly wasn't born to be a banker, although Ronald William George Barker does sound a bit like a banker's name, doesn't it? It's somewhat appropriate, then, that one of Ronald Barker's first stabs at employment was in fact in a bank. A fortuitous move, for it was here that young Ronald met a colleague who persuaded him to have a go at local amateur dramatics 'just for something to do socially'. What was on offer was the chance to paint some scenery and meet some girls. The latter appealed more to Ronald (indeed he met his first serious girlfriend at the local Theatre Players) but very soon the play was the thing. Acting, so often referred to by those in the profession as a bug, did indeed bite, although this was by no means young Ronald's first experience of the theatre.

•••

Ronnie Barker was born on 25 September 1929, in the town of Bedford, the middle child of three (neatly sandwiched between two girls), to mother Edith and father Leonard.

'My mother was just a housewife. In the First World War she worked as a young girl in munitions, but she was a housewife, right through, housewife and mother. We were a normal sort of loving family – no fall-outs. I don't have any bad memories of childhood at all. I don't have any wonderful memories, but it seemed that it was all fine. Parents and siblings, we were all very good with each other.'

His parents had married in 1925 and his elder sister, Vera, came along in 1926. At the age of four, two major events occurred in young Ronald's life. Another sibling arrived – sister Eileen – and his father's job as an oil clerk saw the family relocate first to Ilford, and then to Oxford, where Ronald spent the rest of his childhood. His father may have been named Leonard, but everyone called him Tim. The reason why is something that seems lost in the mists of time, it just was. 'He was always called Tim. I never heard anyone call him Leonard. Leonard William Barker, known as Tim.'

Although Ronnie was the first actor his family ever produced, his father Tim had been prone to the occasional theatrical moment. He used to don a straw boater and entertain his children by performing an old music hall song entitled 'I'm Not All There'. (Years later Ronnie discovered this was Eric Morecambe's party piece when he was a child.) Tim Barker occasionally performed his routine at local amateur affairs in the same manner, but by the time the family had relocated to Oxford, he had hung up his boater, his act remaining but a distant memory for young Ronald.

Also hiding out in the back of his father's wardrobe was a pierrot costume. Ronnie occasionally crept into the wardrobe and dressed up in the outfit. He remembers Tim as a pleasant man with a good sense of humour, often delighting his son with such quips as 'Money doesn't buy happiness but it lets you be miserable in comfort.'

Much in the same way that Leonard was called Tim, Ronnie's mother Edith was known as Cis, so named because she was the youngest sister in the family. Ronnie's maternal grandfather was a gas plumber; his father's father was a master butcher. However, given Tim's job as a clerk for Shell Mex, the family now considered itself to be upper working-class. Such delineations were still very important in Britain at that time.

Soon the family moved near to the Cowley Road in Oxford – again the result of Tim being relocated for work. During the school holidays, Ronnie and his sisters would go back to visit aunts and grandparents in Bedford. In between scrumping apples, Ronnie would watch his elder sister Vera and her friends putting on shows in their relatives' back gardens, charging a farthing a time for admission. Amidst the high kicks and songs, Ronnie freely admits a seed may have been planted; it was, after all, his first experience of watching someone perform, of seeing someone pretending to be someone else. (Later, in Oxford, Ronnie would carry on the tradition of back yard shows.)

In Oxford, Tim Barker began taking the family to the theatre. 'We would stand in the long queue. There was a queue for ninepence and a queue for one and threepence and if they ran out of ninepence tickets we went home. That's how much money we could afford. It's funny how many comedians, actor-comedians, come from working-class backgrounds. It's amazing. I don't know what generates it in a working-class environment but it seems they've got to have something to laugh at. It must be a way out.'

The first time they did actually get in to see a play was early in the Second World War when Geoffrey Kerr's *Cottage to Let* was touring provincial theatres. It starred Alastair Sim, who by that time had a clutch of film roles under his belt and would, indeed, also appear in the screen version of *Cottage to Let*, as would a young George Cole, then a protégé of Sim. Cole also featured in the production Barker and family saw, and would go on to make almost a dozen movies with Sim, including the famous St Trinian's films, before becoming a very familiar face on TV in the early eighties playing the scheming Arthur Daley in the *Minder* series with Dennis Waterman. Ronnie, however, remembers Cole as a fresh-faced youth. 'George Cole was just a lad then, who lived with Sim and his wife.'

Sim was to return the compliment some years later, coming to see Ronald Barker in a production of *Listen to the Wind* at the Oxford Playhouse. He even took the time to drop by backstage, much to the young actor's surprise.

An appearance at the theatre by Celia Johnson prompted Ronald to ask for his first autograph, queuing up outside the stage door to do so.

The Barkers also used to go to the pantos. 'Pantos were wonderful, they really were,' he recalls. 'We were in the "gods" there.' These were seats so named because they were situated right at the very top of the theatre. 'I was a bit frightened to walk along the front row because it was such a steep drop. You couldn't believe it.'

As well as the theatre, Ronnie remembers going to the cinema as a child and being absolutely captivated by the antics on screen. The first film his parents took him to see was the Hollywood adaptation of Noel Coward's *Bitter Sweet*, with Nelson Eddy and Jeanette MacDonald. 'And I remember seeing *Flash Gordon's Trip to Mars*. That frightened me. The clay men came out of the wall.'

Ingrid Bergman was his first real love, courtesy of *For Whom the Bell Tolls*; she was quickly replaced in his affections by Marlene Dietrich in *The Blue Angel*.

An Irish lady living nearby also fuelled his imagination by providing young Ronald with batches of American comics featuring the likes of Tarzan, Buck Rogers and Terry and the Pirates. These wonderfully graphic pieces of work almost certainly contributed to Ronnie's later love of paper ephemera and illustration, something that was to become a lifelong passion.

•••

He recalls his childhood as a happy time, marred by no ructions or family tensions, apart from the occasional wet sock. 'I played a lot of marbles and I was obsessed with brooks and streams. I used to get into a lot of trouble coming home with wet feet and wet socks because I'd been in the streams looking for newts. I used to catch one or two. I used to go snake hunting as well and catch some. Just grass snakes, but I once caught one that was three foot six long, which is very big. I was fascinated by the way they crawled. They used to give off a terrible smell when they were caught because that was their defence. It was actually gas, they would do it to gas small creatures. I used to do all that down by the river at Sandford near Oxford. It sounds idyllic but there was not a lot of countryside because we were in Oxford, in Cowley. But there was enough. Streams and one or two fields.'

Ronnie's younger sister Eileen would often tag along – the prerogative of the younger sibling and often the curse of the older.

Ronnie took one of his grass snakes into school one day to show his class. Keeping it in his desk, the class were treated to an unexpected showing when its head popped up through the inkwell. The result was a caning for young Barker.

•••

Ronnie Barker told his first joke in public at the age of eight. 'There was then a gap of about ten years before I made my next.' It happened by chance during a poetry recital.

'It was in my junior school, Donnington Junior at Cornwallis Road in Cowley. We were standing up and reciting the poems we were supposed to have learned or read, and a boy called Thornton stood up and his poem was something about a windmill. He said, "The windmill cuts through the air, cuts through the air, cuts through the air." And I said, "He'll be bald in a minute with all that 'air cutting'." It went down well, except with the master. He didn't actually do anything to me but he did reprimand me, I remember.'

This incident aside, it was, for the most part, a quiet childhood, one exception being Ronald's singing in the St James Church choir.

'There were no singing lessons as such. I was not following notes and I couldn't read music. I still can't read music, so I just learnt the harmonies. I was fascinated by the harmonies, church harmonies. That's what I liked about it. When my voice broke I was bass, but before that I was treble, but being treble you hear all round you the basses and the tenors singing their thing and that's what went into my head.'

•••

One major trauma in Ronnie's childhood occurred at the age of eight when he contracted a kidney infection, nephritis, which led to four months in the Radcliffe Hospital in Oxford. At first he was served bowls of barley sugar sweets and orange juice, but his diet took a turn for the worse and he was forced to endure rice pudding every day for the next four months – he has never eaten it since. True, there was one inexplicable afternoon when jelly turned up in its place, and Christmas pudding on Christmas day, but mostly it was rice pudding.

In an attempt to cheer him up at Christmas, the nursing staff made Ronnie the star of the ward's Christmas show, dressing him up as Mickey Mouse – ears and all. Young Ronald used to draw Mickey Mouse during his hospital stay, which was probably where the idea came from. He was in full costume when, unexpectedly, his family arrived to wish him a Happy Christmas. Clearly their boy was on the mend.

•••

After his recuperation, Ronnie attended the City of Oxford High School, and recalls finding the name of former pupil T.E. Lawrence in one of his textbooks. Discovering that you were sharing a textbook used by Lawrence of Arabia was hugely exciting, and sharing a textbook with a war hero was made even more poignant by the war that was now raging across the world. The war meant that school plays were off the cards, although Ronald did get to read the role of Shylock in an English class read-through of Shakespeare's *The Merchant of Venice*. Trips to the theatre or the movies were also curtailed for a time because, at the start of the war, theatres and cinemas were closed amid fears that many could perish inside during bombing raids, but they swiftly reopened when the authorities realised the propaganda value of patriotic films and newsreels. If the theatre trips were now becoming rarer, however, Ronnie was quickly developing an avid interest in radio, tuning in with 20 million others in Britain to what is rated as the most popular radio comedy series of all time – *ITMA*. 'I was 12 or 13, I think that's when I started to appreciate funny line comedy. Radio was the thing and you never missed a minute of it. I was a big admirer of Tommy Handley and *ITMA* [*It's That Man Again*] as it was called: the Handley show.'

Tommy Handley was a veteran radio comedy star by the Second World War, having served his apprenticeship as a variety and music hall performer. The anarchic and innovative *ITMA* show ran for ten years from 1939 and relied on his slick, quick delivery to pack more laughs into its 20-minute broadcast than would previously have been thought possible. So was it Tommy Handley who inspired young Ronnie to take up comedy? Was he mimicking Handley to entertain his friends? 'I started to enjoy radio comedy then. I must have been vaguely amusing when I was a teenager I guess, but I was never known as the life and soul of the party.'

As Ronnie remembers it, the radio was a constant companion in those days. Other favourite shows included *Stand Easy with Charlie Chester* and *Up The Pole*, with the double act Jewell and Warris.

•••

But, of course, the War itself made for a less enjoyable constant throughout Ronnie's time at school. He vividly remembers the sensation of sitting in his back garden on top of his family's brown, metal Morrison shelter. 'In 1939 I was ten. So starting at grammar school coincided exactly with the war. I joined them in September 1939, and left in 1945. There wasn't much disruption in Oxford, though – we had one bomb – but the word was that Hitler had said leave Oxford alone, so there was very little activity really. Occasionally you saw Italian prisoners being taken round, doing jobs, later in the war. Rationing of course affected us enormously, as it did everyone else, but nothing dramatic happened. We followed the news of the war always, mainly on the radio. We always listened to the 6 o'clock news, but there was no practical effect on people in Oxford.'

There was however an impact on Ronnie's family. His father Leonard was thirty-three when war broke out, just within the age range to be called up. He was given two choices. 'My father was told that either he could join the army, although he was a bit old for it, or he could learn how to drive a petrol tanker. That was the option he took. So he saw more of the war than he might have done in the army, because he had to drive tankers full of petrol to Southampton, which was being bombed regularly. He said that was scary.'

The Barkers spent many nights in their Morrison Shelter, in response to the howling air-raid sirens. But, despite the presence of two nearby air force bases, young Ronnie saw little of the aerial war apart from the occasional bomber flying overhead. 'Upper Hayford and Brize Norton airbases were around Oxford but they were a distance from us really. We'd see planes but no dogfights or anything. So it's strange to say, but it was quite a peaceful war. And I was never worried about being called up because no-one thought it could go on for eight years.'

Towards the end of the Second World War, Ronald Barker acted out of character. He was generally considered to be a good pupil. True, against the masters' wishes he had played football behind bomb shelters (with a lookout always on hand to warn them if a teacher was coming), and at one stage even caught the gambling bug courtesy of an elite pontoon circle. But there was one more extreme instance of rebellion.

Barker played truant. Over the years, children have bunked off for many reasons, few of them good; as far as he was concerned, Ronald was justified. He was going to the pictures to see his idol Laurence Olivier in the screen version of *Henry V*. He was only missing games, so it didn't seem like such a big deal. That he had already seen the film once (on a school trip shortly before) was hardly the point.

•••

On leaving school after the war, Ronnie studied as an architect. 'I was trying to get away from school. I was always very young in my form, the second youngest, so I was barely 15 when I went up into the sixth form, having done my "O"-levels – they were called school certificate then – at 14, which is at least a year younger than anyone else. I didn't know what to do, which way to go, what to follow. I liked languages so I started to learn Spanish because I'd done French and I'd done German and I'd done Latin (not that I can speak Latin), but I was already doing those. So I went for Spanish and I suddenly thought, I'm never going to use this, why am I kicking my heels in this sixth form when I don't intend to do the higher school certificate?

'Then I heard about this architect school and I used to love drawing and I thought architecture was about drawing. But I was vastly wrong about that. It's about physics and maths and all sorts of things I hate. I never took physics at school. People were much cleverer at it than I and there were very few places for it.'

Among his class mates were Ian and Alistair Smith, whom Ronnie recalls well. 'I went for six months then I gave it up because I realized I wasn't good enough, because they were so good and they were in the same form. I realized it was an overcrowded profession so I should walk out now. And I did, I walked out, left all my equipment there, my brushes and pens and drawing boards. And it was the best thing I ever did in my life, I think.'

Barker would meet up with Alistair and Ian again a few years down the line, when their sister Margaret Smith joined the company at the Oxford Playhouse. Margaret was one of the few actors Ronald ever offered advice to. 'If I were you,' he told her, 'I'd give up.' Maggie Smith now has two Oscars to her name.

•••

Giving up architecture was what turned Barker into a banker. He 'inherited' his older sister Vera's job in the local Westminster Bank, Cowley Road branch. 'Vera always wanted to be a nurse and she got what she needed to pass and became a nurse and went off to

Cambridge. So I took her job in the bank, having just walked out of the architectural school. I knew it was much worse staying on at the architectural school than going into a bank because at the bank I was just treading water really. I was simply going in there as a job for money.'

The work was dull but at least it led to his debut on the stage, albeit in the Theatre Players' local amateur productions. 'Of course acting was a much more overcrowded profession than architecture, but I didn't go into acting straight away. I went into the bank for 18 months as a convenience. I felt I had to earn something every week. Very soon afterwards I was encouraged to go into the amateur company. As soon as I did that, I thought, that's what I want to do.'

It was here that Ronald fell in love for the first time. 'There was a girl I used to go with in the Theatre Players for about 18 months, but never sexually. She was not inclined to permit that. But I was in love with her. I thought I was.'

The Theatre Players would spend three months rehearsing a play, meeting regularly in a room above a local furniture warehouse. Ronnie made his amateur debut in *A Murder Has Been Arranged* by Emlyn Williams. He played the music director in this play-within-a-play, which ensured that for most of it, he had his back to the audience – one way to avoid nerves.

Over the next year, *Arms and the Man*, *Blue Goose* and *Night Must Fall* followed. On these occasions Barker faced the crowd.

While he was with the Players, Ronnie came under the guiding hand of the troupe's leader, an elderly lady named Margarethe Bayliss. She obviously saw a burgeoning talent in Barker and arranged for him to audition for the Young Vic Theatre School, an ambitious move for a 17-year-old bank clerk, and one that precipitated a journey to London in 1947. 'I arrived at the station and I was allowed to splash out on a taxi, which was a luxury. I remember being on stage for the one or two minutes that I was there. For the audition I did "Now is the winter of our discontent" from *Richard III* and I did a bit from *Falstaff* and I failed. George Devine was in charge of it all. I was just 17. I told George that later, when he employed me at the

Royal Court. I said, "You failed me at The Young Vic School." He said, "That was a bit of a mess, old boy."' Not that it deterred the young actor from pursuing the stage as a career. That he persisted was partly down to his patron in Oxford.

'Mrs Bayliss was a marvellous little woman, she was very tiny. I'd only been on the stage six months or so when she suggested I audition for the school. She must have seen something in me and she was so pleased when I eventually got to the Oxford Playhouse a few years later, and then she died during the time I was there. She was so sweet, such a kind woman, not the pushy, ambitious sort, like a stage mother. She wasn't like that. She was just a very sweet lady. Anyway, I came back and carried on being an amateur.'

•••

At least two of Ronnie's friends were pleased that he failed the Young Vic audition, and they celebrated that night in style. 'I had two very close friends called Ivor Humphris and Mike Ford. To celebrate the fact that I'd failed to get into the Young Vic we bought a bottle of gin and we sat and drank this bottle of gin with lime juice. We were none of us used to drinking in any way, and we drank the lot.

'That was in my house in Cowley. I remember Ivor trying to get on his bike to go home that night, and he put his leg over and fell straight off the other side. My father was a bit annoyed about it all, of course. I shall always remember that. I can see it happening now. I remember Ivor saying, "We're nearly down to London" because on the bottle, it said "London Gin".

'I had known Michael Ford when I was at school. He lived quite near the school. He was a member of the Players, as was Ivor Humphris.'

But this wasn't the first time that they trod the boards together. 'We used to do plays in someone's back garden way before the Theatre Players, when I was about 14,' says Ronnie, of the time that echoed the earlier performances of his sister Vera and her friends. 'Mike Ford was the sound man, he was my age, and he had a microphone and he sat in the garden shed, like it was a little studio.

He could look out, with his microphone planted somewhere, and we did strange plays. We did a version of *Cinderella* which I may have written. Then we did a play that featured a character who was a sort of ancestor of Lord Rustless, whom I played. Each of the plays lasted about 12 minutes with a 35-minute interval to serve all the lemonade and things.'

•••

A trip to see the Manchester Repertory Company, based for some reason in the County Theatre in Aylesbury, soon added fuel to Barker's theatrical fire. The play they saw was *At the Villa Rose*, a murder thriller set in the South of France. 'The first time I went there, we sat in the stalls. It was the first rep I'd seen and I thought it was wonderful.'

The next day the young bank clerk wrote to the company asking for work and included a photo. When he heard nothing from them, he wrote again, asking for the photo back. This got him an audition.

He auditioned for the company's director Horace Wentworth by reading in six different accents, a natural talent that had been encouraged by his penchant for radio comedy. Wentworth hired him on the spot, at the princely sum of £2 10s a week. But the suddenness of this offer to work as an assistant to the assistant stage manager caused Barker some consternation, as he had to work out a week's notice at the bank. Wentworth gave him the week though, and the following Monday, Ronald Barker began his life as a theatre professional.

He worked out his last week at the bank, arriving at his regular Theatre Players rehearsal that Thursday night to inform Mrs Bayliss. She was delighted and by the following weekend Barker was housed in Aylesbury. Before leaving he spoke with his parents about his chosen profession. His mother just didn't seem to comprehend such a decision; his father was also unsure, but more practically so. 'My father said, "I'm not going to give you a penny; if you can make your living like that, fine." He was very easy about it. Very equitable. He said, "If that's what you want to do, do it, but I'm not going to support you." He probably couldn't support me at the time.'

In the days before moving he was comforted by a flyer from the Manchester company that boasted the legend, 'The Aylesbury Repertory Company, presented by Mr Armitage Owen, A Different Play Every Week.' Aylesbury seemed like a different world to young Ronald. It was, after all, the first time he'd lived away from home. 'I was in digs in a landlady's little cottage. It was very cold, with no heating in the bedrooms. A bit dismal it was, I remember. And it hadn't got a bath so at the weekends I would go back to my parents' house to have a bath. It was 23 miles on the bus and it took about an hour and a half in those days to travel 23 miles.'

After paying for his digs and other sundries, Ronnie subsisted on 1s, 6d. a week during his early days in Aylesbury.

Another custom of repertory theatre was that the cast had to provide their own clothes. 'I had one suit. One blue striped suit, not chalk, a pin-striped suit and that's what you were required to have and a sports jacket and trousers and shoes. We did period stuff sometimes and they hired costumes for that.

'Alan James, one of the lead actors, had two suits, a green one and an orange one. He used to say to Horace, the director, sitting in the middle of the rehearsal, "Shall I wear the green or the orange, Horace?" And the director would always say, "Better wear the green, I think." It was an appalling state of affairs really. One day Alan had taken a few drinks the night before, and although he lived only across the road at the Old Beams Café, he didn't turn up to rehearsal. After about 20 minutes Horace said to me, "Ronnie, you'd better go over and see where Alan is, he's obviously overslept." I went over and there he was, fast asleep, lying on the top of the bed in his orange suit. He had to get up and come and rehearse in that orange suit.'

•••

Ronald joined the Manchester Repertory Company on 8 November 1948; the first production he worked on was to be the farce, *He Walked in Her Sleep*. The following week it was J.M. Barrie's *Quality Street*. A shudder of fear and excitement ran through young Ronald as he realized *Quality Street* would mark his professional stage debut, the custom in rep being that the backstage boys got to fill in the smaller parts. It was 1948 and Barker found himself cast in the small role of Lieutenant Spicer.

'I was very scared that first night. And doing it all the week was strange. By the Thursday I knew it all backwards though, I was fine. I only had one scene and it was on a front cloth, in front of the scenery. I remember it being very unfamiliar. I wasn't unfamiliar with the lines, because I made sure that I knew them, but it was unfamiliar saying them. Very strange.

'I'm tempted to say Aylesbury wasn't at all as good as my amateur work. Mind you, you had four months to rehearse an amateur play.'

Barker worked as an assistant stage manager, the theatrical term for general dogsbody, largely involved in making sure that all the props were present and correct. 'I had to go and get the props and all that on this big barrow that I used to push around, it was pretty hard work. It was very difficult to get props because the theatre wouldn't pay for anything to be hired. So you had to borrow it and you had to gain the good will of these people and if you broke anything, of course, you paid for it. So you had to be very careful you didn't, and the furniture we used was so tatty. Really, really tatty.'

Scripts often came in the form of that player's individual lines on typed pages, with the preceding three words of the previous performer's dialogue to act as a cue. Needless to say, mistakes were frequent, but they soldiered on, and it was an invaluable experience. 'It was different mainly because of the work rate, which was amazing. I think most young actors today would say, "I can't do that, I need three weeks' rehearsal." But you didn't have that luxury. You had one week's rehearsal and you'd opened the night before in another play. Then on the Tuesday, following the Monday first night, you started the next play. So you were performing in a play and rehearsing a different play at the same time and I was also on props so I was also thinking of the play after that. I could only learn my lines in bed at night. We rehearsed in the mornings and I was busy with the props in the afternoon. Rehearsal time was ridiculous. You did about ten hours in all for the whole play and then on you went. That was the main difference then, that you suddenly had to throw yourself onto a moving vehicle. You're nervous on the first night when you start a new play on the Monday. You think, do I know it? Am I going to get through it? Are all the other people going to get through it? Are they going to give me bum cues and I shan't know what to say? But by Tuesday or Wednesday, at the latest, everyone knows exactly what they're doing.

'It was wonderful training. People used to say at the time that rep was a bit dangerous because you got into habits, because of the quickness. But I think that was a good thing for me because when we did *The Two Ronnies* we only rehearsed for a week. Mind you it wasn't a two-and-a-half-hour play, but it had to be more concentrated and more precise because of television of course. But I think rep was a good training to have to get it into your head. It was certainly good for learning.'

That's not to say it was all plain sailing. Among the many problems Barker encountered in those initial weeks on a professional stage was what on earth he could do with his hands. 'You felt wrong doing some things because you really don't do that in life, you don't have your arms here or there. Where do you have your hands? "Not in your pockets, Barker!" Horace used to say. "Hands not in the pockets, please!" But I don't know what to do with them Horace! "Just let them be, they'll find their way." He was very autocratic, an old actor.'

•••

One of Barker's many roles at Aylesbury was that of the fly-chomping Renfield in *Dracula*, a production that neatly demonstrated the rigours of life in rep. 'We did *Dracula* and I was ASM at the same time and I was playing Renfield, the maniac who eats flies. He opens the play. I remember I was also doing the music, 78 records, so I had to put on the music, call "Stand By, Curtain Up", take out the music and run down the stairs, curtain up and I was on the stage eating flies. It was a terrible four seconds.'

By his second production, *When We Are Married*, Barker felt completely at home on the stage, the hectic work rate having rapidly assimilated him into the group. It was not long however, before he was to discover the thing that would become his life's work – comedy.

'It was the fourth week of my professional career and I thought, "That's it, I want to be funny." It was when I played the chauffeur in *Miranda*, who had some funny lines. That was the first funny part I played. I played a sort of funny part in *When We Are Married* which was the second thing I did, as Gerald, the juvenile. He has some lines but the fun was in the situation. But it was actually getting a laugh on a funny line as Charles the chauffeur in *Miranda* that did it. I suddenly heard this big laugh and I thought, "God, that's marvellous, it's wonderful." I suddenly realized that's what I want to do. Whether I said that to myself consciously or not, that's what I felt. From then on I was looking for the comedy parts. You got what you were given in rep of course, especially in that sort of rep because there were only certain people who could do certain things. We had one other juvenile chap. There always used to be the juvenile and the character juvenile and usually that's what you played. But that was when I thought I wanted to do comedy. By the end of the first month in December 1948, I'd already decided that I wanted to play the funny parts. After that I played a lot of serious parts, but I was hoping the comedy parts would be given to me.'

The feeling of that first laugh was something that stayed with Ronnie throughout his career. 'I've always been surprised by these situation things. It even used to happen in something like *Porridge*. You knew there'd be a laugh but you didn't know how big it would be, because often the situation laughs are bigger than the line laughs because the whole thing has come together. It's fascinating, all that is to do with timing I guess, because you know the laughs have to come. That's the beauty of doing a play. Second or third night you know where everything is. You don't on television. First night is your last night. You go on with the first night nerves and you come off and say, "Right, what's tomorrow?" And you wish to God you could go back, and say to yourself, "I could've sorted that out."'

It wasn't just the thrill of winning the laugh in those Aylesbury days, or the joy of judging and delivering the timing for Barker; he was discovering an innate ability for comedy, something within him that just understood 'funny'.

•••

It was not only Barker's professional life that was developing in Aylesbury, so was his personal life. Having recovered from his first love at the Theatre Players, Ronald found himself deeply attracted to a young woman called Jane, one of the many female students who assisted at the rep. At the age of 19, Ronald was still a virgin, a situation he wanted to rectify. He got the impression that Jane might just be the one to help him do so. One night, Alan James slipped him a packet with a knowing smile. It was a condom, or French letter as they were generally referred to in those days. Fortuitously, the landlady of Jane's digs was away that night, and so first fumblings were duly begun... and interrupted by Jane's disapproving roommate Juliet. Ronald was caught with his pants down when she came in for a glass of milk.

Shortly after this incident Ronnie was cast in a play for the student girls. His major scene was opposite a still-disapproving Juliet. It was then that a strange thing happened – Ronnie discovered his feelings for Jane were led by lust, but suddenly he was falling in love with Juliet. Much to his surprise his feelings were reciprocated and they became lovers. It was for a time, albeit brief, a serious relationship and led to an engagement. (Although Ronnie had been similarly 'engaged' to Jane, another fleeting experience.) As his time at Aylesbury passed, Ronnie took over as head stage manager and saw his salary rise to the princely sum of £5 a week. Juliet became his Assistant Stage Manager.

•••

Ronnie featured in numerous other productions during his stint at Aylesbury and soon, like the other performers around him, began to establish a reputation with the locals. 'In rep the personality was what they came to see. John Moffat was a great favourite at Oxford and people used to go and say, "I wonder what John Moffat is going to be this week?" I was there for four years, and after two years I was popular and playing important parts, so they would come to see not only you, but also four or five other people in the show that they liked. They were interested in the personalities of the people, and what they were going to disguise themselves as this particular week.'

•••

Having spent part of childhood going to panto in Oxford, Ronnie got his first experience playing in one over Christmas in 1948 in Aylesbury. It was *Little Red Riding Hood*. 'I think you simply translated what you'd seen into what you'd got to do. I knew the genre, I knew the surrounding, the background to pantos and how they are done and you suddenly think, "Ah, well, that's what I must do." I haven't been in many. But you've seen them, it's what you do, it's parrot fashion really.'

The following week he found himself cast in three roles, including those of Billy Bones and Ben Gunn, in *Treasure Island*. Billy Bones died on stage towards the end of the first act, which required Barker to lie still collapsed on a table for the remaining five minutes or so of action. One night as he lay supine on the stage, he could smell burning. It was his wig. The candle on the table had set fire to it. Thankfully a fellow cast member came to his rescue and put the fire out before Billy Bones was forced to unexpectedly resurrect and run for the fire bucket.

•••

Ronald's first starring role at Aylesbury was also to be his last. He took the lead in their production of *The Guinea Pig* by W. Chetham Strode. 'I was about 19, playing a 14-year-old schoolboy. It was a very good part, Richard Attenborough later played it in the film version. It was exciting, but next week you knew you'd have only three lines. At that time you wanted to be playing lead roles all the time. You wanted to have as good a part as you could get each week. I'd only been in the business a matter of weeks, when I played it.' In its day, *The Guinea Pig* was a controversial play, which required the young actor to say the word 'arse' on stage. His mother wasn't too happy, but Barker was when he learned that Armitage Owen, the overall boss of their rep company was transferring the production to the Pavilion Theatre in Rhyl, in North Wales, and he was going with it.

The players relocated, with Juliet as ASM due to follow shortly. Ronnie's digs were situated only three minutes away from the theatre – he would always arrive just in time, having got it down to a fine art. Juliet stayed with Ronnie for several happy weeks, but it soon became obvious that the company was not doing as well as it should, or as it needed to do. During those otherwise happy weeks, the spectre of the imminent closure hung over their heads. And then the axe finally fell. The Armitage Owen Original Manchester Repertory Company was disbanded and Ronald Barker went back home to Oxford, as an unemployed actor.

A month or so later, Juliet joined him for a visit, but those few days were to signal the end of the relationship.

•••

Ronald was back at home with his parents and seeking further employment. It was during this period that Ronnie was turned down for a job as a redcoat at Butlin's. 'I thought to myself "I'm an actor now." That was what I was going to do. But I had six months after that before I got another job. I went home and I was working as a hospital porter up at the Wingfield Hospital in Oxford. It doesn't exist now. The Wingfield that is, Oxford is still there.'

During his hospital stint, Ronnie worked with a number of polio cases, something that distressed him so much that for the first week there, he found himself unable to eat. Even under these circum-stances, Ronnie found the need to retreat into character – when people asked him his name, he would tell them he was 'Charlie'. 'Ronald Barker' was the character he was saving for the stage; Charlie could empty the bed pans.

'It was only a few months but I just remember thinking it was unfortunate and I was unhappy about it and I thought, "I must keep trying to get a job." So I kept answering adverts in the *Stage*.

'I wasn't particularly aware of my parents being over-supportive or very generous because at that time it was my home, and they were my parents, and I went back to them and naturally they would support me. It didn't occur to me that it was very good of them to carry on giving me food and shelter, it was my right I thought, not in an arrogant way, but that's my home, that's where I live, I'll go there.

'If my parents ever argued about it, my mother would have been on my side. But my father didn't say, "Give it up, you've tried." He might have thought, "Right, now he's a hospital porter." He maybe thought, "He's tried and he's had a bit of fun and done it." But I was still writing away every week for acting work.

'It was a strange period because it just seemed to go on from week to week and each week I got the *Stage* and each week I wrote off for jobs. Sometimes I got replies from travelling reps. One I did get said, "We do *Wuthering Heights* on Monday nights, *Rebecca* on Tuesday and Wednesday. You can start next week, your salary is £5 and you must have a good wardrobe. You must have this and that." I didn't even answer that. I thought, "I can't go there. All those classic plays, one after the other every night and I'd be straight in playing Giles or something in *Rebecca*." Oh God, the things you escape by the skin of your teeth.'

•••

After his six-month hiatus, Barker's next professional stint was with the Mime Theatre Company. He answered an advert in the *Stage* that read 'Enthusiastic people to start a mime company', and travelled back down to London, to Haverstock Hill, for his first training sessions. 'We had four weeks' training. Mime was absolutely new to me. Clifford Williams ran the company then. He later became a director at Stratford and was quite important. He was an ex-dancer with the Ballet Rambert, and he knew a lot about mime and he decided to take this company round the country. I wish he hadn't! We were performing all these folk tales and we did a lot of shows in schools.

'There were comic bits in it and I embellished it a bit, but it was folk stories and dances and a mishmash that we took round to schools and I'm sure they didn't appreciate it at all because it wasn't worth appreciating, I didn't think. I wasn't pleased with the content of it at all. But you'd said you'd do it and you were there and you were getting £6 a week for about three weeks and then it went down to £3 a week, then it went to 30 bob [£1.50] a week. I knew we weren't getting bookings. He'd say, "We're working Monday, we're working Thursday and then the following Tuesday," and then you were hanging about with no money at all.'

It would be fair to call this period the low point of his career, accompanied as it was by a heavy dose of flu... 'I was in Cardiff, at 22 Clare Street, and I got the flu and I only had a loaf of bread, no-one brought me any food or anything, the landlady was not interested. She was a proper, typical, money-grabbing landlady, and there was no heating. I was in bed, I had the flu and this loaf of bread by the side of me and I was picking at it. That was my lowest ebb, it was really my lowest ebb.'

After a further largely fruitless four-month stab at bringing mime to the masses, the company collapsed somewhere near Land's End, leaving Barker with a rather inauspicious journey home. 'Then I had to walk home! I walked home from Penzance. The company folded and we'd got just enough money for five tickets home but there were six of us so we drew straws and I, of course, drew the short straw. So off I went. I slept in a hedge all night. I slept in a youth hostel. I had five shillings [25p]. I suppose I could have phoned home to get some money, but it didn't occur to me. I thought, "I've said I'll manage on my own" and this was 1950 and when you're 19, 20, you can do it.'

Ronald arrived back in Oxford just in time to attend his older sister Vera's wedding the next day.

•••

A quick trawl through the *Stage* soon secured some stage management work at Frank H. Fortescue's Famous Players, a rep company based in Bramhall in Cheshire. 'It wasn't that long between jobs this time. I got that quite quickly, in about three or four weeks. It reminded me of Aylesbury again, only it was more established than

Aylesbury was. Fortescue had about eight or nine companies all round the north and so you felt you were under some umbrella of safety. You didn't feel that you were going to get the sack or the company was going to collapse. So it was good.'

Ronnie – still billed as Ronald – was there to replace an aspiring young actor by the name of Roy Dotrice, who went on to have a very successful career in British theatre and television. The leading lady at the time – who had little time for young Ronald – was Patricia Pilkington; she would later reinvent herself as Pat Phoenix, and become a major star as Elsie Tanner in *Coronation Street*.

It was there at Bramhall that Barker was to meet one of the most influential men in his career. Glenn Melvyn was the company's leading man and the man that Barker claims 'was to teach me everything I ever learned about comedy'.

'I would enjoy watching him very much. He was very satisfying to watch as a performer. I suppose one does consciously think, "now I'm going to watch this man and learn something", but I don't remember ever doing that with anyone, saying I can learn something from this man I'm going to watch. Never. I watch a performer because he or she is funny or because he's very moving or I will want to watch him because I want to watch him. There's no question of my setting out to learn from him, but I obviously did.'

As well as having a professional relationship, Barker and Melvyn became fast friends and a night in the pub would often be followed by a lift home after which they would sit in Melvyn's car, harmonizing into the small hours. This type of impromptu sing-along was incorporated into a production of *Too Young to Marry*, in which Barker played a drunken Scotsman. By the end of the run the two had added ten minutes to the show's running time, purely through ad-libbing.

'Mike and Ivor were very close, but with Glenn, it was a very strong friendship. Without a hint or a whiff of any sort of homosexuality! That frightens me, homosexuality, I'm appalled. I would be disgusted at it. I'm quite happy for it to go on around me, but if someone said something to me I would be appalled. So it wasn't that.

There was no ghost of a chance that it would be. He was a mate. He was about 35 I think. He had young children. He was playing leading men and had the role of Maxim de Winter in *Rebecca*. But he would also play these hilarious characters. A very funny man.'

•••

Within a few years, Melvyn would be starring in the West End in *The Love Match*, a play he had originally written for Arthur Askey, and would have his own television series in 1959 called *I'm Not Bothered*. Barker would get his first television acting and writing experience on that show and would later repay the debt to Melvyn, casting him in 'The Fastest Gun in Finchley' episode of *The Ronnie Barker Playhouse* (in 1968).

It was Glenn Melvyn who taught him the comedy stutter he later used to such effect in *Open All Hours*, an acknowledgement that Barker has always been keen to stress. 'We did a play together later, around 1955. He'd already written *The Love Match* with Arthur Askey and starred at the Palace Theatre. He was there for two years playing opposite Askey in this stuttering part. Then he wrote this play called *Hot Water* which also had a stuttering character. Askey couldn't go on tour with it, or wouldn't go on tour with it and Glenn said to me, "I will play Askey's part and I would like you to play my part." So I consciously observed him then, for the voice and the accent, which I used to find very funny the way he did it.'

•••

Oxford however still held an allure for the young actor. As well as it being his home town, Ronald had long admired the company at the Oxford Playhouse. Among the many performers he had seen at the theatre was a young Tony Hancock. 'I saw Hancock in the pantomime, with Frank Shelley, who was one of the three men I say furthered my career. Hancock was a very thin ugly sister and very funny, and John Moffat, who was a favourite there, was also in it. Tony Hancock just seemed to have shown up, I don't know how he got there. He was obviously just an actor who branched out into comedy, rather like I did I suppose. You never hear it referred to, though. I was reading a thing recently about Hancock's life, but it never mentioned that. Because I was such a fan of John Moffat, Tony Hancock didn't stick out as much as if I'd gone with an open mind. Moffat was the epitome of wit and clever characterisation which, naturally, I liked. So my eyes were on him most of the time.'

When Barker learned in 1951 that two of his old friends from amateur days were working backstage at the Playhouse, Oxford became irresistible. He realized this could be the opportunity he was waiting for. 'Ivor Humphris was working there, scene shifting, and Mike Ford was doing the sound. Ivor said, "You ought to try and get here," and he said, "I'll get Mike, because Mike knows Frank better than me, to have a word with Frank Shelley and see if he'll see you." Mike was successful in getting an interview for me.'

Ronald decided to go for broke in order to get the job, even if it meant lying to his then boss. A week back home to see family effectively meant missing at least two weeks' worth of shows in rep, but it was agreed and Barker travelled back to Oxford. 'That was just to go home to do an audition, well not an audition, more of an interview with Frank Shelley at the Playhouse. I told the company director after I got back. I always thought of the Playhouse as being a wonderful place. Oxford was my Mecca. Living in Oxford. I used to go there even before I left school, and see things, see their pantos. I always thought how wonderful if I could work there.'

The only job available was on the publicity side of things though, and Frank Shelley gave Ronnie the chance to go away and think up three good publicity ideas. He returned next day with a dozen and landed the job, even though it meant cutting his current salary in half, and remaining behind the scenes.

'I took the job because I thought, "I must get to the Playhouse." When he offered me a job he said, "I haven't got any acting jobs but I need a man on publicity" and Frank was mad on publicity, there was no need for him to be. He'd already got one guy on publicity but he said, "I want another." I thought, "If I don't take this job I'm not going to get connected with the theatre. It's very possible that if I take this job I will be offered a small part now and again." Because I knew the productions there, I'd seen many of them, and sometimes there were 35 people in them. I thought, these are all people called in from the outer suburbs of Oxford, whom he knows. I know two or three of them, I can see them now, guys that occasionally came in. I thought I was bound to do something. I told Frank, when I was being interviewed, what I'd done.

'And then suddenly this part came up and it was a wonderful part, not very big, but it was very, very sympathetic, it was a young violinist and I think it was the best performance I ever gave at the Playhouse. I didn't know how long I was going to be there, but I think it was the best thing I ever did, because I was so delighted to get this job.'

Later at the Playhouse, Barker was to land a role in *Rebecca*, this time as the butler, a demotion from the role he had played in the same play back at Bramhall, for which he was soon compensated in the shape of the lead role of Danny in *Night Must Fall*. He also took the lead role of Hercule Poirot in a trio of Agatha Christie whodunnits – *Black Coffee*, *Peril at End House* and *Alibi*.

•••

Poirot may have been a dream job for the young actor, but he did not always agree with the way the theatre was run. 'At the Playhouse, we used to go free to the Wednesday matinees and, especially on light-hearted musical shows, matinees were always an opportunity to mess about, because nobody cared about matinees, quite wrongly. I've always disagreed with matinees. I don't think there should ever be matinees ever, because they ruin the evening's performance. You get neither one thing nor the other on that day, and actors need time. They shouldn't have to do two shows on Wednesday and two on Saturday. It's too much and they're never financially rewarding to the impresarios, the owners, the producers – they just do it because they can. They don't have to pay more and they've got all these actors doing nothing in the afternoon so they say, "We may as well stick a show on, might get 30 or 40 people in, old ladies." It's always a terrible house. Playing comedy to a matinee is really awful. I've always said, "No matinees." When we did *Two Ronnies* at the Palladium I said, "Six shows a week", which they didn't like. But that's when we were at the height of our power.'

•••

There was of course another spectre hanging over Barker at this point – the possibility of putting his burgeoning acting career on hold in exchange for two years of National Service. However his childhood bout of nephritis, coupled with an operation he had at the age of 15 for a tubercular gland, ensured that he was not eligible. Barker cites the latter operation and its results as the beginning of his burgeoning weight. The closest he came to wearing uniform was appearing in the play *Carrington VC*.

By now Barker had made an impression on Shelley, his fellow cast members and the local critics and audience alike. It was to signify the end of his run in the publicity department. Having found his way out of distributing handbills and onto the Playhouse stage, Barker spent four years at Oxford. It was here he gave that bad advice to Maggie Smith and, in early 1955, received some equally dubious advice from Peter Hall, then a bright young hope of British theatre, paying his pre-West End dues. The brightness of the young hope sometimes outshone his wisdom.

'You and I will never get on, Ron. You have to be queer to get on,' was how Hall summed up his and Ronnie's future prospects, over a couple of pints down at an Oxford pub popular with the actors and stage crew of the nearby Oxford Playhouse. Peter Hall was not only to go on and have a profound effect on British theatre, as one of its most respected figures, but he also had a profound effect on Ronnie Barker's career. He was the man who took Ronnie to the West End in 1955, and, around thirty years later, he was the man responsible for Barker's retiring at the height of his fame and popularity.

'I thought how strangely out of touch and in another world that remark is now. But he said it, and we both proved him wrong. Peter Hall was the man who caused me to retire because he wrote to me, a couple of years before I retired, it was about 1986, and he said,

"Would you come to the National to do *Henry IV 1* and *2*, to play Falstaff?" Which was a wonderful offer. "Let me know when you'll be available." Which was another wonderful thing because in other words it meant whenever you're ready, we'll do it. I asked how long it would be. He said, "We'll rehearse eight to ten weeks for the two plays, you'll only play about four times a week because we'll be in repertory...' I lived in Pinner then, and I said to myself, "Now what time should I leave to deal with the traffic?" Then I did a mental double take and said to myself, "Wait a minute. If your first priority when you've been offered this wonderful part at the National Theatre is how you're going to get through the traffic, you really shouldn't be in this business anymore. Your priorities have drifted right away from the business, they now are to be comfortable and not stressed going through traffic." I wrote to Peter and said, "Thank you for your offer, I've considered it and I'm going to retire." I didn't retire the next week, I planned it and it happened 18 months later. But that really was the time when I thought, "Look, you've had enough. You really have no more ambition left."'

•••

Sir Peter Hall says: 'What I remember about him right from the beginning at Oxford was that he was an extraordinarily gifted actor. The thing that struck me was that he had the gift of total relaxation. It's what all actors strive for. And allied to that, he had immaculate comic timing. Absolutely immaculate. And I think in all his comedy, all his acting, right from the very beginning, you had an awareness of the performer, a rather genial but rather cryptic personality, commenting on what he's saying. I just thought he was going to have a spectacular acting career. If you'd said to me then he was going to become a great comic, and a comic writer, I probably wouldn't have known what you were talking about. I always regarded him as a great actor. And still do. The measure of his comedy was that he was absolutely true. He completely inhabited what it was he was being, even if it was a north country charlady.'

Barker was more than happy to stay at the Playhouse, rarely thinking about looking beyond its boundaries. 'It never occurred to me to think beyond the Playhouse. The West End didn't figure in anything.' However the arrival of Hall, fresh from his London success, in what would turn out to be Barker's last year in Oxford, revised that opinion. Among Hall's early productions was a music hall piece, in which he cast Barker as the chairman, introducing the acts (which included Maggie Smith and Eileen Atkins). This was Barker's first experience of playing comedy of this sort directly to an audience, and involved a good deal of ad-libbing on the actor's part. Needless to say, despite the nerves, he loved it.

'In the last year there, my horizons certainly did begin to expand because Peter Hall arrived. He'd just done something in London, his first production ever in London, and another company merged with us called the Elizabethan Players. In fact most people got the sack. Derek Francis and I didn't get the sack and so we were there with the Elizabethan Players. We had various directors down from that. We had Lionel Harris and Hugh Goldie and various people, and so you began to think these are London men and you began to think in terms of maybe going to London.'

It wasn't just backstage luminaries that were expanding Barker's horizons. He was also beginning to attract the attention of some of his idols.

'Alistair Sim turned up backstage one day and offered me a job. He asked me to be in the play he was doing. I didn't go because by then I'd already agreed to do Glenn Melvyn's *Hot Water* play (the follow-up to *The Love Match*) on tour, doing the stuttering character. I had to turn down Alistair Sim. But he was lovely. I used to admire him very much. He said to me, when I met him years later in the BBC's Acton rehearsal rooms canteen, he was sitting there, he said, "Ooh, I think you're wonderful, you're one of my favourite actors, you really are, you really are. You and The Goodies." I said, "Talk about handing a compliment with one hand and taking it away with the other. You and The Goodies!" He hadn't remembered and then I reminded him that he'd been round to see me in Oxford. "Oh, was that you I came to see? Ooh!"'

Ronnie may have missed out on working with Alistair Sim, but the combined influences of Glenn Melvyn and Peter Hall were ultimately to tempt him away from his beloved Oxford. He toured first with Melvyn in *Hot Water* from January to May 1955 as the stuttering second lead Wally; then when Hall was asked to direct a production of Eugene O'Neill's *Mourning Becomes Electra* at the Arts Theatre in London in June of that year, he asked Barker to join him.

CHAPTER 2

The World's a Stage

I looked cross the water, and what did I see,
Standing on the sea front at Frome,
A gal with a bust that measured fifty-three,
Looked like St Peter's in Rome.

Her name was Harriet –
A stripper at the Hippodrome,
Swing low, sweet Harriet,
Took four men to carry her home.

The words are from a song written by Ronnie for *The Two Ronnies* TV show, although that was still more than 15 years away when he arrived in London in 1955. His new life in the capital, where the rejuvenation following the devastation of the Second World War was now picking up pace, was vastly different from sleepy Oxford. Ronnie's not prepared to admit whether Harriet the Hippodrome stripper ever actually existed or whether he was one of the four who carried her home, but cosmopolitan London was buzzing with all things new and it was an enormously exciting place for the young actor. Rationing was all but over, although petrol was one of the commodities still restricted and, while the rock 'n' roll revolution had not yet erupted, blue jeans were the latest fashion item. At the cinema, Marilyn Monroe was starring in *The Seven Year Itch* and in the theatre *The Mousetrap* was into its third year while there was avant-garde new comedy with the Cambridge Footlights revue *Between the Lines* starring Jonathan Miller.

•••

By the time he made his West End debut, Ronnie Barker had already appeared in around 350 productions and was ready to move on to bigger and better things in the capital. 'London was where everybody wanted to be. It was a milestone. I was glad because at the Playhouse, the rut was setting in. I'd been living at home for four years, so Peter Hall took me away from that.'

Life in the capital city moved too fast for any possible rut to develop. Following *Mourning Becomes Electra* at the Arts Theatre Club, Peter Hall moved Ronald into the West End for his next production, *Summertime*, at the Apollo. Dirk Bogarde and Geraldine McEwan were the leads. Bogarde was already a big star, having appeared in almost two dozen movies since 1939, including the first of his 'Doctors' films in which he starred as the hapless Simon Sparrow. Geraldine McEwan was less experienced but also well established, having made her first film, *There Was a Young Lady*, two years earlier. In awe of such distinguished company, Ronnie was, nevertheless, overjoyed to have the opportunity to play alongside such stars.

'I don't remember thinking that I wanted to be a big star in the West End. I wanted to work, and I remember saying "I'm very happy to be a feed. I don't want to carry a show, I don't want to be the best, the most important man. I like to be the second best, the feed."'

•••

Later that same year, Hall started work on a production of Vivian Ellis's *Listen to the Wind*, a play he had recently staged at Oxford and one that was to create a unique opportunity for the young Barker, just beginning to make his name in the London theatre world.

'At Oxford I had a part in the first act and a small part in the second act. But a good part in the first, a sort of mad gypsy song and dance. Peter said, "It's a pity you can't play the gypsy man again." And I said, "Well why can't I?" He said, "What do you mean, you're in *Summertime*?" I said, "But I'm only in the third act there... I could do the first act of this one at the Arts, then I've got all of the second act to nip round and get ready for the next one. I can do a composite make-up – one's a yokel and one's a gypsy." He said, "It hasn't been done for years." It was last done in 1935 or something. So he told me to go home and work out the times, which were different, especially Saturday matinees, so I went home and worked out a time sheet. It was a bit of a rush on Saturdays, I remember. It was only four minutes away through Gerrard Street and onto Shaftesbury Avenue.'

'He's a phenomenal hard worker,' says Peter Hall. 'And we simply couldn't not have him in *Listen to the Wind*, he'd been so marvellous in it in Oxford.'

Playing two different roles in two different plays, with a four-minute dash in between, proved in no way a strain for the young actor. In many ways, it was something that led him to explore his approach to characterization, something that would become a trademark of his career.

'I've never had that problem of separating characters. I can do *Porridge* now, immediately followed by Arkwright, immediately followed by anyone you mention. Because, you see, I'm of the opinion that a lot of characters that people play are quite shallow. I don't mean the person is shallow or the actor is shallow, but you lay it on like a thin layer of icing, on top of you. So it's easy to just shift along, I find. I had no problem at all, so I did it.

'My aim is not to find myself in the role but to lose myself within the role. I find it very difficult to take in or take on the theory that some actors have about a journey through a character. When I start a character I'm at the winning post already, at the end. I'm ready. I've never delved into characters that way. I seem to just know straight away what the character should be and how I want to play it. As many have said, "Ronnie Barker turns up and he's got the character on the first rehearsal and he's playing it" and that is really true. I have to admit to that. It's the same with the lines. I nearly always get the lines very early on so that I know exactly what I'm doing and I know what the other people are doing. It sounds as though there's no depth to the characters but that is not true. They have a depth. I have a sort of memory of them all the time. But I would never lose myself in the character. I don't think I ever had a big enough role in West End theatre to be able to do that. I never played a lead in anything. If you're playing the lead in something like a Chekhov play, something which has that intellectual stimulus, you could probably decide to play it like that, but when you're doing musicals and small parts in plays you don't, you play to your other actors. I used to think every audience is exactly the same. You don't think about the audience. You don't consider them at all. You make sure that they can hear you, that's one thing, but apart from that you don't think of them as a body, as an existing person or persons, it's just the noise. It's somehow a sort of wall you're throwing your jokes at and it makes a noise as it comes back.

'I'm quoting Tony Hopkins, but he says the right things: "Acting's easy, it's easy," he says. "You turn up and know your lines and don't speak when other people are speaking." That is his theory and that's the way he works. That's the way I say I work, but there will be times within that you actually are going deeper than that, you've got something in your mind somewhere that you're using. But on the face of it if someone hands me a character and says, "That's what you're playing, you're playing the Archduke Ferdinand in something," then you are the Archduke Ferdinand. You become him. You become him very quickly.

'Acting comes from the head. People say if you want to cry you think of something terrible from your childhood or your pet dog dying. It's a sense of memory. The heart doesn't think at all. The heart is a pump and people say, "this breaks my heart," but actually it's doing something to your head, really. A broken heart is a severe depression.'

Ronald Barker performed 22 shows a week and was paid the princely sum of £27 for his efforts – £15 a week for *Summertime*, and a further £12 a week for his gypsy man at the Arts Theatre. 'It was ridiculous, but that was a wonderful moment.' This unintentional piece of theatrical grandstanding paid off in spades. Having played two roles at once, Barker was now being offered several others, moving first into a production of *Double Image* at the Savoy Theatre, in 1957. This was an opportunity for Ronnie to work for and meet his idol Laurence Olivier. *Double Image* was being 'presented' by Olivier and his then wife Vivien Leigh. Richard Attenborough was the lead, or rather the two leads, given that he played twin brothers in the show. Attenborough had made his film debut in *In Which We Serve* in 1942 and had been the first star in *The Mousetrap*. It was he who introduced Ronnie to Olivier at one of the show's parties. It was a momentous occasion for at least one of them. Years later, at an awards do where Ronnie was himself picking up a gong, he met up with Olivier again, the knighted legend telling him, 'I just wanted to say – I've always admired you.'

•••

A short break from the West End in late 1956 proved equally fortuitous, when Barker met young actress/ASM Joy Tubb in a Cambridge production of Somerset Maugham's *The Letter*. '*Summertime* had finished and I knew a man called Anthony Knowles who ran the Buckstone Club, a watering hole for actors in the West End. He also put on shows for tours and he'd do special weeks in places and we went to Cambridge with a double bill of a play called *The Letter*, by

Somerset Maugham and Wolf Mankowitz's *The Bespoke Overcoat*. Joy was stage director there. One was looking for any sort of work then and it was a nice part. And it was lucky that I did it, because that was where I met Joy.'

Joy's family had roots in the theatre. Her grandmother had wanted to see all her daughters on the stage, and Joy's aunt had been a Tiller Girl before moving on to the Folies Bergére in Paris. Joy had grown up in that environment. She became a secretary for the Rank organization. She was in the company's amateur dramatics society but gave it up for a job at the New Theatre, Bromley, which turned out to have no pay attached. Her family helped her out until the end of the first month, when the theatre realized how indispensable she had become and started paying her a wage. She quickly worked her way up to the position of stage manager.

During the run of *The Bespoke Overcoat*, Ronnie had to eat a great amount of chopped liver on stage every night, a dish he detested. Joy, in her role as stage manager, would make a stiff chocolate blancmange every night as a substitute for the liver. It was years later that Ronnie confessed to her he couldn't stand blancmange either.

Joy was seeing another actor in the show at the time, but Ronnie was seriously smitten, a feeling that was soon reciprocated. He proposed to her over dinner at the Royal Court Theatre in Sloane Square. She accepted – but double-checked next day to make sure it hadn't been the wine talking.

Ronnie and Joy were married the following year on 8 July 1957. With both of them broke it was a small wedding – ham and lettuce in a restaurant in Stanmore as Ronnie recalls it. They moved into his current not-overly-large flat in Hampstead Hill Gardens.

'Joy Tubb she was then. She was glad to get rid of her name, she's always said that. We went to a BBC party recently and they had all the names and she was down as Joy Tubb again. She said, "I got rid of that name 40 years ago."'

Among the many things they had in common was their love of Laurence Olivier. As a star-struck teenager, Joy had stood outside Olivier's house for hours on end in hope of catching a glimpse of him. As an actor Barker later said he always approached his characters by starting with the make-up – 'If it's good enough for Olivier, it's good enough for me. He used to do it that way. It's not necessarily hiding, it's assuming a disguise. It may be a very thin disguise or it may be a complete Quasimodo. When people ask me this, I always say, "Olivier did this and I was a great admirer of his, I still am a great admirer of his." It's always been my way to start a character, with the face, the make-up and the voice. Tics and things may come, they may not, but the voice is always important to me – that, and the make-up.'

Olivier permeated the newly married Barkers' life offstage as well as on. On 23 October 1959, their first son was born. They named him Laurence. 'Olivier was always my idol, my wife was a great fan so naturally our first son was named Laurence.'

•••

Barker was quickly back in the West End, courtesy of Peter Hall again, this time in *Camino Real* at the Phoenix. But by now theatre was not the only outlet for Barker's burgeoning talents.

Radio comedy was something that young Ronald Barker had grown up on. Listening to the radio had nurtured both his talent for characters, voices and accents and his fondness for line comedy. By now, radio comedy had moved on somewhat, with programmes like *The Goon Show* breaking new ground and Ray Galton and Alan Simpson writing material that turned the Tony Hancock first seen by Ronnie in Oxford into a major star with *Hancock's Half Hour*. Radio was, as yet, relatively untroubled by its upstart sibling television, although independent television had now begun broadcasting. Hughie Green was presenting his *Double Your Money* TV game show and Eamonn Andrews had a new show called *This Is Your Life*. As a response to ITV's opening broadcast speeches from the Guildhall in London on 22 September 1955, BBC television aired the *Donald Duck Story* and on radio there was the unmissable death in a fire of Grace Archer, one of the main characters in the radio drama *The Archers*. While there was great excitement about the developments in television, it wasn't an avenue down which Ronnie considered steering his career at that point.

'The first time I saw a television it was this eight-inch screen in a big wooden box and the first thing I saw on it was the coronation of King George, so that would have been 1937. Then it was closed down because of the war.

'When ITV launched I didn't really think of there being any more opportunities for me because I was in theatre, and I'd only just got to the West End then, in 1955. There wasn't an immediate thought of another avenue. It was way above my head at the time. I had no idea that I would make my living out of it eventually.

'Going to the West End was the move up that I wanted. It was a foot on the lowest rung of the ladder, actual success. Although I'd had great success comparatively at Oxford, I'd done very well, this was the real thing. I really did think I was on my way. I saw the West End as a ladder but I didn't see stepping off that ladder on to the television ladder. I didn't think of television for a long time.'

Television may not have featured on Ronnie's horizon but he was inadvertently manoeuvring himself in the right direction. Now to some degree established on the London theatre scene, Barker's move into radio happened swiftly. His first radio appearance was as a regular supporting player on *The Floggits* in 1956, mere months after arriving in the capital. The show starred Elsie and Doris Waters as Gert and Daisy Floggit, characters the duo had been playing on radio since the early 1930s. Their latest show featured Anthony Newley, Joan Sims, Hugh Paddick and the newly christened 'Ronnie' Barker. 'The director Alastair Scott-Johnson did that, without telling me. The first *Radio Times* I was in, it was Ronnie. I thought, "Ronnie", is that all right? He said he thought it sounded more friendly, more chummy. I'm glad he did. I was still Ronald in a lot of the plays. Ronald's a bit pompous really. It's a funny name.'

Ronnie's stint on *The Floggits* was to prove short-lived, however. 'Tony Newley and I got sacked from that because we were getting too many laughs. It's funny because I always thought Hancock did the same thing, he got rid of all the comedians round him. We said this to Elsie and Doris or at least the producer said it, "This is your show, girls. These fellas will get laughs from you, of course they will, but that makes a funny show. You must have a funny show." And they replied, "Why can't we have funny lines?" "You do have funny lines but you can't have these characters' lines, you can't have these catchphrases that men come on and say." God knows why but catchphrases do make people laugh – "And it's goodnight from him" – extraordinary. But anyway they got rid of us.'

Not that the distinctive radio talents of Barker were left out in the cold for long.

'After *The Floggits* I did *Variety Playhouse*. That was an extraordinary show. Leslie Crowther and I, or Ted Ray and I, did the low comedy, and the opera singers from Covent Garden would come on. It was a wonderful mishmash of a show, variety in its true sense I suppose, a real mixture. But we loved it, especially Leslie. We used to arrive Sunday and he was very tired, he'd been working very hard, and we would sit up in the stalls and I remember looking round as this wonderful aria was being sung and tears were pouring down his face. He was a very emotional fellow anyway. I miss him. (Crowther passed away in 1996.) He was a great friend. But it was a great show and we used to say, "We're being paid for this as well?" Our work was far from onerous because you got a script in front of you and all you had to do was stand there and read it, wonderful. That's why radio's such a doddle.' This popular combination of Crowther, Barker and Whitfield soon spun off into its own series.

'I did *Crowther's Crowd* later with Leslie and with June Whitfield. That was sketches again.

'Leslie wrote for them, I didn't. Obviously you add bits, you add gags, but you only have about three hours to rehearse it so you don't get much time. Actually we'd put a bit in after rehearsal, and just didn't tell the producer.'

•••

For all the fun he was having on radio, Ronnie was still playing it straight in the West End, in a Royal Court production of *Lysistrata*.

'*Lysistrata* was an extraordinary performance. It was directed by a Greek man called Minos Volanakis and he liked certain scenes and didn't like the others. So he'd only rehearse scenes that he liked, which was a bit upsetting for those of us who considered ourselves not exactly old pros, but certainly professionals. Jimmy Grout was in it, Natasha Parry and Joan Greenwood, too.'

Again, Ronnie found himself in illustrious company. Respected actor James Grout was already established and went on to have a glittering career, in one of his many roles becoming known to millions as the irascible Chief Inspector Strange in *Inspector Morse*. Natasha Parry was then a Shakespearean actress with numerous film credits and Joan Greenwood had delighted audiences with her performances in classic movies such as *Kind Hearts and Coronets*, *Whisky Galore!* and *The Man in the White Suit*. In 1995 *Empire* magazine readers voted her one of their top 100 sexiest movie stars of all time. The quality of the cast, however, was offset by the eccentricity of its director. 'Minos wouldn't join the scenes; there were 14 scenes and he wouldn't join one to the other. So you'd finished the scene and I'd be over this side of the stage and Neil McCarthy or someone would be over there and we'd go to the next scene and we'd all be in different places. I said, "Minos are you ever going to put these together?" and he said, "Oh yes." But it came to the dress rehearsal and it still wasn't done. So I said to Jimmy Grout, "What are we going to do?" And he said, "We'd better do it ourselves."

'So I asked the others if it would be all right if Jimmy and I worked out the links and they said, "Yes, please do." And Minos never even noticed when he had a run-through. We'd done it all!

'Jimmy was very funny because it was considered an immoral and maybe disgusting play, about these women denying the men any sexual whatevers if they carried on fighting because they wanted to stop the war. There were a lot of phallic jokes in it. One night from the gallery a sort of snowstorm of leaflets came floating down saying that this play was disgusting and Jimmy Grout was on the stage and he looked up and watched this snow storm and then he said, "The Gods are angry." I wish I'd said that.'

•••

It was during the run of *Lysistrata* that Ronnie was to discover one of the other passions of his life. He was sharing a dressing room with fellow actor Peter Bull. Having accidentally ruined one of the post-cards tucked in to Bull's mirror, Ronnie went to a nearby stall selling similar cards at a penny a time. He bought 100, meaning to give them to Bull, but became so entranced by these pieces of Victoriana that he kept 50 of them for himself. His collection now stands at 55,000.

'I'm a very nostalgic person. I collect many things to do with nostalgia. I collect cigarette cards for instance, and I certainly collect the old postcards. I collect old coins and stamps because I used to collect stamps as a boy and loved it. And paper work. I have theatre programmes, illustrated sheet music, I have lantern slides, I have stereoscopic photo viewers, everything that can be loosely termed paper ephemera. And I love illustrations. I've got copies of the summer and Christmas issues of *Tatler* and *Punch* that were wonderfully illustrated in colour. I collect illustrated books.'

•••

Having found success on radio, Ronnie Barker found himself dipping his toes in the emergent waters of television in 1959, courtesy of an old friend. Having successfully played in *The Love Match* and its sequel, Glenn Melvyn was offered his own show, *I'm Not Bothered*, and he asked his old friend and colleague Ronnie Barker to join him. *I'm Not Bothered* was to prove a vital stepping stone in Ronnie's career. Not only did it offer him the first chance to work before a camera in a medium he came to dominate, it also allowed him to try his hand at writing comedy material for the first time, which was something he would continue to do – under a series of pseudonyms – for the entirety of his career.

'He [Melvyn] had a TV series of his own where he was a theatrical agent. In one scene, the door opened and three men came in, one jumped on the other's shoulders, one produced a unicycle, so there were three of them all riding on this unicycle and they rode all round this office. And he looked at his assistant and said, "I wonder what they do?" It was wonderful. Then he asked if I would like to play a part. He also asked if I would like to do some ghost-writing, which was, I suppose, the first time I wrote anything. I got £50 a script for that, which was a bit of a joke, but it was good for me then because I had no money.

'He asked if I would like to be in it and I said yes. I was terrified because I'd heard that if you moved one inch to the right or left on television, you were out of shot. Which was rubbish of course. I don't know who told me that. I was terrified about this but when I got there I found I was playing a patient in bed and I didn't have to move. So I was very relieved.'

Ronnie wrote three scripts for the show, all of which were attributed to Melvyn himself.

'I only did about three and I wasn't writing right away. He just said if you've got an idea for a script, write it. So I wrote three. I remember us working with the very experienced director Henry Kendall. He was in his later years, I suppose. He wasn't working as much as he had been in his heyday, but he directed one of these that I was in and he didn't know that I'd written it because Glenn didn't tell anyone. He just said, "Will you write it and I'll put my name to it, is that all right?" I said, "Yes, fine." Anyway, mine came up and he directed it. In the bar afterwards I said, "That went very well, Mr Kendall, didn't it?" And he said, "Bit of quality in the writing old boy." I still couldn't tell him, but I was very delighted with that. That was my first praise for my writing. Amazing.'

Writing was an interesting experience for Barker, but not a particularly easy one.

'It's never been easy. I never enjoyed the actual physical act of writing. When it works it's wonderful, like in a *Two Ronnies* sketch, or the little silent films. When it works and you hear the audience laugh, you're very pleased and very proud of it. But actually getting it on to paper I find very painful. I very rarely rewrite anything. I rewrite it all in my head before I put it all down on paper. Some people will put something down, then go back and fiddle with it til they get it right. I do it all in longhand, I don't have a typewriter, so I very rarely wrote anything before I sorted it out in my head. I found it was a painful process.'

It would be another eight or nine years before Barker wrote for television once more. And when he did no-one would know it was him then, either.

•••

Although he was now dabbling in radio and television, Ronnie dreamt of movies. First though, it was a break on television that Ronnie received from a certain London casting agent. 'I was cast by a man called Ronnie Curtis. All us actors used to go into the Arts Theatre snack bar which was just below the Arts Theatre at the time, it was a place where everyone met, all the out-of-work actors. Ronnie Curtis was a cross-eyed talent scout/agent who had an office three doors away. He used to come into the Arts Theatre and look round and pick someone. He'd say, "You!" And you never knew who he was picking. Michael Caine used to be there, Sean Connery used to be there, Ian Hendry and Roger Moore, sometimes. All these young men were waiting for a day's work. But he came in and pointed at me this time and said, "I want to talk to you."'

This led to Ronnie's first work on screen – a low-down-the-list guest spot on *Sailor of Fortune*, an English TV series starring Canadian-born Lorne Greene, later the star of *Bonanza*. It involved Ronnie travelling to a location in the Home Counties, playing a cowering waiter and receiving £7 for his one day's work.

A short while later, the short-sighted Curtis was again picking Ronnie out of the crowd, this time for a role – ironically another waiter, although this time the head waiter – in his movie debut, a 1958 film called *Wonderful Things*, a vehicle for a young singer named Frankie Vaughan, who starred as a Portuguese fisherman off to London to earn his fortune.

'He said, "I want you to be a head waiter in a new film." It was two days' work, over a week, which means you're available for a week and they can pick any two days. So off I went and there I was enjoying my first screen experience, which was extraordinary. It was the debut of Frankie Vaughan as a young he-man star *and* it was the first time I ever appeared on the big screen.'

If the glamour of the movie world had left him cast simply as a head waiter, it was on radio that Ronnie was to find the first of a multi-part breakthrough. In 1958, writer Laurie Wyman had decided to build a series around rising comic actor Jon Pertwee, who'd recently scored a success with his own radio show *Pertwee's Progress*. Pertwee had served in the navy and it was quickly decided to build the show around the senior service. The rest of the cast were assembled, including Dennis Price, Michael Bates and Leslie Phillips. As Wyman told the *Radio Times*, 'I felt we needed an idiot and there was no-one better at playing idiots than Leslie Phillips.' Ronnie Barker signed on for duty in the supporting role of Able Seaman Johnson, but was soon sharing the limelight with Pertwee, their interactions often providing the comic highlights of the show that had been christened *The Navy Lark*.

'He was wonderful. I loved Jon. I thought he was a very good actor, I don't think he acted enough. Of course he got into *Doctor Who*, which was wonderful for him, but he got stuck with it a bit, I thought. But I thoroughly enjoyed working with him on stage. We only stole the show in as much as we only said the lines that were in the script of course. I notice that they've recently reissued *The Navy Lark* on cassette and CD and the billing used to be Leslie Phillips, Jon Pertwee and Stephen Murray in *The Navy Lark*, with Michael Bates, Ronnie Barker and Tenniel Evans. But now I notice on the cassette sleeve it says Jon Pertwee, Ronnie Barker, Stephen Murray and Leslie Phillips, so they've promoted me.'

•••

The series was set aboard the HMS *Troutbridge*, stationed in Portsmouth, and within three weeks of its first broadcast on 27 March 1959, the show was such a success that the film rights were sold. (In the somewhat uninspired movie version that followed, only the services of Leslie Philips were retained.) By the second series,

Price had left and was replaced by Stephen Murray, who remained on board for the show's remaining – and at the time record-breaking – $17\frac{1}{2}$-year run. By the second series, Seaman Johnson's role was expanding, becoming a favourite with the audience and consequently, the script writers. His oft repeated, 'You're rotten you are' was all but a catchphrase. In the show's fifth series, it briefly became *The TV Lark*, with the crew commandeering a TV station – Troutbridge Commercial Television. The idea ran its course and after ten weeks they were back to the boat.

Overall – on radio at least – *The Navy Lark* was a huge success, and Ronnie remained with the show until his appearances on *Frost on Sunday* made him unavailable for the show's recordings. 'I was the first one to leave. I was in it for seven years. I started in '59 and I left in '66.'

•••

It was all going too well, of course. 'Then I went into *Irma La Douce*, which drove me mad.' Ronnie landed the role of Roberto in the 1958 West End production of *Irma La Douce*, which featured an all-star cast including John Neville, Clive Revill, Keith Michell, Julian Orchard and Elizabeth Seal. It proved, much to Ronnie's distress, to be a huge hit. Normally for any actor, such a guaranteed gig would be a good thing, but Barker found it soul-destroying to be tied into a run that, for him, lasted two years. He even got to the point where he was physically ill before going on stage some nights.

'It's very difficult to explain how awful it is because it's not like saying people go to work every day for years. You have to do everything exactly as you did it before. You can't change the lines slightly if you're bored with them. You can in a stand-up act. Ronnie Corbett does his act, he puts bits in, takes bits out, does what he likes. But with this, you must not waver at all, a) because you've got all the other people round you and b) you're not in a position to be able to judge what is better or worse. That's the author or the director's job. So it was the fact you had to sit down in the same place, do the same thing, say the same line, sing the same number... it was fine for the first six or nine months I suppose. Everyone gets bored and I'd been told by the producer Donald Albery, "We can't give you a year's contract on paper. But believe me if you want to leave after a year and you've got something to go to, I will let you go." Just over a year later, a musical version of *Sweeney Todd* came along and they wanted me to play Todd in it. So I went to Albery's manager and said that Mr Albery had said this and she said, "No he wouldn't have said that, he wouldn't have." I said, "But he did, he told me, gentleman's agreement as it were." And she said, "I'm sorry but it's not on paper." I was furious.'

Six months later however, Barker found his way out. The play was transferring to Broadway and Clive Revill, who played the narrator of the piece, was going with it. Ronnie had been understudying his role and was expected to take over. It was a bigger role and naturally meant more money. But Ronnie opted not to go.

'I thought, "Well, why should I do that?" I explained, "It's a much harder part, much more energetic, he does a lot more changes. I'm comfortable where I am thank you," knowing very well that this would rock the boat a bit. So about a fortnight later they said that we were supposed to be going in ten days and they had no-one to play it. So I said, "Say to Mr Albery that I will play it for six weeks while you find someone else, provided he lets me out of the show altogether." Blackmail it was really. He said, "Fine but you won't work for me again." I said, "I'll have to risk that." And I was out, but it was such a relief and I never signed anything again like that.

'It was just the length of time with *Irma*. I don't think it's allowed now. I think management these days are only allowed to sign you for a year then they ask you if you want to stay in or not. In those days it was for the run of the play. Some people were in it for four and a half years, couldn't get out. Julian Orchard – lovely man, he was in *Futtock's End* – was in it for 4¼ years. Drives you mad. Some people can do it. I think one man was in *The Mousetrap* for 15 years or something – but other people go mad. I know.

'Even after three months you can have enough. We did *The Two Ronnies* at the Palladium for three months and even then I said, "You know, I'm not sorry it's coming to an end," although the money was very good, we were on a percentage and all that. And it was lovely to be at the Palladium. I must be the only person ever to start my variety career by topping the bill at the London Palladium. It's extraordinary isn't it? I'm sure no-one else has done that.'

•••

Barker's desire to leave a successful West End show was indicative of how he ran his career, right up until the end. Indeed, it was more a reflection of character than of career-building. At architecture school, he had laid down his pens and walked when he realized it wasn't the best thing for him; despite being six months unemployed as an actor and working as a hospital porter, he had turned down the occasional acting job. Here he was in a major success in London's theatreland, yet he knew the time was right to leave. In his later career, Barker would exhibit the same sense of control, the very quality that he himself says made him a difficult man to direct. It wasn't arrogance, as much as assuredness. A strong understanding and belief in his own abilities, the very thing that would lead him to retire at the peak of his success. Comics say it simpler – it was timing.

Life during *Irma La Douce* wasn't all bad however. Over the course of its run, Barker's wife Joy gave birth to Laurence and TV and film work was fast coming Ronnie's way. He was still juggling radio work on *The Navy Lark*, and the occasional guest spot on ex-Goon Michael Bentine's *Round the Bend*, and had added another West End role, this time in a production of Chekhov's *Platonov*. By now, he was by no means a famous face, but his voice was instantly recognisable thanks to *The Navy Lark* and, more importantly, he was beginning to be known within the industry as a reliable, talented and extremely funny performer.

He appeared on television again in a live schools' broadcast of extracts from *Macbeth*. 'My first time playing Shakespeare was for schools' television. I played second murderer in *Macbeth* and it was a 20-minute excerpt. I had two lines. And the funny thing is, in those days they couldn't record anything. So you did this piece, it lasted for

20 minutes, you had a 5-minute break then you did it all again, live on television, twice. The schools could watch one bit or they could watch the other bit. That was a very strange feeling.'

Ronnie was also briefly seen on the popular early evening *Tonight* programme, a current affairs magazine show. Ronnie and Prunella Scales (later to become a firm TV favourite as Basil Fawlty's wife Sybil) appeared as a human cartoon strip.

'Cliff Michelmore fronted it. It happened at 6 o'clock and it was always live. We were dressed in cardboard all the time. I had a cardboard moustache and a cardboard hat and she had a cardboard boater on. She was a schoolgirl and it just had little jokes, like a cartoon strip would have.

'Then a producer named Jimmy Gilbert rang my agent and said he was looking for a man to replace Richard Waring in a Stanley Baxter show. There'd been a television show called *On the Bright Side* with Stanley Baxter and Betty Marsden, and Richard Waring was the feed in that. He said he was looking for a chubby chap to take over because they were going to do a stage version of it. And he asked, "Where can I see Ronnie working?" My agent said, "You can't see him working but you can go to a radio show and watch him working from the audience. So you can hear him and see him playing different characters." One day they turned up and he'd brought Stanley Baxter with him and they watched it and they both decided I should do it. So I did the stage version, *On the Brighter Side*. That's how I got to know Jimmy Gilbert. Although he was a TV person he was also producing the stage version.'

Noted British comedy writer Barry Cryer, who would later write for Barker and others on *The Frost Report*, recalls seeing Ronnie in this early show. 'I met Ronnie in Leeds, my home town. He was on tour with Stanley Baxter. I'd worked on the series *On the Bright Side*, and Ronnie was in the stage show of it. Stanley was obviously the star, but he said, "Watch out for this one, he's stealing it all." Stanley spotted it right off.'

•••

Producer Jimmy Gilbert had also 'spotted it' and wanted Ronnie for more TV work. It might still have been in its relative infancy at this time, but this was, nevertheless, something of a golden age for television, especially in terms of its writers. Hancock had successfully transferred his *Half Hour* to the medium, courtesy of the work of Ray Galton and Alan Simpson. Another team of writers, Frank Muir and Dennis Norden, were also coming into their own, writing a series for the blustery, moustached comedy actor Jimmy Edwards, already a huge star on radio courtesy of *Take It From Here*, which also featured a young June Whitfield.

The 'Playhouse' format was dominant, in which the name performer would star in a series of half-hour shows, playing a different character in a different situation each week. *The Seven Faces of Jim* was Muir and Norden's first vehicle for Edwards and it proved to be a vital link in bringing Ronnie Barker fully into the medium he would one day, literally, set up shop in.

'Jimmy Gilbert said, "There's one line in one of the Jimmy Edwards' shows I'm going to do. Would you like to come and do it?"' recalls Barker. '"It's only one line, it's an announcer," but he said, "it's quite funny because the caption comes up underneath you, saying it's Judith Chalmers." This was when she was a newsreader. I said, "Fine." Then the next week, he said, "There's two or three lines here you could do," so I said, "Fine." Terence Alexander was in it and he was playing the villain, called Sidney Figgins. Anyway, the next day he rang through and said he was very ill. Frank Muir and Dennis Norden, who wrote it, said, "We think Ronnie could do this part." And I said, "Can I do it Welsh?" They said, "Why?" So I said, "That covers the class." He was supposed to be rather grand and well-to-do but he's not. So they said that was a good idea. I played it Welsh and that went well. I was then in the series.

'And then in the second series I became a regular and it was the three of us, June Whitfield and me, supporting Jimmy. That was my first real television and after that people began to spot me and from there I started to get the other television offers.'

•••

Fame was certainly beckoning, but ever the chameleon, Ronnie was having none of it.

'I certainly wasn't well known in the street because nobody saw my face. I was known just as a voice, I suppose, and when you were going for a job and you said, "I play Able Seaman Johnson in *The Navy Lark*," then you were known. But no, even when I started television it was a while before people said, "Are you that feller with Jimmy Edwards?"'

•••

In 1962 there was a further extension to the Barker family when their daughter Charlotte was born on the last day of January. Jimmy Edwards's TV series was also renewed for a second season that year. Now titled *Six More Faces of Jim*, Ronnie was made a co-star alongside June Whitfield. The first episode saw him cast as Ron Glum, the Glum family having been one of Edwards's biggest hits on the radio. 'My first impression of Ronnie was that he was rather talented,' recalled June Whitfield. 'He was always spot-on with all his characters. He automatically picked something that was appropriate and amusing. We played all kinds of different roles in that. I think Ronnie enjoyed the variety of it all.' The *Six More Faces of Jim* of 1962 became 1963's *More Faces of Jim* and Ronnie Barker's own face was well on its way to becoming well known.

•••

For an actor who cites Laurence Olivier as an idol, Ronnie Barker has never really had an overwhelming desire to play Shakespeare (despite the odd turn on schools' television). Yet in 1962, sandwiched neatly between Jimmy Edwards's various *Faces*, he was cast in a Royal Court production of *A Midsummer Night's Dream*. It was a prestigious production, featuring the debut professional performance of two members of the great British acting family, the Redgraves. Lynn, daughter of Sir Michael and younger sister to Vanessa, appeared alongside her older brother Corin, who played Lysander in the production. Corin had already worked at the Royal Court, however, having made his directorial debut there with *The Scarecrow* the previous year. Other cast members included Nicol Williamson, now a distinguished actor but then fresh out of Dundee Rep, and Rita Tushingham, who had won a 'Best Newcomer' British Academy Award for her performance in the movie *A Taste of Honey* in 1961. Also among the cast was David Warner, who would go on to win great acclaim as Hamlet in the 1969 production, but to whom Ronnie offered the advice, 'You shouldn't be in this business. You're not cut out for it.' Advising other actors was never Ronnie's strong suit.

This was one of Ronnie's rare stabs at the bard. Ironically, his only other attempt at things iambic would be a decade later in a BBC television production of the very same play, this time cast as a heavily made-up Bottom. 'I never hankered after Shakespeare. I never felt I had to prove myself that way. Then again, I was never offered it. We never did any at Oxford. I saw *Hamlet* done at Oxford, but that was before I worked there.'

By now, radio and television were buttering the Barker family's bread, but movies still held an allure, offering as they did a touch of glamour. 'I suppose they were glamorous. I was pleased to be in them. Pleased to see them on the big screen. But they're even glamorous to me now. If I had been working and someone had offered me a big part, like Bob Hoskins has been offered, those sort of parts in American movies and things, I would still find them glamorous.'

•••

Throughout the early 1960s, Ronnie became one of what could almost be termed a floating repertory company, in terms of British movies. The same faces showed up all the time, rarely leading, but always supporting ably. If it wasn't Bernard Cribbins it was Eric Sykes. If it wasn't Eric it was Leslie Phillips. Or indeed Ronnie Barker. Made in 1962, *Kill or Cure* was one such vehicle, featuring as it did, Barker, Sykes, Dennis Price, Terry Thomas and Lionel Jeffries. 'I remember sitting talking to Lionel Jeffries, who was a grumbler, maybe, or gloomy; it was comic gloom really and he said, "Aren't things expensive these days?" I said, "Yes they are." I said, "It costs me £100 a week just for housekeeping, just for running my house." "Two hundred and fifty it costs me," he said. Those are the little bits you remember, strange little things like that. *Kill or Cure* was a good old British B picture – I was a policeman in it. It was about a murder in a health resort, we just wandered through it. Of course making any film then was different and interesting.'

Despite being a regular voice on one of radio's best-loved shows, Barker was convinced it had no impact in getting him seen on the big screen. 'Certainly not. It must have been my agent. I certainly wasn't trading on any reputation, I didn't have any reputation then. My reputation only really started with *The Frost Report*, a bit, but *The Two Ronnies* of course was the one.' However, work kept pouring in. 'I did a *Harry Secombe Show*. We did a couple of sketches, me and Harry.'

•••

Movies may have held an allure, television may have felt most natural, but the theatre kept the offers of work coming in. Ronnie starred as Bob Acres in *All in Love*, a musical version of Sheridan's *The Rivals*, before taking on the role of Lord Slingsby-Craddock in *Mr Whatnot*, by a young British playwright called Alan Ayckbourn.

'That was done at the Arts Theatre. It was about a piano-tuner who never spoke. I don't know if he was dumb, he was a young man, Chaplin-esque really, because a lot of it was physical. And everything was done without props. It was a very strange piece, it was lovely. Very funny. Certain props, action props, were left out. We had a tennis match on the stage and there was no ball. It took a lot of rehearsing. I was the umpire and at one point I'd picked up a news-paper and was reading it and Alan, who was directing, said it would be nice if the ball hit that paper. And I said, "Well, why doesn't it split it right down the middle?" It got a very good laugh. It was very strange and quite surreal. A bit *Alice in Wonderland* in places – we were having a picnic in the garden and suddenly war broke out, we were attacked by the enemy and we were lobbing buns over the hedge. No props of course.'

Ask Barker if the role of Lord Slingsby-Craddock was a prototype for one of his most enduring creations, Lord Rustless, and he answers the question before it's finished.

'Yes he was. Absolutely. He was Lord Rustless mark one, definitely. I did a character at Oxford rep and it was a part that was supposed to be done by a woman and Frank Shelley, who was running Oxford rep and was God there, said, "No we won't play it as a woman, because we haven't any women. Ronnie, you can play it as an old man." So I started doing this old chap and it was very successful and it worked very well. That character stayed at the back of my mind and he became Lord Rustless, because I enjoyed playing him so much. He's also in *The Picnic* and *By the Sea*, but he just mutters in those. He's not called Lord Rustless, no-one's called anything. But to me he was Rustless. He was one of my favourite characters. When I did *Hark at Barker* – that was him, albeit with sketches. Alan Ayckbourn wrote all the links for that show but I don't think he admits it. He called himself Peter Caulfield, but I don't know whether he would like people to know that was him or not. He liked the character in *Mr Whatnot*, so he knew what the character was about. Rustless was really giving a lecture to the audience on a subject, such as "communication" or "servants" or something and he would illustrate it with sketches, which enabled me to pay lots of different parts.'

•••

Lord Rustless did in fact make his first appearance by name in Ronnie's 1968 series *The Ronnie Barker Playhouse*, before being spun off into 1969's *Hark at Barker*, and the 1972 sitcom *His Lordship Entertains*. Although the character he played in *Futtock's End* was called General Futtock, Ronnie freely admits that this too was Rustless, as was the nameless figure in the *Two Ronnies'* specials *The Picnic* and *By the Sea*.

Ronnie, meanwhile, cites the actor Fred Emney as the inspiration for his characterization. Emney had been working on stage since the age of 15 and was a variety star by the time TV came along, even appearing in some pre-war BBC broadcasts. He had his own BBC TV shows in the 1950s, *Emney Enterprises* and *The Fred Emney Show* among others.

'Rustless doesn't sound like him, but he has that same wonderful character in that he'd sit back and let the world go by and nothing affected him. I love that sort of comedy, the way he did it, very, very laid back he was. I used to see him at the Oxford Theatre. I was at the Playhouse and we were allowed to go to the matinees at the New Theatre for free, so we were always there. We saw wonderful plays. There was one called *Blue for a Boy*, which had Fred Emney and Richard Hearne in. I remember him in the middle of a song this woman was singing to him, he put his hand in his coat and took out a bag of chips in newspaper and started eating his chips all through the number. Then he offered her a chip. That's what he did, he did strange things like that.'

•••

In 1963 Ronnie was introduced to two people he would come to share his life with. The first was fictional, the second was serving drinks, standing – if you believe Barker's more prosaic recollections – on a crate so he could actually see over the bar he was tending.

The latter was Ronnie Corbett. The former was Norman Stanley Fletcher. At the time, of course, Ronnie failed to recognize the importance of both meetings, particularly given that he met Fletch under another name.

Years later, while filming *Porridge*, Ronnie Barker was surprised by an old publicity photo of himself from the 1963 Charlie Drake movie *The Cracksman*. The look was the same, the prison uniform was the same, the hair was the same. Snout in his pocket, gum in his mouth – take away the scar on his face and this was Fletcher as a boy (although tellingly Fletcher did sport a facial scar for the first few episodes of *Porridge*), doing stir for the first time in the life of a 'habitual criminal who accepts arrest as an occupational hazard, and presumably accepts imprisonment in the same casual manner'. Looking back, Ronnie realizes that the seeds of his performance as Fletcher were sown in *The Cracksman*.

'We had a frightening time in that, I remember. We were doing a night scene, it was snowing and we had to climb a 20-foot wall, the three of us that were escaping – Percy Herbert, Jack Rodney and me. Plus Charlie. We had this vast ladder and we had to pick it up, push it against the wall and run up it. On the other side of the wall was scaffolding built up to about five feet from the top that we jumped onto. I was terrified and I think Jack was and Percy might have been scared as well but he didn't show it. We could only shoot it once because it was very late and it was getting light. Peter Graham Scott was the director and he said, "We have to get this shot and we've only got one go at it." So we ran up this ladder and Percy jumped over the top and Jack went up next and I was the last one to go up. I got to the top and I looked over and Jack and Percy were shouting, "Don't jump", because the scaffolding was swaying from side to side. But I had to go, and I did and God, it was frightening. So much in films happens like that because it's thrown together. You're working against a schedule all the time.

'In *The Two Ronnies* you'd find you'd have to get a certain shot at a certain time. And of course unions then were much stronger, they would pull the plugs out if you ran over. But that was never scary like this.

'Also in *The Cracksman* I had to hit a man on the head with a prop which was supposed to break and it didn't break the first time. And I had to hit him harder. But nonetheless they said that we had to get the shot.'

•••

So much in comedy you find is fate, coincidence, that in retrospect you find yourself asking a number of 'What ifs?' What if Mrs Marx had had girls? What if Eric's mum hadn't spotted a teenage Ernie? What if solicitor Bob Mortimer hadn't been drunk enough to heckle Vic Reeves that night in a pub in South London? And what if Ronnie Barker, West End actor and semi-known television face, hadn't popped in one night for a drink at the Buxton, an actors' drinking club just off Shaftesbury Avenue? He might never have met the bartender, a between-jobs Scottish performer who shared a forename with Mr Barker.

Ronnie Corbett hailed from Edinburgh. As he served Ronnie a drink, they spent a few moments talking about this and that, actors shooting the breeze. Both, of course, had no idea that in a few short years, upwards of twenty million people would be doing the same thing with them on a weekly basis.

'It was a theatrical club, you could have lunch and dinner there and the bar could be said to be open till about 3.30 a.m. It should have closed at II p.m. but it was one of those sort of places that I think the police didn't bother with. It wasn't sleazy, it was just an actors' drinking club and the actors simply carried on drinking halfway through the night. I used to go in and there he was behind the bar. He had a part-time job there. That's where I met him first. Then, he was just the man who was serving. I knew who he was, I knew he was an actor, but we didn't become chums then. We first became chums when we met three years later when Jimmy Gilbert, again, contributed me and Ronnie Corbett to *The Frost Show*. Ronnie Corbett and John Cleese were suggested by David Frost. David had seen Ronnie when he was working with Danny LaRue at Danny LaRue's club. And then Jimmy Gilbert put me in, and that's when Ronnie and I teamed up because they were all a bit university and we were grammar school boys. Everyone goes to university now, but thirty years ago, university was considered a cut above. So they were a bit grand, especially John Cleese who was very grand. He looked down on Ronnie, and Ronnie was right down there. John was nice, but nevertheless, we felt that he and David were "them", and we were "us". There was no enmity or no real distance, but if you had to group together in twos, naturally Ronnie and I would go together as John and David did. But as to me and Ronnie, we just met the one time.'

It wasn't that big an event of course, but Ronnie Corbett remembers it equally vividly: 'He was doing quite a lot of radio shows like *The Navy Lark* at that time. I don't think we thought about it in any momentous way but we knew each other a bit because I had worked with his wife Joy in a pantomime in Bromley where she was the stage manager. So I'd known her before and she was with him when he used to come down for supper sometimes.' In a few short years these two casual acquaintances would become one of the nation's best-loved double acts.

•••

Following a brief appearance in *Doctor in Distress* – 'I had one line and it was shot at Windsor railway station. I came up behind James Robertson Justice, he sneezed, I said, "That's a nasty cold, you should see a doctor." He said, "I am a doctor!" That was it' – Ronnie found himself back on radio with his close friend Leslie Crowther, as a regular player (alongside *Seven Faces of Jim* alumnus June Whitfield) in *Crowther's Crowd*. The three had of course previously worked as a trio on *Variety Playhouse* and the *Radio Times* of the day described this new show thus: 'They are three students out to reform the world – Leslie the medical student, June the drama student, and Ronnie a trainee at a school for chefs. Thanks to the miracle of radio, listeners can join their summit conferences at El Aroma coffee bar in Bloomsbury... they'll argue about anything and illustrate their points with impersonations.'

'It was really a sort of continuation from *Variety Playhouse*,' remembers June Whitfield. 'We were very much a team at that time, but people drift on to different things so that was to be the end of that, sadly.'

•••

A role in the movie *Father Came Too* not only saw Ronnie reunited with Leslie Phillips, Stanley Baxter and James Robertson Justice, but in the character of a country cowboy builder, he found yet another blueprint for the role of Norman Stanley Fletcher.

'With *Father Came Too* I was on the film right the way through. That was the biggest part I ever played in a film, except for *Porridge*. I was a country builder, a bit of a tatty builder. Leslie Phillips and Stanley Baxter had done *The Fast Lady* and this was a sequel to it. I had Kenneth Cope and various people in my group, I was the foreman. I played it exactly like Johnson in *The Navy Lark*. Which I started to tend to do. You do, you set out by never wanting to play the same character again, but eventually you start saying that is a good character, an easy character for me to put on. So you start to get a group of characters and you finish up with *The Two Ronnies* maybe having twelve people that you play. But that was enjoyable. Same director as *The Cracksman*, Peter Graham Scott. James Robertson Justice was rather fussy. On this one he insisted on a lot of things being done by a double, like walking down a step. He was standing underneath a beam in the cottage and he said, "I can't do this, my neck's aching."'

•••

In 1964 another movie, the dialogue-free *A Home of Your Own*, was to prove equally influential.

'I play the man who was laying the cement and everyone kept going over it, running over it. I fell into it. I had this great sequence where I suddenly threw everything down and I danced on it. I did ballet steps, I did swimming, I did everything in it. There again, you could only do everything once because of the costume. That was all done on a shoestring as well but of course it gave me the idea, having seen it, that these silent things really work; I should do this. So *Futtock's End* was the first one I did (in 1970) and it was directed by Bob Kellett, who also directed *A Home of Your Own*.'

Films kept offering themselves up, even if truth be told Barker's inclination was rapidly heading towards the smaller screen. Harry H. Corbett, meanwhile, was trying to move the other way. Having hit the big time on TV's *Steptoe and Son*, he was looking to expand his horizons, and move beyond the limitations of what was usually perceived to be a one-hit wonder. His first stab at this was a movie called *The Bargee*. In support to the already established television star was the ever-reliable Ronnie Barker.

'I suppose that was one of the biggest parts I had because I played Harry Corbett's cousin who ran the narrow boats. We had ten weeks on the narrow boats. I had to have my hair dyed black to match

Harry Corbett's. Eric Sykes was in that as well, written by Galton and Simpson, through their connection to *Steptoe*. Hugh Griffiths was the heavy. We rehearsed a scene where I was trying to get him drunk to keep him out of the house while Harry Corbett had it away with his daughter. But he eventually drinks me under the table. I said some line and burped in the rehearsal and Hugh looked at me and said, "You gonna burp there?" I said, "Yes." So we did the take and about two lines before I burped, he burped. I said, "You knew I was going to burp there." He said, "I know, but I just felt it, it just came out." Bloody liar! But he was a very good liar, a strong personality. Richard Briers was in that, and so was Brian Wilde who was eventually to appear in *Porridge* as Barrowclough.'

Barker admits that despite the glamour of film, he was already more interested in the box in the corner of the living room.

'I was never primarily interested in films. By then I think I'd realized that television was my market place. I thought that's where I should be. You see television is the only place where you can get a series. You don't get a series of films. You don't say, "I've got a good film series, I'm doing *Terminator 1, 2, 3* and *4*. You do one film at a time. And also I knew it was a much bigger market. Television was somehow more parochial, more cosy, I suppose. I never had vaulting ambition, as they say in the Scottish play, I believe. I just loved working and I wanted to be successful, I wanted to earn money. I wanted to be well known. But I thought television, it's British for a start, and I've never thought of anything outside Britain as being my métier at all. I thought if you make it big here... Films were lovely if they came along and, fine, I would accept them and I'd do them. But television seemed to be the thing to work at. The thing to conquer and, touch wood, I think I managed it.'

•••

Ronnie's work on television in 1964 was also to prove highly instrumental in his career. Eric Sykes was one of the first comics of his generation who, alongside the likes of Tony Hancock and Benny Hill, realized the full potential of television. By this time, Sykes was a mainstay of television, with a series designed to showcase his talents in sitcom format.

Displaying his penchant for playing older characters ('I was this terrible tramp'), Ronnie guest-starred as a hard-to-lose tramp in one episode of the show, *Sykes and the Log Cabin*. Throughout his career, Ronnie has portrayed a variety of often unrecognizable characters. It harks back to the notion that he disguises himself in the role, rather than using elements of his own personality to allow audiences to see him in that role. Whether through the use of accent, a speech impediment or make-up, Barker slides into the role, often playing outside of his own age range and background. The tramp in this one episode of Sykes was no exception. 'People ask how you do this. And you can never answer them. The only answer is that it's your job and you get used to it. And the same with playing an old man I suppose. I never made a study of it. All through my life I've never consciously studied people to get characters, but obviously a lot of it rubs off on you subconsciously. You pick it up without knowing it. You look at the old chaps in a pub and you suddenly get a character.'

It was while working on Sykes that Ronnie first met a young BBC producer and director by the name of Sydney Lotterby, who would go on to perform those duties for Ronnie on *Porridge*, *Open All Hours* and *The Magnificent Evans*.

•••

By 1965, Ronnie Barker was a known figure on both television and radio, with what appeared to be a blossoming film career, albeit in supporting roles. Having worked in these various mediums, he now knew in which one he felt most comfortable. So it was to television that Ronnie Barker devoted himself, appearing in a variety of roles. These included that of Spettigue in a production of rep favourite *Charley's Aunt*, top-lining Danny LaRue and Australian actress Coral Browne (who would later marry American horror film star Vincent Price, after he'd murdered her in the 1973 movie *Theatre of Blood*).

'We filmed *Charley's Aunt* in Oxford and we stayed at the Randolph. Coral Browne changed her room three times and we'd only been there an hour. She was such a funny woman, very witty and very grand. Danny of course, being Danny, would only play it as a beautiful woman, which doesn't quite fit the thing. It should be a little rugby player. John Mills was ideal when he played it. Frankie Howerd did it, Arthur Askey did it. But Danny looked wonderful although I felt he was miscast, although he did play it very well. I played it in Oxford. I played the college servant then, who has 24 entrances. This time, though, I was playing the lover, the one they laugh at. He was the figure of fun.'

Ronnie also played Jerry Cruncher in the BBC's Sunday afternoon adaptation of Charles Dickens's *A Tale of Two Cities*. 'I enjoyed that. I played Jerry Cruncher, who was a real Dickensian character, with a crew cut I remember, chopped-off hair. I was a bank messenger but I was also a grave robber. I remember saying to Joan Craft who was the director, "I've summed this character up. He doesn't know whether to take the money or open the box." She couldn't understand that for a bit, it was the great catchphrase of that quiz show *Take Your Pick*. I also had to sit on a horse in it. That was a first.'

•••

Having co-starred with Cyril Fletcher in the radio comedy *Not to Worry*, Ronnie was rewarded with his first top billing in the 1965 show *Let's Face It*.

'It was because I was in *Not to Worry* and the director John Fawcett Wilson took a shine to me and he suggested they should do a series for me as well. It was a normal run-of-the-mill sketch show, written by everybody. By today's standards I wouldn't want it to be heard now. There are very few things I feel that about. I don't even feel it about *The Navy Lark* because that was quite good stuff, quite fruity, meaty stuff. Very broad comedy, but good lines. But I should think *Let's Face It* was very ordinary. I remember a lot of puns. I had to keep cutting out puns. It was OK, and it certainly gave me the first top billing.'

•••

Headlining roles also came along on television courtesy of *Gaslight Theatre*. The show was based around a touring Victorian repertory company, which each week performed classic melodramas, live on BBC2. Adapted by Alec Clunes, the six hour-long shows also featured the likes of Warren Mitchell, Alfred Marks and Patricia Routledge. It gave Ronnie the opportunity to play everything from 'an American dastard' to a 'a revolting Dutch miner' to 'Shawnegenwam' a North American Native in the wonderfully titled *The Blood-Craz'd Scourge of the Redskin Wilderness, or What You Will*.

'That was marvellous and it was never kept. They wiped the tapes. It wasn't exactly live, but it was done live, at the Shepherd's Bush theatre. Alec Clunes – Martin Clunes's father – was a Shakespearean actor in his own right. I was supposed to be the manager of the company. There was no backstage to it so none of this was known, it was just simply presenting these melodramas. But they were done live to an audience and at one point I was playing the old gypsyish male lead in *Maria Martin* and thirty seconds later I was playing his son, who was blond. It was the same man in that the manager was playing both parts so I had to do this costume and make-up change in 30 seconds. On stage all this crowd gathered round this gypsy and sort of chanted and wailed and I was off changing.

'They had models like they used to have in Victorian times. There was a chase across into the distance: the policeman chased this man off stage and further down on came these puppets that went across, then smaller puppets came across, and then tiny puppets came across. It was very funny.

'Alec Clunes also said, because he was a great historian on these things, that these plays used to have modern songs in them. Even if they were doing something in say 1870 and it was supposed to take place in 1750, it would still have modern 1870 music hall songs in it as well. Like a panto I suppose. So we were singing things like "Hot Time in the Old Town Tonight".

'In one of the plays I played a Welsh Red Indian and also a sort of James Cagney cowboy. He had a blond curly wig as well. I looked hopelessly mutton dressed as lamb. Patricia Routledge was in one called *Three Cheers for the Red, White and Blue*. We did *Sweeney Todd, Maria Martin* and we did one called *The Worst Woman in London* in which I played Lord Rustless really. But a wonderful part, and sang "A Bachelor Gay Am I", which was quite anachronistic.'

•••

Gaslight Theatre was also to afford Ronnie one of his few stoops to temperament.

'Alec Clunes would come in on the first day and we would read an hour-long piece and it would come in at two hours. Then he'd say, "I'll come in the morning with cuts." He'd come in the next morning and we would read these cuts which were like – "Don't say, 'I've never been so disgusted in my life,' say, 'I'm disgusted.'" And we'd read it all again and we'd find it lasted one hour 50 minutes. This happened for three weeks and eventually in the fourth week, we read it and it came to two hours. I stood up – I've never done this before or since – and Warren Mitchell always remembers it, I said, "OK Alec, it's two hours. When it's an hour, give us a ring and I'll come in again." And I walked out. I was amazed at my own courage then. I remember their faces as I went out, they were frozen. Even Alfred Marks didn't have anything to say, which is very unusual. Warren said afterwards, "I don't know how you did that, but it worked." The same evening Alec rang me up and said, "Ronnie you're absolutely right, it's no use going on like this, why don't you cut it?" This particular piece had a subplot in it that ran all the way through and Bill Owen and Megs Jenkins were cast. But it had nothing to do with the rest of the play, so I cut them right out, and rang Alec and said, "Megs and Bill have gone completely. Is that OK? Can you tell them?" And they went and it was down to about an hour and ten minutes, so I cut another ten minutes and it was OK. After that he used to say, "Will you cut them?" I enjoyed that and it was comparatively easy.'

Working on the scripts for *Gaslight Theatre* was the first time Ronnie had put pen to paper since his days with Glenn Melvyn. Yet instinctively he knew how to make things work, a talent that would eventually see him have a hand in most of the material he subsequently played. Ronnie has often spoken of his fondness for old gags. 'I've always said old jokes are only old jokes if you've heard them before. You can have a joke from 1895 and, if you haven't heard it before, it's a new joke to you. It has to be funny, and so often they aren't. But some of them are. That's what it is. I find it's universal. If a joke is funny it stays funny for ever.' Ronnie's next screen venture gave him plenty of opportunity to exploit that fondness.

Before the Fringe was a show based around old-time music hall jokes and sketches, many of which were performed by Ronnie in tandem with the actress Beryl Reid. 'We called it *Before the Fringe* because they were such old sketches. It was all old sketches that had been done in the West End, and *Beyond the Fringe* had started by then. I did that with Beryl Reid, funny lady, very scatterbrained, very way-out sense of humour.'

The show's title referred to the stage revue *Beyond the Fringe*, the 1960 production featuring the combined talents of Peter Cook, Dudley Moore, Jonathan Miller and Alan Bennett, that had effectively turned British comedy on its head. In *Before the Fringe*, Ronnie Barker paid tribute to what had gone before. But it would be a graduate of the so-called Oxbridge comedy mafia, a man who owed his career to both the comedic and indeed social advancements made by the *Beyond the Fringe* troupe, who would finally make a star out of Ronnie Barker.

CHAPTER 3

I Look Up To Him

Good evening. Equality. The Government White Paper on the Equal Society was published today. Its main provisions are as follows:

From 1 April 1981, everyone must be of equal height. This height will be three feet above the saloon bar for men and two feet under the hair dryer for women. Anyone found shorter than the equal height will be looked down on. He will then be sent to a Government height-inducing camp, where he will stand in a barrel of manure until he's tall enough to step out without catching anything on the rusty nail at the top. Anyone found taller than the equal height will be required to carry lead weights in the trouser pockets and wear very short braces. This will cause a stoop and, inevitably, a few boy sopranos.

The monologue Ronnie wrote to be presented by him as a 'government spokesman' in *The Two Ronnies* ably demonstrates nothing whatsoever except that inequality exists in society and always will. The answer? Whenever possible, ignore it and it simply won't matter. Both Barker and Corbett, by no means equal in any way themselves, were about to become embroiled in a social and professional situation of inequality where their best course of action would be to take no real action at all and simply get on with doing what they do best.

•••

David Frost was something of a phenomenon. While his Cambridge contemporary Peter Cook was shepherding the British 'satire boom' via his London nightclub, The Establishment, Frost was packaging it wholesale and serving it up into the mainstream courtesy of television. As the front man of both *That Was The Week That Was* (TW3) in 1962–3 and *Not So Much a Programme, More a Way of Life* in 1964, he had established himself as a unique force in British television, equally comfortable cracking gags or interviewing leading politicians. This was stylish modern television entertainment to suit the mood of the sixties, now in full swing. By 1965 television had taken over from radio in the corner of the living room. The day-to-day trauma of living in Weatherfield had been enthralling the nation for five years in *Coronation Street* and in Sebastopol Terrace, Eric Sykes had been causing havoc with his 'twin sister' Hattie Jacques for nine series of *Sykes and a...* Sykes certainly held the middle ground, with his cosy style of comedy washing harmlessly over his docile audience, but the sixties were all about innovation, and humour with a sharper edge, humour that made TV audiences sit up and pay attention, was what the younger, vibrant market wanted.

In March 1966, David Frost launched his new series, *The Frost Report*, designed as an irreverent look at one particular topic each week. There was a wealth of subject material from which the satirists could choose. Harold Wilson's Labour administration was declaring itself the people's government at one moment and freezing the people's wages the next. Rock 'n' roll had come and gone, with Elvis trading in his rebel image for that of a movie matinee idol. Rock and pop were now the order of the day with the Beatles and the Stones taking over the world and London becoming the coolest place on the planet. Suddenly everyone knew where Vietnam was and the cold war was growing ever more chilling.

Although it remained topical in nature, *The Frost Report* steered clear of the 'this morning's headlines' approach of *Not So Much a Programme...* It concentrated more on topical themes and featured a number of sketches for which Frost assembled a team of three – John Cleese, Ronnie Corbett and Ronnie Barker. 'David Frost brought me along,' recalls Ronnie Corbett, 'because he had seen me quite a lot in nightclubs, where I was performing with others, like Barry Cryer. We were at a club called Winston's in Clifford Street, and David was stepping out with a girl in the show called Jenny Logan. So he used to come in there quite a lot and saw me. Ronnie B was a lot better known than either John or I.'

As Ronnie Barker noted, not sharing the university background of Frost and Cleese, the two Ronnies naturally drifted together. 'That linked us, it's true,' agrees Corbett. 'Also the fact that we were much more experienced theatrical performers than both of them, Ronnie in particular. We'd knocked about a bit. John used to get very, very nervous at doing live television, but Ronnie and I didn't. I think it's also funny that both Ronnie and I were brought up and raised in big university towns, Oxford and Edinburgh, with the university glowering over both of us, although we didn't attend it. There was a comfort thing between us, I'd say.'

'University then was very different,' agrees Barker. 'There was a university and there was a town and they didn't seem to mix much, although of course when I was at the Playhouse it was very different because there was a very famous coffee bar there that was always full of students and actors. I used to meet a few of the undergraduates there. Ned Sherrin was certainly one, and a man called Brian Tesler who is big in television now was another, and a man who is big in the theatre now, Michael Codron, I know he was there. I first met Maggie Smith there, of course. So I met a lot of university people. Kenneth

Tynan was there – very strange man, he used to dye his hair yellow. He looked like a skull with yellow hair!'

'I was coming back from America,' remembers John Cleese, 'and I came back safe in the knowledge that Mr Frost wanted me to join these two people called Ronnie Barker and Ronnie Corbett, neither of whom I'd ever heard of, of course. It was terrifying because it was live. I was surrounded by entirely nice people who were friendly, supportive, cheerful, helpful, couldn't have been nicer. I think I learned a little bit, particularly from Ronnie Corbett, which might surprise people because Barker is a great actor but Corbett had moments of timing that were absolutely extraordinary. Ronnie Barker could just play anyone or anything; Ronnie Corbett had a narrower range but his timing was extraordinary.'

'It was a wonderful combination,' agrees Barry Cryer, one of the show's writers. 'I always say that Ronnie Barker was the actor who was rather good at comedy, and Ronnie Corbett was the comic who was a rather good actor. They met in the middle and it was perfect. Jimmy Gilbert, the producer, wasn't too thrilled with Ronnie Corbett, but David was and had seen him in nightclubs with Danny LaRue. David opted for Ronnie Corbett and Jimmy Gilbert opted for Ronnie Barker. *The Frost Report* really got them all going as performers.'

•••

Having taken the leap of accepting Frost's offer, Barker was pleased with the show and its results, particularly in its broad approach to its weekly topic, whether it be 'class', 'law', or whatever. Barker recalls: 'I think David made a positive move to be more across the board, he made a conscious effort to not be so satirical but to have an edge, a kind of attitude. All three of us had a rapport. We were all extremely comfortable with each other. And the material that was coming forward was also well thought out and cared for, with an attitude. *TW3* and *Not So Much a Programme, More a Way of Life* were political programmes. Ours may have appeared to be a sort of topical and pointed show, but it wasn't. I think it was just humour. The things that David read out on the clipboard, that we later did as news items in *The Two Ronnies*, may have sounded topical, but they weren't at all topical. People used to say in *The Two Ronnies* you sat there and you did all those topical jokes. And I'd say you pick one topical joke out – there isn't one! That's why you can show them 20 years later and they're not dated, except you might get, 'the Prime Minister Harold Wilson . . .' or something. We shouldn't even have done that at the time, but we did. But the jokes were not to do with current affairs at all. I think that *The Frost Report* may have given that impression, but it wasn't.'

•••

In retrospect, *The Frost Report* can be seen as a hugely important breeding ground for modern British comedy. 'It was the place to be,' says Barry Cryer. 'I always say, if you're lucky and you don't realize it, you don't deserve it. We all grafted away, but to be around Frost in that era was to be in just the right place.'

In addition to its own numerous successes, *The Frost Report* indirectly begat *Monty Python's Flying Circus*, given that its extensive team of writers included future Pythons Graham Chapman, Eric Idle, Terry Jones and Michael Palin (as well as writer-performer Cleese). It also put the two Ronnies together for the first time, beginning an on-screen partnership that would last for another two decades. In addition, *The Frost Report*, which ran for two seasons, produced numerous classic sketches, perhaps the most famous of which remains John Law's biting take on class. Physicalized by the distinct difference in height of the three central performers, the tall Cleese played upper class, the medium Barker personified middle class and the diminutive Corbett was the flat-capped working class.

'Someone obviously saw that our heights were very funny. You could put a plank across between Ronnie Corbett's head and John Cleese's head and my head would touch it as well. We were absolutely in a straight line. So they thought upper class, middle class, lower class and that's where the whole "I look up to him", "I look down on him" came from. That was the whole premise of the sketch, because there weren't funny lines in it. And then I wrote about three others, about work and other things, trying to get more laughs in them, more jokes, because I couldn't use the looking up or looking down idea anymore, we'd done that. But that is the one that everyone remembers and I sort of wish they didn't show that one so much, I wish they'd show something else, but probably not much of *The Frost Report* still exists at all. I remember John did the funny walks thing, before *Python*, before the "Ministry of Silly Walks", he did that first in *The Frost Report*.'

The Frost Report not only gave Ronnie B his first on-screen experience with Ronnie C, it also allowed him to develop what would become one of his trademarks in *The Two Ronnies* – the monologue.

'John Cleese started by doing monologues, he would be the headmaster talking to his pupils and so on. There was one – as the Chancellor of the Exchequer – which John couldn't do for some reason and the producer Jimmy Gilbert said, "Let Ronnie do this one for a change." And of course I never looked back. I always did all the monologues straight through *The Two Ronnies*, all those spokesmen. That started by accident because John couldn't do it.

'Often the three of us were in sketches because the boys who were writing it were all the Python chaps, Terry Jones, Michael Palin, Graham Chapman, John himself was writing, Marty Feldman occasionally wrote stuff, Eric Idle certainly wrote stuff. So it was three people in a sketch mainly. But sometimes there were two people in a sketch and sometimes I would do a sketch with John Cleese. It wasn't a fixed thing, it wasn't that any two-handed sketch was done by the two Ronnies.'

•••

Shortly before beginning his stint on *The Frost Report*, Ronnie appeared with two other products of the Fringe, Peter Cook and Dudley Moore, in *Not Only... but Also...* A hugely inventive sketch show, *Not Only...* showcased the talents of Cook and Moore probably better than anything in their subsequent careers, and each week featured a guest who would take part in the regular feature 'Poets Cornered'. Pete, Dud and said guest – in this instance Ronnie

Barker – sat suspended over a tank of gunge, and attempted to speak in rhyming couplets.

'They sat on either side, on very tall chairs, above a pool full of gunge. These chairs were operated from the gallery upstairs. I was a bit scared of it to be honest. I don't know why I took it on. Dudley Moore would always start, and you had to speak in rhyming couplets. Whenever the bell went the next person had to take over. He would say, "As I was going down the road one dark and windy day, I saw a man the other side . . ." and then the button would go and someone else would carry on. It was frightening because you were trying desperately to make this rhyme and terrified of going into this unknown pool. Peter Cook was so clever that he would try and involve you in a risqué rhyme. I don't know how I got to it but I was about to say, "The cabin boy stood fearlessly, his back glued to the mast," and I was going to say, "I shall not turn around he said till Oscar Wilde has passed." That was the line I had. I got as far as his back glued to the mast and I said, "I shall not . . ." and the button went and I went in. I was furious. I'd arranged to take my glasses off when I went in so I came up and I said, "I've lost my glasses," and Dudley was distraught and he jumped in with me. Afterwards, I said to Jimmy Gilbert who was directing, "Jimmy I thought you pushed the button when you stumbled or failed to deliver. I was going great guns, I was about to give you a laugh." And he said, "We always drop the guest in first, and I thought it had gone on long enough." I was furious. But it was a wonderful experience. Afterwards we went up to their usual haunt in Hampstead for a party. I enjoyed the evening very much. They were great lads.'

•••

In between appearing on *The Frost Report*, Ronnie was being kept extremely busy by a number of other appearances. There were two films for the Children's Film Foundation – *Runaway Railway* and *Ghost of a Chance*. 'I did two – Bernard Cribbins was in *Ghost of a Chance* and we played poker in that one. *Runaway Railway* was dear old Sydney Tafler and children of all sizes and sorts. We did them for a very reduced fee. There was never too much pressure. A lot of people were available and did it, so it was an easy time. No strain at all.'

He also delivered guest star turns in two of television's most popular dramas, *The Saint* and *The Avengers*. *The Saint* starred Roger Moore and had been running for three years. *The Saint*'s creator, Leslie Charteris, had sold the TV rights in 1961 and the first of 71 black-and-white followed by 47 colour episodes was screened from 1962. The show, and Roger Moore, became a huge hit internationally, especially in the USA, up to its termination in 1969. While *The Saint* was action/adventure drama, in a relatively traditional mould familiar to viewers all over the world, *The Avengers* was something from another planet entirely. The escapades which starred secret agent John Steed (played by Patrick Macnee) and his female assistant, at this time Mrs Emma Peel (Diana Rigg), were psychological, psychedelic and sometimes simply downright silly but the series suited the mood of the sixties so well that it is still fondly remembered by legions of fans.

Ronnie's role in *The Saint* saw him tipping the nod to French comedy star Jacques Tati and the character Tati had created for a classic series of movies, *Monsieur Hulot*. Playing a bumbling French detective, Ronnie managed to clatter into props on set almost whenever he moved, and not always on purpose.

'He just happened to be a bit clumsy is all it is, although he was more like a Hulot than a Clouseau. I always used to think Tati was a funny man. But it was just a coincidence that I kept knocking into things. There's one scene where I'm supposed to be listening to something in a restaurant and I turn and bump into a lamp and catch it and I sat down and I knocked the table by accident and it rocked from side to side but it didn't fall. And they said, "How the hell did you do that?" It was just pure accident. I sort of stared at it and used it. It was a small part really. I was the assistant. You're always going to be the assistant if you're the funny bloke. The inspector was always walking out of doors and letting them swing in my face, that sort of thing... and that's the sum total of my comic contribution to *The Saint*.'

The Avengers episode, 'The Hidden Tiger', saw Ronnie cast as a mysterious cat fancier named Cheshire. The character could almost have been a forerunner of the numerous spokesmen he later played on *The Two Ronnies*, as Cheshire was the head of P.U.R.R.R. – 'The Philanthropic Union for the Rescue, Relief and Recuperation of Cats'. *The Avengers* was a much better part. My character was obsessed with cats. I got on very well with Diana Rigg, she was a nice lady and always a big fan of mine afterwards, she said.'

•••

Another television appearance holds less happy memories for Ronnie. His old friend Leslie Crowther had asked him to appear on his popular children's show *Crackerjack*; that same week his son Laurence was taken ill with measles.

'I went to do the programme on the Monday and when I got home my son was much worse. The doctor had come and said he'd got pneumonia. So he was rushed into the hospital and put in an oxygen tent and I sat there all night. At one point the nurse couldn't change the oxygen and I had to summon up the strength of ten men to open the new oxygen tank. I got home in the early morning. I remember this so vividly, by the time Friday came and the show was on, my son, who was then six, and had been so looking forward to seeing me on *Crackerjack,* was in the oxygen tent. I was sitting next to his bed and it was showing in the ward, and I cried. I remember crying and thinking, "Poor little sod, he was looking forward to this and now look at him." But he came through all right. I did a little drawing of him, he was getting better but he was still in the tent – and I've still got it. His little wan face was so thin... It was a very, very moving moment, me thinking, "he's not going to survive this," him so look-ing forward to seeing me on *Crackerjack* and there it was on and he couldn't even see it. That was very upsetting for me.'

•••

Following the recovery of his first-born, television had more in store for Barker. *Foreign Affairs* offered Ronnie his first stab at proper weekly situation comedy. Debuting on 8 September 1966 (shortly after the end of *The Frost Report*'s first run), and written by Johnnie Mortimer and Brian Cooke, the show was based around the exploits of the Foreign Office's Dennis Proudfoot, played by *Navy Lark* regular Leslie Phillips. Ronnie played the role of Russian Ambassador Grischa Petrovitch, Proudfoot's chess-playing opposite number.

'I remember Frank Muir, who was head of light entertainment at the time at the BBC, came up to me and said, "We've got this idea we think you'd be right for." I remember them coming on to the stage when we were doing *Frost Report* at the Shepherd's Bush Empire, and saying, "Leslie Phillips wants to do it and you know him, and we think you could play the Russian." I was pleased with that because that was a step forward. And it was fun to do it with Leslie because he's a very funny man. I'd worked so long with him in *The Navy Lark* that I knew his every move and he knew mine.'

Although it ostensibly dealt with Cold War issues, the emphasis was firmly on Phillips's girl-chasing and the show was not exactly a classic, lasting just one brief six-week run, although Barker did not object too much to its rapid demise.

'Some people could be over-exposed I always thought. I think Harry H. Corbett was over-exposed (as Harold Steptoe in *Steptoe and Son*), and so was Warren Mitchell (in the hugely popular BBC sitcom *Til Death Us Do Part*). They stayed too long in their series, so they could never do anything else. They used to play wonderful character parts in films then, but after Alf Garnett, Warren was always Alf Garnett and still is. That was very instrumental in me coming out of *Porridge*. I think I successfully dodged the typecasting curse, maybe only just because of the history, I suppose. They knew I could be different people.'

•••

Making 1967's *The Man Outside* was probably as close to Hollywood as Ronnie Barker ever got. It starred Hollywood's very own (yet improbably named) Van Heflin and received American distribution. Ronnie's role was confined to the movie's first reel, but for that time he shared the screen alone with Heflin, picking up a few tips on screen acting along the way.

'It was glamorous to do that film. Van Heflin had been a big star and was still a name to be reckoned with. He was a marvellous man, I liked him. He was a real, real pro. Knew everything. He said, "Ronnie don't ever take a drag on a cigarette in a close-up, and don't ever take a drink in a close-up." I said, "Why not?" He said, "They will never be able to edit it because you will not be doing exactly the same thing in the other shot and you will lose the close-up. If you do that, your close-up will not be in." And I used to watch him and he never did. Very clever. I loved that. That was a taste of the American movies. My only one.

'For the first ten minutes of the film it was Van Heflin and me, which meant you had meaty scenes together rather than just flitting through the film.'

•••

The second series of *The Frost Report* proved even more successful than the first, picking up the Golden Rose of Montreux award at the prestigious European television festival. As adept as he was before the camera, David Frost was equally skilled in the business side of making television. His own Paradine Productions took charge of the show and each of its principal performers was also signed to Paradine, effectively ensuring Frost's involvement with Ronnie up until the fifth season of *The Two Ronnies*. 'David always had that business sense. Ronnie and I were quite the reverse. It was always enough for us to do the work. Basically we didn't want to be management. He set Ronnie C up with a series (*The Corbett Follies*), he did a series with me (*The Ronnie Barker Playhouse*), produced by Marty Feldman and written by Graham Chapman, Eric Idle and Barry Cryer. And then he also did *At Last the 1948 Show* with John Cleese. And we were also in all of the live *Frost on Sundays* as well. So he really got us all started.'

One of Frost's most astute moves was to relocate to the 'other side', commercial television. Here the programme morphed into

Frost on Sunday, an equally successful mix of Frost's ever-developing clipboard-grasping monologues, and comedy sketches. Cleese had tired of performing and opted out this time round, leaving room for the occasional appearance of writer Michael Palin. 'John wanted to write and he was getting a bit nervous of performing as well,' Barker recalls. 'He used to be very white and pale and worried before he went on *The Frost Report* and he said, "I don't really like performing, I'd rather write," and so that's when he left.'

Another addition to the cast was Josephine Tewson, with whom Ronnie was concurrently co-starring in the West End production of Tom Stoppard's *The Real Inspector Hound*.

'It was a very funny play, a very weird play. I met her in that, which also starred Richard Briers, who has always remained a great friend. We had a great time in that. He's one of those people who just make you laugh because of who and what they are, the better you know them the funnier you find them. The same things make us laugh. He loves Eric Morecambe and Tommy Cooper and those sort of things. Josephine was very good in that, a good character woman. Which is why we had her in *Frost on Sunday*.' 'The two Ronnies were doing the sketches on *Frost* and they had to have somebody else there to play the woman,' Ms Tewson explains. 'So when they needed a girl, and a versatile one at that, Ronnie said, "There's this girl and she's playing Mrs Drudge. As she's got to be there during the week doing the play, she's going to be available on Sunday." When the play came off they then put me under contract. I got to know Ronnie quite well just going backwards and forwards from Wembley Park where the studios were to the theatre.'

'You've got to have someone you can rely on,' says Barker, 'and I was always on the lookout for someone who knew their lines the next day in rehearsals.

'Another time a woman named Gerry Raymonde wrote me a five-page letter – this was in *Two Ronnies* – she was in some summer season and she was fed up. It was a moaning letter but in a very funny way and she said she wanted to be on television. "I see all these women on television and I could knock them into a cocked hat." I wrote back and said, "Come and show us what you can do then." She showed up and she did half an hour and she did everything. She did funny walks, she was a comical character woman, she sang, she did impersonations, she did funny lines, she did *Two Ronnies* news items in front of us – the Two Ronnies were sitting there watching her do it! Great courage. I said, "I think you're marvellous," and the next week she was in a sketch and she was often in sketches after that. You knew you could rely on her.

'Jo was the same, she knows what she's doing. You do work with people you know because you haven't got time to experiment, ever, with those sort of things. People have been accused, not only us, but lots of people have been accused of using the same people all the time. And the reason is you know you can rely on them, you don't have to worry about them. And you've only got a few days to rehearse and they can only do it once and it's got to be right. It would be lovely to try different people in different things, but you haven't got the luxury of that because it's on television and you're as good as your supporting cast. Even if you're very good and everyone else is rotten, the show will be rotten. Like with Hancock, he needed all those people to make him look even funnier.'

Jo Tewson recalled one telling conversation she had with Ronnie as they waited for the tube to get them to their performance of *The Real Inspector Hound.*

'The train was late and I thought we might miss the half-hour call at the Criterion that night and I said, "Well, the show must go on." "Why?" he said, "Why must the show go on?" "Well it must," I said. "No, no, no, Jo. Nobody's going to bother if we're not there. The world's not going to come to an end if we don't do the show tonight." That's anathema to me, but he's not like that at all. He is so balanced. I remember while we were doing *Frost on Sunday* he was offered a good Shakespearean part on BBC2, something you give your eye teeth to play and something he hadn't done before, but he was saying, "Oh, isn't it a pity. They've offered me this but I can't do it because it's during the school holidays." And I said, "What do you mean you can't do it during the school holidays?" and he said, "I always go down to Littlehampton with Joy and the kids." I was thinking, there are trains Ronnie, but he just said, "No, I don't do this during the school holidays." He was totally balanced. He knew the value of having his wife and children and he knew he had to have this holiday. I think that's marvellous. He'd absolutely got it right and very few actors do.'

•••

Frost on Sunday was an hour-long show, which featured on average around five sketches of approximately two minutes in length. Despite boasting one of the most impressive writing teams in all of television, Ronnie felt that the material was not always as strong as it could be. And thus was a man named Gerald Wiley born.

'When you're doing 26 weeks you start to find bits that maybe you don't want to say, that aren't that good. So then we started interfering with it. This is where the Gerald Wiley story starts. We used to have four or five sketches a week, and five sketches of two minutes is much more difficult to find than one sketch of ten minutes, because they've all got to have an idea and a tag and funny lines in the middle. And we weren't getting enough stuff. I remember going to David at the end of one show, and it hadn't gone well, but David was always so optimistic, he said, "What a wonderful show that was." I said, "No it was bloody dreadful, David. It was terrible, the scripts were awful." Ronnie Corbett looked at me thinking I was sticking my neck out here and could be out on my ear. But I felt I had to say it, we must somehow do better that this.

'People weren't writing stuff for us. I decided that I would write something, I had a couple of ideas and I decided I would write them and send them in under an assumed name. I spoke to my agent who said, "You'll have to send them through me, I'll have to pretend I'm this man's agent as well." So I picked this name Gerald Wiley, because most people who have a pseudonym have a glamorous name like Rock Armstrong or something wonderful. So I picked a really ugly name that no-one would dream of choosing as their pseudonym. Then I said, "Supposing they want to see me?" And my agent said,

"I'll tell them you're a bit of a recluse, an older man I'll say, but you've seen the shows and thought you might try your hand." So in came the scripts and the producer said, "I've got two new scripts in from another writer, must be something to do with David. A man named Wiley." We laughed, I laughed, and we sat and read the scripts and he asked what we thought. Ronnie C said, "Well, they're not bad, I think we ought to try them." I was very pleased secretly. For the next three weeks we did sketches by Gerald Wiley, as well as other sketches.'

Ronnie had chosen to work under a pseudonym so the cast and crew would be brutally honest over the material and not try to cushion the performer/writer's ego. He found out how well this worked in the fourth week when Wiley's material was deemed to be well below par by all those concerned. 'I was pleased really because that was exactly what I wanted. I wanted complete anonymity. I wanted people to choose them only if they liked them. If Ronnie Corbett for instance came up and said, "I've written this sketch," and you didn't like it you'd say, "It's very good Ron, it's excellent," while knowing you didn't want to do it. I couldn't have that. So that's why I kept it up through the whole of the first series, which was about 26 episodes long, a long series. Sometimes they were rejected but most were done.' 'One sketch was about a ventriloquist,' recalls Ronnie Corbett, 'and it really died, the first Gerald Wiley to go down the pan. We came off and Ronnie said, "Well he let us down there didn't he?" and I was defending him, "Be fair he's done so many."'

•••

Keeping Wiley a secret from the rest of the *Frost* crew was taking Ronnie to ridiculous lengths, at one point instructing his agent to appease Frank Muir's desire to know more by setting up a meeting, then later calling back to cancel it. 'I went to see Frank for something else at the arranged time and he said, "What are you doing here?" I said I'd just come to ask him about something. He said he was expecting Gerald Wiley. I said, "What, you mean our writer? Oh, I'm sorry I shouldn't have interrupted." It was nearly a terrible mess, but it resolved itself.'

Ronnie C, too, was eager to know more about Wiley, and was keen to buy the rights to some of his sketches so he could use them in his act. He unknowingly contacted his colleague via the agent, an opportunity that Ronnie B couldn't help but exploit.

'We did a sketch called the "Doctor's Waiting Room" which featured Ronnie almost entirely, and he wanted to do it in a summer show, because he used to do summer shows and pantos. He said, "Do you think he'll sell it to me?" I said, "Write to him, you know he's with my agent anyway." The agent said, "I've had a letter from Ronnie Corbett asking if he can buy the sketch." I said, "Charge him £250 for it." So Ronnie came in and said, "He wants £250 for it." I told him, "That's rubbish. Don't pay it. It's not worth that."

'Anyway, it was Christmas time and I said to my agent, "Send it to Ronnie Corbett and say Mr Wiley would be very grateful if you would accept this sketch with his compliments, free of charge. Because you've done such marvellous work with his sketches and made them look so funny on screen." Ronnie came to me, "He's given it to me, he's given me the sketch." I said, "Oh, that's nice of him." A short while later, half a dozen crystal goblets arrived from Ronnie Corbett, all inscribed with the initials "GW" for "all the many sketches you've given me and for giving me that sketch". Of course I took them and said, "Well thanks for the glasses Ronnie," afterwards.'

As Ronnie Corbett confirms, after a while, the *Frost* crew began to doubt the existence of Wiley, convinced that he must be another writer.

'I suppose it was a comment and a judgement of how good the material was, that it must have been written by an expert. We knew it wasn't written by somebody who'd just started writing. There was more than a bit of quality about it. All our lives we've never done anything, any sketches that were just sent in by somebody unknown. But we thought it was good writing so he must be in writing of some sort. Then somebody ran a book to try and guess who he was. The most illustrious names were in there – Tom Stoppard, Noël Coward was still alive so his name was down there, Rattigan, Willis Hall, Keith Waterhouse, Frank Muir.

'Given that it came through his agent, Ronnie used to visualise this character as being possibly a novelist or short story writer or playwright, possibly gay; that was the rumour he put out. And we all fed on it. On a Sunday afternoon before the show Ronnie did come in to my dressing room and say to me, "I have to tell you. I'm Gerald Wiley."'

Wiley's true identity could remain a secret no longer.

'I wrote a letter – I had Wiley notepaper printed and everything – saying that Gerald Wiley would like to entertain the cast of *Frost on Sunday* at the Chinese restaurant opposite the studio. All the writers turned up as well because there were bets going on as to who he was. It said that Gerald Wiley would be there to meet you. Then the time came and Frank Muir was late. I was there already and Frank Muir came in and they all applauded him as he entered, and he said, "It's not me, it's not me." When everyone was there I got up and said, "Can I just say something before we start? It's me. I'm Gerald Wiley." And David Frost said, "It *is* you. I wondered about that."'

The majority of the *Frost* writers attended that illustrious dinner at the Chinese restaurant in Wembley, including Barry Cryer, who recalls the moment.

'I'd no idea who he was because we'd run out of theories and Ronnie Barker had already lied. He'd denied it. We knew Gerald Wiley's agent, but we didn't really tie it up that it was also Ronnie's agent. Frank Muir was the boss at the time so we thought it might be Frank Muir having a little bit of fun. Then we thought it was Tom Stoppard, who was with the same agent. Frank Muir actually popped into the Chinese restaurant and we all went, "Hey – it's you," but he said, "No I can't stay. I just popped in." Then Ronnie Barker stood up and said, "It's me," to cries of derision and "Sit down" and "Piss off". So he sat down. Then he got up again shortly afterwards and said "I'm sorry, no. It was me," and I stood up and said the toast is, "Nobody loves a smartarse." I didn't think it was Ron. I'd be lying if I said in hindsight I thought it was him. I must say though, I thought it was a very Freudian choice of pen name – "Wiley".'

Barker was pleased by the success of his subterfuge but in many ways regretted being revealed, even if he was the instigator of that revelation. 'Frost was the only one who had guessed it. It was out then. From that moment I wished it hadn't been out because with *The Two Ronnies* I was writing stuff and they were saying, "Oh that's very good," so I was back in the situation I didn't want to be in. If it [the mystery of Wiley's identity] had continued all my life it would've been better.'

In many ways, it did continue for all of Ronnie's life, though. Gerald Wiley lived on as a writer for *The Two Ronnies*, penning the vast majority of their serials. Other pseudonyms – Jonathan Cobbold, Jack Goetz, Dave Huggett and Larry Keith, Bob Ferris – all graced the works of Ronnie Barker. All were, of course, Ronnie himself. 'They were used for the public, because everyone in the biz knew it was me. I don't like "produced by Charlie Chaplin, music by Charlie Chaplin, starring Charlie Chaplin". Or Orson Welles. Orson Welles and Charlie Chaplin would put their names on things five times if they could. So that's why I used other names, just to put the ordinary punter off, who didn't really care who wrote a thing. I didn't really want to put my name on things more than once.'

After the earlier occasions writing for Glenn Melvyn and reworking the scripts for *Gaslight Theatre*, Ronnie felt instinctively that writing comedy material was something he was capable of doing.

'What I don't want to sound in any way is big-headed, but I never had to think about timing a laugh. I never came off a stage and thought I'd mistimed a line. I never had to do that because I said it how I say it. That's why it's always been difficult for me to take direction. That also applies to writing or rewriting comedy. People say that something could be better written. But I say, "Well, I can't write it any better because I've written it already and I've written it in the best way I think it can be." I was always like that in acting. If a director pointed out something like, "Maybe you've hit the wrong inflection," I can take something like that. But if somebody says, "You shouldn't be feeling what you're feeling there," I would say, "I can't change that." So I was a difficult person to direct in a way.'

...

Showbiz partnerships are often referred to as a marriage. The 'marriage' between Ronnie B and Ronnie C lasted for 22 years. In all that time, you'd expect there to have been arguments, falling outs, negotiations, reconciliations. According to both men though, this was never the case. It was a good, strong marriage, kept alive no doubt by the fact that they always had parallel, and equally successful, solo careers. They never fell out, although they came close once, when Ronnie C had been picked as a candidate for *This Is Your Life*.

During work on *Frost on Sunday*, a sketch appeared that featured an ordinary man who was convinced that he was going to be on *This Is Your Life*.

'He was an ordinary little man and Josephine Tewson played his wife, saying, "They're not after you, why would they be after you?" He'd say, "I don't know, I think they are after me." He had various funny explanations why he thought that – the man in the supermarket's looking at me oddly – all sorts of things. The tag of the sketch had him saying he was frightened to go out and her replying, "Don't be silly it's only Taffy coming round to see you, you're only going to the pub." There's a knock on the door and Eamonn Andrews comes in as Taffy and they go off down the pub. That sketch came in and I said to the producer that he had to have Eamonn Andrews doing it or the sketch was nothing. He was told Eamonn Andrews wouldn't do it, so we put the sketch aside.

'Then, a few weeks later, Thames Television said they wanted to do Ronnie Corbett's *This Is Your Life*, and asked, "How do you suggest we pick him up, how do you think we can work this?" Immediately I thought of this sketch and I told them about it and they said, "That sounds wonderful. Of course Eamonn will do it." It was the last of the series and they said this couldn't be better. The producer, Phil Casson, and I were in cahoots and said to Ronnie, "As it's the end of the series we thought we might try Eamonn again. I think he might do it because it's the end of the series and he owes David a few favours." So Ronnie said, "Fine, fine." But he was already cast in another sketch, because one of us played the main part and one of us played the feed part, we swapped round. Phil said, "As you're going to play the lead in the Eamonn Andrews sketch, Ronnie B will have to play the lead in the sketch you've been rehearsing." Now that was a sketch that Ronnie C was very fond of. And so he thought that somehow this was a trick to get him. He lost confidence or something.'

'He fiddled me into a role that was palpably not right for me,' confirms Corbett, 'and took that role for himself. I thought for the first time that this was a mistake, that I should be playing that role, and it was funnier. He was trying to do something funny here. I walked out of the room and came home and said to my wife Anne, "I'm being manipulated and I don't think it's right."'

'It was the only moment that we've ever had that was slightly worrying for him,' says Ronnie B. 'Not for me because I knew what we were up to. But he became distanced from me a bit. He said, "Why are they doing this?" And his wife said, "Oh, ride it out. You're doing so well together, the both of you, I'm sure he's not doing that." He was a bit distant. But he did it.

'We were friends all right, it wasn't a tiff or anything, but I could feel a little distancing. Came the day and we were sitting there and we were all ready and geared up and Ronnie went out to the canteen. When he came back he said, "There are Thames Television vans everywhere." I thought, "'Oh, Christ, why have they showed themselves?" But I said, "What does that mean?" He said, "I wonder if it's a *This Is Your Life*?" I said, "It must be David Frost. I'll go and find out." I went outside and saw the vans there and walked about for five minutes and went back and said, "It is, it's David. The rumour is that it's David Frost." Ronnie said, "Of course, it could be one of us," and that was the best moment I've ever had of thinking on my feet. I said, "No, it couldn't be one of us." Ronnie said, "Why not?" "Because the other one would know." And he said, "Oh yeah. Well that's a relief." I knew I must say something and he fell for it straight away. If he'd thought about it of course he could've said, "Well perhaps you do know," but he didn't. It was such a surprise for him. You could see it on the screen, he turns to me and says, "You bastard," which is, I

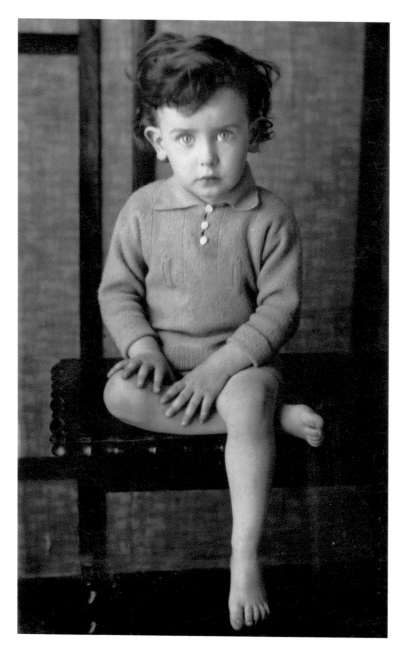

Ronald William George Barker takes an early opportunity to get familiar with the camera.

(*clockwise from top*)
Ronnie on the right, his father Leonard (known as Tim)
and Ronnie's elder sister Vera.
Ronald – a young actor in the making.
School photo, at the age of nine.

(from top)
Ronnie *(centre, seated)* with *(from left)* Bill Fraser, Walter Carr and Warren Mitchell in
'The £2000 A Year Man' episode of *Gaslight Theatre*.
The two Ronnies in drag to sing 'Mad Dogs and Englishmen' for *The Coward Revue*.

(from top)
Ronnie dons head waiter tux, opposite Frankie Vaughn,
in *Wonderful Things* (1958), Barker's film debut.
Ronnie builds alongside *Navy Lark* alumnus Leslie Phillips and
Stanley Baxter in 1963's *Father Came Too.*

Norman Stanley Fletcher as a younger man? Ronnie doing porridge for the first time in 1963's *The Cracksman*.

'I look up to him' – the always visually satisfying combination of Corbett, Barker and Cleese, from *The Frost Report* (1966).

(clockwise from top)
With friend and early mentor, Glenn Melvyn in an episode of *The Ronnie Barker Playhouse* (1968) entitled 'The Fastest Gun In Finchley'.
Ronnie takes a break in the control room after supervising another episode of *The Two Ronnies*.
Bigger movies; bigger stars – Ronnie with Van Heflin, in *The Man Outside* (1967).

(*clockwise from top left*)
Ronnie delivers a sermon from the pulpit in *The Ronnie Barker Yearbook* (1971).
Ronnie bares his Bottom – in a 1972 TV production of *A Midsummer Night's Dream*.
Ronnie and the late Roy Castle do their best Laurel and Hardy (lifelong heroes for Ronnie) in
'Another Fine Mess', an episode from 1973's *Seven of One* series.

think, the most frequent word used on *This Is Your Life*. They usually turn to somebody and say, "You bastard." That was wonderful. It was one of my proudest moments for thinking on my feet.'

Years later, plans to feature Ronnie B on the show would be scuppered when he found a piece of paper his wife had left lying around with an unknown phone number on. He dialled the number and was put through to a researcher for *This Is Your Life*.

•••

While working on *The Bargee* back in 1964, Ronnie decided to spend his time between set-ups writing a song. 'I had a lot of time sitting in a caravan and I suddenly thought I'd write an Edwardian music hall song. I don't know what made me do it, but I just started and I wrote one called "Not Too Tall and Not Too Short".'

Verse 1
I haven't been out with a girl for years –
Now maybe you think I'm slow.
No, that's not the reason: I'll tell you why –
I'm particular, you know.
Some girls are two a penny,
And others a halfpenny each.
I don't want them – the girl I seek
Must be a perfect peach.

Chorus
Not too tall and not too short,
Not too thick or thin;
She must come out where she should come out ,
And go in where she should go in;
She mustn't have much too much behind,
Or much too little in front;
If ever I have a girl again,
That's the girl I want.

Verse 2

I heard about a girl called May,
She sounded quite a catch.
'She's only five foot five,' they said,
'With golden hair to match.'
But when I met her in the woods
I knew I'd been sold a pup;
'Cos she was taller lying down
Than when she was standing up.

Repeat chorus
Not too tall... etc.

Verse 3

Then I met Rachel Rosenbloom,
An Irish girl from Wales.
She had a face like a summer's morn,
And a shape like a bag of nails.
'Could I only see your face,' I said
'I never more would roam.
So bring your dear sweet face to me,
And leave your body at home.'

Repeat chorus
Not too tall... etc.

Verse 4

At last I met my heart's desire,
A girl called Annie Moore.
She walked in beauty as the night,
With legs right down to the floor.
I pressed my suit, she creased her frock,
We had a splendid spree –
She was the girl I'd been looking for,
Now her husband is looking for me.

Repeat chorus
Not too tall... etc.

'I probably did it because I'm interested in that kind of thing and I collect old music and old song sheets, so I must have been thinking of that and I wrote three verses and a chorus in about four hours. I showed it to Galton and Simpson and I remember Ray Galton said, "Not bad, not bad, it's all right." I thought, "Maybe it's all right, maybe it's very good," I didn't know. I started to write and eventually I wrote seven songs.'

These included such titles as 'They Tell Me There's A Lot Of It About', 'Billy Pratt's Bananas' and 'Black Pudding March'. During his stint on *Frost on Sunday*, Ronnie showed some of these to Laurie Holloway, the show's musical arranger. 'I told him about the songs and he asked if I had got the music for them. I said, "I've got it in my head." So he and I sat down and put the dots on paper, he wrote them out and said, "Have you got any more?" I wrote another seven so we had 14 and he suggested we could make an album.' The result was titled *A Pint of Old and Filthy*.

'The title indicates that some of them were old and some of them were filthy. Or both. I don't know how successful they were, but they were published and I enjoyed it very much. A couple of people have subsequently asked if they can do the numbers in their act.'

This was not Ronnie's only foray into recording. 'I did another record later called *Ronnie Barker's Unbroken British Record*, that contained a lot of *Frost* material and *Two Ronnies* material. I enjoyed that. I enjoy most things. There's not much I didn't enjoy really. Being in a play for a long time is about the only thing I didn't enjoy about the business, and filming in the freezing January weather at midnight. And lying in the gutter in Doncaster. I think that's the coldest I've ever been in my life. With a dustbin on my head, playing Arkwright who had fallen off a ladder going up to Nurse Gladys's room. I lay there for a quarter of an hour because it was very difficult to light. All the local people in their houses were trying to sleep. That was one of the unpleasant things, but there were very few.'

•••

David Frost and his Paradine Production company was eager to nurture the talents he had discovered on his own shows. The next two years were to prove a remarkably prolific period for Barker, introducing various characters and further developing a number of comedy ideas that would stay with him. He also celebrated the arrival of another Barker when Joy gave birth to their third child, Adam, on 29 December 1967.

In 1968, his first top billing on television, *The Ronnie Barker Playhouse*, took a leaf out of Jimmy Edwards's book and featured Ronnie in six separate one-off half-hour sitcoms, each in many ways a potential pilot for a future series. It was yet another opportunity for Ronnie to show his considerable range, playing among others, a Welsh champion reciter of verse, an aged aristocrat, an escapologist, a bashful Scotsman and a silent monk. Two of the episodes were penned by the *Foreign Affairs* team of Mortimer and Cooke, three of them by the playwright Alun Owen, one of which – 'Ah, There You Are' – finally put a name to Barker's eccentric aristo character he had been playing in various guises since childhood – Lord Rustless.

•••

Ever since *A Home of your Own* in 1964, Ronnie had been toying with the idea of writing a similar dialogue-free film himself. The result was 1970's *Futtock's End*.

'You didn't think about it every day or every week or every month, but occasionally I thought that I really must write one of those. I'm sure there's a lot that one can do without any words and I like complicated things. It was a very complicated thing to write. Someone said to me that it must have been very easy because I didn't have to write any dialogue. But it was the hardest thing to write because you have to lace things together. It was a very thick script even though there wasn't a word spoken. I started by writing all sorts of characters and then each one had to have a line on what they were like and what they did, and then they all went off for a weekend and combined.'

The result was a very funny film – Prince Charles counts it as one of his favourites – that allowed Ronnie to indulge his love of filming. And, of course, it gave him yet another chance to play with what was essentially the character of Lord Rustless (although he is referred to as 'General Futtock' in the movie). The film was written in part for actor Michael Hordern, whom Ronnie knew from a TV advert they had done together for tinned soup.

'We were Mr Crosse and Mr Blackwell. That was the only time I'd met him before that. He was a lovely fellow, very funny, lovely sense of humour and loved to joke. I wrote *Futtock's End* for him and I sent him the script. "I've written this for you, Michael." He said, "I can't do it Ronnie, I'm going to play Lear, I must prepare for Lear and I can't do any other work. But send the script, I'm sure it'll be funny to read." He rang me and said, "I've got to do this." I said, "What about Lear?" He said, "Well naturally I'm doing Lear but I think I can study it," and in fact I've got a home video somewhere of him sitting around learning his lines for Lear where we shot it up in Stanmore at W.S. Gilbert's house.'

The format of the almost silent movies – or the 'grumble and grunt movies' as Ronnie refers to them – was something he would go back to years later in *The Two Ronnies*, making two further films, *The Picnic* (1975) and *By the Sea* (1982).

'I've always loved comedy where everyone in the audience knows what's happened but the actors don't. There's one scene in *Futtock's* where they're all having tea in the garden and the maid brings a plate of cakes and as she puts the tray down one of the cakes falls off and the dog picks it up and runs off with it into the woods. Then a boy grabs the cake and throws it over the wall and it lands in the water. He takes it out, and wrings it out, then throws it again and the dog runs back, drops it, the maid sees it on the floor, picks it up and puts it back on the tray, from where Rustless picks it up and puts it back on his plate. And no-one knows what has happened except the audience.'

In his desire to ensure that his movie would be as good as it could be, *Futtock's End* saw Ronnie all but co-directing with Bob Kellett. 'I know I had a reputation for being very pernickety. "Oh, he wants to do it again." But I knew the reason I had to do it again would be because the audience would see if you didn't do it right. They don't care about the perspective of the sound, what they care about is the person in the foreground. They used to grumble, "He's a bloody nuisance he is." I know they did that because people have told me. But you've got to get it right.'

•••

Back with his Lordship, Rustless (and returning him his rightful name), Ronnie spun him off into his next series, *Hark at Barker*. Running for two seasons in 1969 and 1970, *Hark at Barker* used Rustless as host for a look at a variety of topics from 'females' to 'Britain's military', from 'communications' to 'cooking'. From his country seat of Chrome Hall, his Lordship would expand on the given topic each week, allowing for a series of sketches featuring Ronnie in a number of roles, upwards of fifty or so per series.

'He would be speaking to the camera and he'd say, "Today I want to talk about transport today. I mean it's absolutely a mess . . ." He'd start by saying something like, "My great uncle used to be a bus driver . . ." then you would cut to a sketch of me as a bus driver, or something. The sections were quite lengthy, they weren't just links. I used to think the sketches were almost an intrusion, they almost got in the way of the daft lecture that this man was giving, although I wanted to do them at the time. But this half-hour was a visit to Chrome Hall and the person who owned the place spoke to you about his life. And I thought that the sketches may have intruded a bit.'

Sticking as always with the people he knew and could rely on, Josephine Tewson was added to the cast as Miss Bates, the secretary who was hopelessly in love with Rustless, not that his Lordship ever noticed. Among the other characters was a wizened old gardener by the name of Dithers, a character who would later be played by David Jason, when his Lordship returned to television. 'David wasn't in the first series because the character was simply a lawn mower crashing by,' explains Barker. 'Then you once saw him go by the French windows, but it was always reported in the show, what he was doing.'

•••

Having played around with Rustless for two series, Ronnie was keen to get back to the Playhouse format. The result was *Six Dates with Barker*, Ronnie's last-ever series for ITV. Looking back he reflects that his fondness for trying out different characters every week in this format may well have been inspired by previously working with Jimmy Edwards in a similar manner.

'I wanted to try out different characters. I can only be a character actor because I'm not a leading man. I never looked like a leading man, I wasn't tall and good-looking like a leading man. So I will always be a character actor. I always have been. I was certainly the leading man in *Porridge* and *Open All Hours*. So although I'm a character, I am the leading man. Jimmy was exactly like me really, he was playing all these different characters as a character man, but he was the lead in the show.'

Once again, the show featured six unconnected tales, this time hinged on the fact that each took place at a specific point in history. These ranged from 1899 with Spike Milligan's 'The Phantom Raspberry-Blower of Old London Town' ('which we later expanded into a whole *Two Ronnies* serial, which I wrote most of, using Spike's original script') to the year 2774 with 'All the World's a Stooge'. Which was a curious future vision of a world where humour has become a dominant religion. The latter was penned by Gerald Wiley. 'That starred Michael Hordern and me and featured the very first performance ever of Lesley-Anne Down. She was a 16-year-old child, really.'

Former *Frost* alumnus John Cleese also contributed an episode, 'Come In and Lie Down', one of the few examples of Cleese's solo writing. In it, Barker played a psychiatrist attending to a patient (played by Michael Bates) who is so repressed that he pretends not to be a patient but the window cleaner instead. It has been remarked that the character played by Bates exhibited a lot of the traits that would later characterise Cleese's most famous TV character, Basil Fawlty. More importantly however, *Six Dates with Barker* served the purpose of cementing Ronnie's relationship with the man who, alongside Ronnie C, would become the most significant working partner of his career.

•••

Bernard McKenna's script 'The Odd Job' dealt with a suicidal husband who employs an itinerant to help him go through with his own death, then backs out, only to find the other guy likes to see a job finished. (It was later remade as a movie starring *Python*'s Graham Chapman.) When it came to casting, the producer, Humphrey Barclay, suggested using David Jason, fresh from the TV success of *Do Not Adjust Your Set*. 'I knew David from the show I'd done with him,' says Barclay. 'And I knew he had a remarkable range and a gift for characters, in a very similar way to Ronnie. So putting them together just seemed natural.'

'Certainly from that moment when we first met, it was wonderful,' recalls Ronnie. 'We became soul mates. It's strange because with both him and Ronnie Corbett I've had such a connection, at the same time, really. It's extraordinary. Always work with little men, you see. It really gelled with him.'

Jason recalls landing the role in 'The Odd Job'. 'I was away on holiday on the South Coast. I got a message to call my agent who said they were doing one of the Ronnie Barker things and he was keen to know if I wanted to play a character in it. They wanted to know as soon as possible so they sent the script down to me and I read it and got on the phone instantly and yes, of course, I'd love to do it. There were two super parts and I said, "I expect Ronnie wants me to play the husband does he?" They said, "No he wants you to play Clive, the loony." But I said, "No, you must have got it wrong, that's the funnier part, that's the best part." So I spoke to the producer, "I'd love to do it but I just wanted to clarify something, they're saying they want me to play the odd job man but that's the best part. Ronnie must be doing that, surely." He said, "No, Ronnie wants you to play it," which was amazing. I just couldn't believe it. Then when I played it, it sealed our fate a bit. Ronnie and I so enjoyed working together. I could never understand why he asked me to play what I considered the best part, though.'

Barker and David Jason would continue working together until Ronnie's retirement, having clearly found in each other a rapport and performing relationship that delighted both men.

'There was no finer comedy actor in the country than Ronnie Barker, so when Ronnie Barker said something, you listened,' Jason says about their early joint appearances.

'I was fortunate enough to recognize his talent, because I'd been doing a lot of comedy myself and I could see how far ahead of the game he was, and I thought if I look and inwardly digest, I might just learn something from this guy. With that sort of trust came an ability to enjoy each other's work because he knew that I had instant timing, which is something that Ronnie respected and admired quite a lot because he had it. His timing was so specific that he needed someone who had equally good timing in order to get his material to work. I think what I recognized in Ronnie was his brilliance as a comedy character actor. There weren't many about, there were a lot of comics, but Ronnie was a one-off.'

•••

Although acting as a series of six pilots, *Six Dates with Barker* didn't initially yield another series. However, 17 years later it would come good when Ronnie took Hugh Leonard's script 'The Removals Person' – the tale of a short-sighted furniture removals man named Fred on Coronation Day, 1937 – and transformed it into *Clarence*, his final sitcom. 'That was the first of the *Six Dates with Barker*. He was called Fred then but later I changed it and we used that show as the basis for the first episode of *Clarence*. Jo Tewson was in it the first time and she was in it 20 years later as well. It looked silly to give someone else the writing credit so I bought it from Hugh. The script was the same, we altered one or two lines. Emma Thompson's mother, Phyllida Law, was also in it. In essence, as *Clarence* it was exactly the same. I wrote the rest of the series [penned under his pseudonym of Bob Ferris] in Australia in 1986.'

•••

Most people who have starred in a string of successful TV shows don't get sacked. But the powers that be weren't happy with David Frost, and while they were keen to keep the two Ronnies on, Frost had them contracted to his own company. So sacked they were. It was to prove the most fortuitous of firings. 'I think David Frost was more sacked than we were,' remembers Ronnie Corbett. 'Paradine was sacked. I think there was some political in-fighting between [executive] Stella Richman and David, something like that. Ronnie and I were co-hosting the BAFTA awards live from the Palladium and there was this technical hold-up and we are led to believe that we held the fort quite cleverly while they were off the air and kept the whole thing going until we got back on the air. I don't remember it being particularly earth-shattering, but that is the evening that Bill Cotton asked if there was any chance of getting those two for the BBC.

'Stella Richman couldn't continue with David's contract because of a difference of opinion or something, but she wanted us to stay. We said, "We're sorry but we can't Stella" – she was an authoritative figure – "because we are under contract to Paradine Productions," which was David's company. She said, "I guess it's farewell chaps, we'll have to say goodbye." We said goodbye on the Friday and meanwhile Bill Cotton had been saying, "I think I can get those two fellas." He'd no idea we'd been sacked and thought he snatched us from the jaws of ITV by offering us a contract to do *Two Ronnies* shows. We said, "Um, we'll think about it Bill," but were rubbing our hands with glee. I told him that a while back when we were inducted into the Royal Television Society's Hall of Fame. I was sitting with Bill and I told him this story and he laughed. He thought he'd pinched us from ITV and in fact we'd just been sacked. Timing was everything.'

CHAPTER 4

Good Evening. In a Packed Show Tonight...

Sitting on old boxes on their sunny allotment, the two slow-thinking gardeners ruminated over life and its endless complications.

Ronnie B: You know old Cyril Harris, with the one eye?

Ronnie C: Yes. You don't see much of him lately.

Ronnie B: No, well he don't see much of us either.

Ronnie C: Where did you see him then?

Ronnie B: Up the pictures. He went up to the girl in the box office and says, 'With one eye, I should think you'd let me in for half price.' But she wasn't having it.

Ronnie C: Oh... Did he have to pay full price?

Ronnie B: He had to pay double.

Ronnie C: Double? Why was that then?

Ronnie B: She reckoned it would take him twice as long to see the picture.

Ronnie C: Oh...

Messrs Barker and Corbett were now seen as a pair. They were never a double act, never totally reliant on one another in the traditional sense of a double act, the kind that television loved so much. Some of the most successful mainstream comedy on the small screen came in the form of double acts. Before the advent of wall-to-wall kids' TV, on Saturday mornings children in the 1960s and early '70s were still sitting down to watch the world's most famous double act – Laurel and Hardy. Mike and Bernie Winters, two brothers from Islington, north London, had been appearing together on television since the mid-1950s presenting a variety-based show with comedy sketches interspersed between other acts. Morecambe and Wise had been doing much the same thing, appearing in their own TV show since 1961. In 1971, the year that *The Two Ronnies* TV show first appeared, a double act called Little and Large won the TV talent show, *Opportunity Knocks*. Sid Little and Eddie Large would go on to appear in their own TV show for no less than 14 years.

•••

Television loved double acts and Ronnie was well aware of this. He knew the value of a well-matched – which usually meant mismatched in terms of size, shape or intellect – pairing. As a child he had, after all, listened to one of the all-time great variety double acts, Sheffield cousins Jimmy Jewell and Ben Warriss, in their radio show *Up the Pole*. Warriss played the slick, hard-nosed straight man and Jewell was the simple, gullible one – poles apart but rigidly set in character. This was not to be the way for the pairing of Barker and Corbett.

'We were a pair and all we needed then was a show,' says Barker. 'They were looking for a name and someone in the office said that as we were always called two Ronnies, why not call it *The Two Ronnies*, so we did. It's the simplest title in the world. We were a twosome already and remained it.'

'Obviously we knew them as the two Rons,' adds Barry Cryer, 'but they didn't become *The Two Ronnies* until a few years later when we'd all gone to ITV and then we all came back to the BBC again. It was a natural title.'

•••

A noted collector of paper ephemera, Barker even examined the nature of the name further. 'About 50 years ago there were two people called the two Leslies, but that was the only "twos" I've ever found. I collect Edwardian postcards and I've got one of an act that says "The Ronnies" on it – it's a man and a woman. They were German I think, but the card was in English and I don't know what they did – whether they sang or whatever – but it was very funny to find that.'

•••

The Two Ronnies was devised as a show comprised of a collection of opening news items, sketches and comedy-musical numbers, for two already established and very popular entertainers, both of whom had already proved their worth individually, but whose combination not only seemed to work on screen, but also off screen for the audience. It was to prove to be an enormous hit for the BBC for many years to come.

History already tends to view *The Two Ronnies* as a 'cosy' show; after all, *Monty Python's Flying Circus* was a contemporary and was generally seen as ground-breaking and form-bending in all manner of ways. But it's easy to forget just how innovative the Ronnies were in their day. It remains just about the only other television show that all of the *Python* team actually wrote for, indeed Cleese occasionally appeared during the first season.

'*Python* was an explosion,' says Barker, whose own show followed less than a year and a half later.

'I used to always think it was a cop-out when they couldn't think of an end and someone used to come on and say, "This is very silly and it's gone on long enough." That was a bit of a cop-out, and nowadays with things like *The Fast Show* you just have a character that's funny who comes on. In those days, in *The Two Ronnies*, you had to have a reason to be funny. You had to have something in the script to hang your hat on. It was more of a rigid format, although *Python* broke through that, even though something like the parrot sketch was still an ordinary sketch, it had funny lines, it was a funny situation. It drifted a lot. In the first series it was almost *The Two Ronnies* with different actors. It found its own way as it went; and Terry Gilliam's cartoons helped that.'

One of the Pythons, Eric Idle, with his tongue firmly in his cheek, recalls how different it was writing for the Ronnies. 'If we thought a sketch was a bit old or hackneyed or not very funny we'd just send it to *The Two Ronnies* or Roy Hudd. It went off to them. Dick Vosburgh's phrase to me was always, "Nothing's wasted." I always remembered that.'

•••

There's also a tendency to bracket Ronnie B and Ronnie C with Morecambe and Wise. But Eric and Ernie had started their television career more than a decade beforehand, their background was one of music hall and summer seasons. They were in essence generationally removed from the Ronnies as performers. Ronnie Barker had come from straight acting and had never performed a comedy act as such in his life; Ronnie Corbett was a stand-up, but he was equally at home in London nightclubs as he was at the end of the pier.

Corbett was aware of their differences, but says neither of them ever saw it as an issue.

'We weren't consciously thinking of it. I can't remember any debate over the parts we played in the sketches. It usually stuck out a mile as to what we would do and what we wouldn't do, and we didn't seem to mind either way what we did. It's usually the case that comics are the best feeds anyway. If anything what gently emerged was that Ronnie B was going to be a character comedian, because he had the facility to play parts better than me because he had a range of voices, but also because deep down he always liked to cover himself up a bit, whereas I was quite pleased to be nearly myself. So that's how it has been throughout our lives together. I don't remember an evolution going on but I remember the bond strengthening. We would always agree on what jokes were good enough and which weren't. That was happening, certainly, we were taking more interest in the material and judging it and worrying about it.'

The big differences between the Ronnies and other double acts was that both men worked extensively on solo projects (you never saw Ernie without Eric), but more importantly, in terms of their shows together, both were comics and both were straight men. They could feed or they could deliver, equally, often reversing the roles between them. It's impossible to imagine Ernie without Eric, or Laurel without Hardy, but not Ronnie without Ronnie. 'We were two character men really,' insists Barker. 'It's very difficult to say what a comic is – as opposed to a comedy actor or a character actor. I suppose the definition is the man who gets all the laughs is the comic. Or he works alone and feeds himself. But we didn't really fall into that category. You either called us character actors or you called us comic actors, who worked much better together. I suppose there weren't other people doing it when we started so it was to that extent unusual. But it was an acted piece.'

•••

The format of their show drew heavily not only on the standards of television variety, but also on the work of the *Frost* shows. The musical numbers that became the finale of each show had begun life back on *Frost on Sunday*, courtesy of writer Dick Vosburgh. Ronnie B's monologues had also started on *Frost*, while their opening and closing news items were a direct lift from *Frost*'s 'Continuous Developing Monologue'. 'We borrowed shamelessly from David Frost's clipboard jokes, with his permission, as we were under his aegis then, because we were contracted to Paradine Productions for the first five series of *Ronnies*. The news desk was the thing. I don't think you could name a comedian now who hasn't done news items. But we were the first to do them, apart from David who had a clipboard to announce the news in the *Frost Report* and *Frost on Sunday*. Then we had the serial in the middle and then we had the musical thing at the end. The first one we ever did was "Grouch Marx and Mae West". Dick Vosburgh wrote that, then he did a complete change and did the "Short and Fat Minstrels". The pieces were always based on something that existed.'

•••

The Black and White Minstrel Show had existed for almost twenty years on British television. It was based on what had been known as 'Nigger Minstrel' entertainment in the music halls of the nineteenth and early twentieth century. The act had been brought to the UK by a British entertainer of the late nineteenth century. He had travelled to the States and seen the strange spectacle of white men, 'blacked up', singing songs about America's Deep South. The Black and White Minstrel TV troupe were primarily white entertainers who wore blackface make-up with white lips and eyes in a bizarrely stylized representation of black performers. Their elaborate song and dance routines – often, but not solely, based on Dixie or songs of the Deep South – were interspersed with appearances by comedian/comperes such as Leslie Crowther (who wouldn't wear blackface make-up). The show was so popular that it ran from 1958 until 1978, regularly pulling in UK TV audiences of 16–18 million. At one point, the stage version even found its way into the *Guinness Book of Records* for having been seen by the largest number of people. The whole idea of the Black and White Minstrels would correctly be considered far too socially insensitive and politically incorrect ever to be made today. *The Two Ronnies* version would be considered equally unacceptable, for different reasons. 'We were blacked up so you could never do it now. We had to have a casting session with all these enormous men and women to play the fat minstrels and all these tiny people to play the short ones.' The opening number for the 'Short and Fat Minstrels' was sung to the tune of Robert E. Lee as the female dancers filed on to the stage.

> *Fat men*:   See them shuffling along,
> Hear them singing this song,
> Just bring a big pal,
> A fat gal,

> If she's fat and heavy,
> Get down on the levee.

Short men: (Will you) let those little gals through,
    And if they're small we'll take two.

All: We're short and fat but,
    That won't stop us singing,
    All these songs we're bringing to you.

Swannee River, of course, also featured heavily:

Ronnie B: Way down upon the Swannee River,
    I met Kate Maguire.
    Two onions and a pound of liver,
    That's how she won my desire.

    She knew just how to cook my dinner,
    Oh! Shut my mouth –
    No chance of ever getting thinner,
    Down in the deep-fried South.

    All the steaks were rich and fatty,
    All the beans were tinned.
    That's why my heart is burning ever,
    That's why I'm Gone With The Wind.

The show was not as anarchic as *Monty Python* but was tailored for a more mainstream audience while still shying away from the kind of format adopted by those other, more traditional, TV double acts. 'It was different,' says Ronnie. 'It wasn't just a sketch show. We got the format from the first episode and we talked a lot about how we'd do it beforehand.' 'We sat down and worked out between us a running order for the first show and it never altered,' concurs Ronnie Corbett.

'That's because we were, in a way, so knowledgeable about ourselves, having been around so long, we were experienced, we knew our limitations and our skills. With the opening news items we realized that it was a peculiar position with us that we could talk to an audience, but we couldn't talk to each other as people in front of an audience. Not like Eric and Ernie; we couldn't direct jokes at each other, only at them. "It's goodnight from me and it's goodnight from him," at the end, that was the biggest reference. We knew we couldn't talk to each other that way. So the news item piece meant that we were together in a slightly anaesthetized way, but we were also slightly separate. We knew that Ronnie B would not be himself but he would want to have his solo spot so he had his character man and all those spokesmen. And, because I had started doing it on *The Corbett Follies*, I would do my monologue piece and that would happen in the chair. And because we'd already found very good parody writers, we'd have a musical number to close the show – a finale. Also a film item in the middle because we had facilities to film and we could both act roles, and the rest of the time it would be sketches. So it took on the pattern of all these disparate items and the format never altered really because we knew what we could and couldn't do.

'I think we weren't as different as we looked. People think of the little one and the big fat one, but in fact we were quite similar in our styles. Ronnie always had more vocal skills because he'd been such an excellent character actor in repertory and he is a very good voice man. I wasn't so much that, but we're both pretty good actors, that was the basis of it. I think people see me more as a sort of variety comic doing patter and jokes. But I can also act in the same way as Jack Benny or Bob Hope can act. We could do that and in a way music hall comics in this county hadn't been that good actors before. So we were character actor-comedians really. Basically our skills were very similar, we only looked different.'

'Ronnie Corbett I think to this day was vastly underrated,' adds Barry Cryer, who also wrote for the Ronnies' show, 'because he was a wonderful foil for Ronnie Barker. But Ronnie Corbett was always basically Ronnie Corbett, that's what the comics do, while Ronnie Barker was the man of a thousand faces.'

Quick to point out their independence, in the weeks before the show debuted on the BBC in 1971, Ronnies B and C made their presence known in two one-off specials – *The Ronnie Barker Yearbook*, with special guest Ronnie Corbett, and *Ronnie Corbett in Bed*, with special guest Ronnie Barker.

The idea of branding them as distinctively separate first came from the omnipresent Paradine Productions. 'It might have been a political thing to say, "Here is Ronnie Barker in a show; here is Ronnie Corbett in a show – now we're going to put them together." Whereas Eric and Ernie you see always worked together. That's the only reason we did that.'

'Certainly I remember feeling quite strongly about that,' Ronnie Corbett agrees. 'It introduced us to the BBC as two people. And then we came together. Plus we said we wouldn't do chat shows together, or interviews together. It was in a way prophetic because I had had my independence for too long before Ronnie came along. I was more vaudeville than Ronnie, therefore I was guarding that bit as well. And the more he had successes with *Open All Hours* and *Porridge* the more it insulated us from being bunged together. But when Ronnie did decide to retire, as careful and protective as we had been of our individuality, I still had – not a serious rocky period – but people were saying, "What will he do now on his own?" I had done six series of *Sorry!* and that came to an end at the same time. Suddenly I was chopped down in mid-life in terms of quite a lot of my work. Had I not been so secure in myself it might have affected me more seriously. So it's a good thing we did do that. And it hopefully allowed Ronnie to retire whenever he wanted to, which he did, without feeling "Christ, what will happen to little Ron?"'

•••

The Ronnie Barker Yearbook was scripted by Gerald Wiley, Dick Vosburgh, Eric Idle, John Cleese and Graham Chapman. Cleese also made an appearance, which was more than could be said for the first two of months of the year. 'It's another reason why I was annoyed with Jimmy Gilbert. He was executive producer of the *Ronnie Barker Yearbook* and obviously it started with January, but he said he didn't think we needed the first two items. I said, "You can't cut them!" He said, "Oh yes you can, you can go straight into March." The titles read, "The Ronnie Barker Yearbook – January/February/March", and I thought it looked dreadful. January was something about skating and it consisted of very fast shots of lots of professional skaters falling over on the ice. I thought it would build. It would be funny the faster you cut it. But he wouldn't have it. I think somebody may have whispered in his ear, that it would take us a fortnight to do that. Nowadays you could do it a lot quicker.

'Then Ronnie did *Ronnie Corbett in Bed*. And that was before Madonna. Barry Cryer suggested a good title for it – *Corbett in Orbit* – but Ronnie wouldn't have it.'

•••

Ever since *Irma La Douce*, Ronnie has always taken great care with his contracts, partly to avoid once again finding himself trapped in a long run of anything, but also partly to avoid typecasting.

'We were contracted to David Frost and Paradine Productions, for what I consider to be slightly too long a period, five years. As to the show, we were contracted only show by show. But we knew before we finished year one we were going to do year two.'

•••

When asked to define what made the combination of Barker and Corbett so successful, the former has a few firm thoughts on the subject – but he did have over 20 years to ponder it. 'Fat man/little man,' he says simply, before elaborating. 'You were a straight man, that was the point. I was the straight man sometimes, he was the straight man other times. You never get a double act where two people are being funny at the same time. It would be very difficult writing a sketch with all tags. Even with the Yokels, you've got to have someone say "How's that then?" So when you say, "I've got 200 more bones in my body than you have," someone's got to say, "How's that then?" And you reply, "I had a kipper for me breakfast." You got to have a feed, even someone nodding "Oh really" – that's feeding. So one of us fed and one of us did the jokes. And in a sketch, it swaps over. I would say that joke, then he would say, "I don't eat breakfast" and I would say, "Why?" So I was feeding him the next joke. We fed each other and scored laughs off each other in the sketch. So it was two comics and two straight men.'

•••

With Gerald Wiley's name gracing the credits, right from the off it was clear that Ronnie B was also a power to be reckoned with behind the camera. Wiley wrote all of the show's serials, from the first – a costume drama parody titled 'Hampton Wick' – through to such well-loved classics as 'The Worm that Turned', a futuristic vision of a world where all men were forced to wear dresses and Diana Dors was calling the shots. Dors was at one time branded the 'English Marilyn Monroe' because of her undoubted sex appeal but had, in fact, begun her career long before Marilyn. She had appeared in her first movie in the 1940s as teenage starlet (having changed her name from Mavis Fluck) and went on to become a household name in the UK right up to her death from cancer in 1984. 'The Worm that Turned' relied a great deal on Dors, who played the Commander, making fun of her own former image as a pin-up girl.

'We had a lot of stick about that from the feminists. The idea was suggested by something I read, and the great thing was you had to make all the men absolutely butch. They had to look straight, so they were allowed to wear moustaches, and they just had to wear dresses as a sort of badge really. That was the fun of it. If they'd all been camping about it wouldn't have worked. But we did get a lot of adverse response from a small minority.'

The opening scene in the first episode set the tone as Diana Dors addressed her loyal followers and Ronnie C, as a man called Janet, fussed around in a frock serving coffee.

> *Commander:* Now, ladies, it has been suggested by certain opposition
> factions that men should once again revert to wearing
> trousers and I can see that to you as well as to me this
> whole concept is unthinkable. They must be kept in
> frocks if we are to retain the control which we have
> fought so hard to achieve. Trousers have always been
> the symbol of the male overlord. Here in England,
> trousers were traditionally always worn by the head of
> the family. In those olden days, all women had an image
> of their perfect man.

> *Janet:* Nice strong black one for you, wasn't it?

Also revived was 'The Phantom Raspberry-Blower of Old London Town', adapted by Wiley from Spike Milligan's old script from *Six Dates with Barker*. Milligan did not write directly for *The Two Ronnies*, or for anyone else, but was by now making waves with his own *Q* TV series on the BBC. The first of the *Q* series had appeared in 1969 just before the first of the *Monty Python* series and had the Pythons worried because Milligan had adopted the same kind of unstructured, anarchic format that they favoured. 'The Phantom Raspberry-Blower' had been abandoned at the BBC until Ronnie found it 'lying on a shelf'. 'I thought the younger viewers, especially the kids, would love it, so I thought that would make a serial. I added lots of bits.'

Two of the Ronnies' most successful creations featured in several of their serials over the years – the bumbling detective team of Charley Farley (Corbett) and Piggy Malone (Barker).

'It's been done since: *The Detectives* (a 1990s comedy series starring Jasper Carrott and Robert Powell) was the same thing. I just thought of the names and the chaps. There again, Piggy Malone is Fletcher really, slightly different, he gets on his high horse occasionally, but more or less they're the same man. He's selfish and lazy and Charley Farley is more industrious and keen. I never know when someone asks where the characters come from. They're in your head or you bring them into your head. Sometimes you think about a specific person, but they just appeared.'

In the initial years, Ronnie reckoned he was writing up to 75 per cent of the show each week. 'I wasn't very slow as a writer. I remember writing a *Two Ronnies* sketch we did about an amateur play, I went into my room at 9 o'clock and I came out at 5 o'clock with it completely finished and that was about a 20-minute piece, but it had a lot of physical stuff in it that needed working out. I used to write the musical numbers we did at the end, often in a day. And I might write two sketches a day. But I suppose that was when I was flowing.'

There was the odd occasion when he felt that wasn't the case. Having always written alone, Ronnie considered taking on a partner. 'I tried with Barry Cryer once. This is when I had a sort of mental block when I gave up smoking in '72. We were into the second series of *Two Ronnies* and without a cigarette, I couldn't do anything. It took me about a year to get over it. I used to suck one of those plastic menthol cigarette things. So I asked Barry to come in one day, I think it was to work on the serial I was stuck on, and we had a great time, but at the end there were just two lines on the paper. Afterwards I rang him up and I said, "It's just not going to work, I can't write with people." And I've never tried since. It's something to do with having to discuss a point or argue a point, I think, that I find very time-consuming and not very effective. I let my mind do that, let it discuss things, is this line right? Are we going in the right direction? No, we're not, perhaps we are, no that won't work, no, that's out. So all that can be done in the time it takes to say it, more or less. But writing with someone else, you've got to say all that and he's got to put his argument against it and it's a very difficult thing to define the reason why you feel you should write on your own. It may be, dare I say it, that you think you know better than anyone else. It's a very arrogant thing to say, but it might be true that I think I know better. If you're working with someone else, you have to defer, to a certain extent, to their reasoning and their wishes and therefore their lines. You can't say, "No, that's no good, that's no good." Out of politeness and trying to work together, you'd accept stuff that probably you really didn't think in your heart of hearts was right. How do you know that both people think it's funny? I think it's funny and you say it's funny, you may be not thinking it's funny, but you say it is because there's two of us writing and you wouldn't want to offend.'

•••

One of the key elements of the show's success was the way in which it presented the two performers, linked by their forenames, in an individual light. Ronnie B would make a habit of presenting himself as the spokesman for all and sundry, delivering countless mono-logues that seem to redefine the phrase 'verbal dexterity'. 'I love language. I always have.'

Ronnie C meanwhile had a chair that became a thing of legend, and every weekly would deliver a sterling monologue – in a very dif-ferent style from Barker's – that would appear effortlessly casual, but was indeed a wonderful reinvention of the stand-up's art. 'A man named Spike Mullins wrote them for the first seven series,' recalls Barker in his unofficial role as series editor, 'and then David Renwick wrote them after that. It was difficult to find people to write them. They were always over-long and Ronnie would cut them himself, and then do them, and they were over-long when he did them and they would be cut down again. I never cut them because I thought it wasn't really up to me. The director cut them, he would consult with Ronnie of course.

'Spike Mullins was a curious character, a very funny man, and he had a very whimsical turn of phrase which Ronnie used to use in the early stuff. You find phrases which you'd think were not very funny but were amusing, whimsical. And Ronnie retained the best joke from every week in his stage act – he took one joke every week and he's got an hour and a half of marvellous stuff now.

'When he did them I might very rarely suggest a change, a line or two, but very rarely. We rehearsed Tuesday to Friday, learning all the sketches; then we were in the studio on Saturday and we'd tape it on Sunday.'

•••

Despite his off-screen predominance as a writer, one thing Barker never wrote was the show's trademark opening news items. 'We used to read about 200 every week to pick 20. And sometimes it was difficult picking 20, because we were very ruthless over it and if one of us wasn't sure about something, it was out. So we'd reduce the 200 to 20 and those 20 we would use and some of those would get cut. We used to get down to about 14 or 16. We never knew who'd written anything, so no favouritism went on.' Those decisions were always made equally between Barker and Corbett. 'In any script, any sketch, particularly the news items, if one of us didn't like it, there was no argument, it was out. If I'd written some stuff and Ronnie knew I'd written it, he'd say, "I don't like that line there, I don't like saying that line," and I'd say, "take it out". I'd have to say "take it out" and I would willingly say it, not just have to say it, because that keeps it clean, we know that everything left in has been approved by both performers and that's very important. Sometimes you might disagree with the choice in your head, but you would never say it. If he would say, "I don't like that line," you'd look at it and say, "I can sort of see why you don't, I thought it was funny at the time but I can see why you don't think it's right. Take it out." So it was very rare that I would have a grudge against a line being taken out that I thought was wonderful. He would only want to alter a line if it was a bad gag or he thought a weak joke.'

'His scripts are very precise,' says Peter Hall. 'Very immaculate, very particular. And they relate to his extraordinary ability as an actor to time accurately in the way he says a line. I think the writer and the actor coalesce in their precision, because although he's an anarchic comedian is some respects, as a performer he's about precision.'

•••

No one, not even Wiley, worked as a staff writer on the *Ronnies*, but if some people thought that Wiley/Barker had an easy ride, they were badly mistaken. 'Even not-so-good Ronnie B was better than most other people at their best,' says Corbett. 'I think there might have been an atmosphere occasionally with writers who were trying to get stuff on the show, thinking that Ronnie's stuff got preferential treatment. That maybe was felt. I don't think it was justified.' All material was submitted freelance and therefore there was no obligation to use anything just because someone was on staff and only the best material would get through. Around a third more was filmed than was ever broadcast, with Ronnie B keeping a close eye on the editing of the show as well, something that didn't always endear him to the BBC. Largely at Barker's insistence, the Ronnies made a rule of recording their entire series before any of it was broadcast so they could edit and arrange each week's show to make it as strong as it could be.

'I had a big row with Bill Cotton when he was head of light entertainment. He wanted to put a *Two Ronnies* show out when we'd only done three episodes out of eight, and I said, "You can't put it out Bill, because we must do the whole eight and then we put all the sketches in a pile and sort out a balanced show and throw out what we don't want." He said, "I'm sure these shows will be fine." I said, "No, please don't, because it will mess it up." He agreed eventually, so after that we always did a pile of things and we could sort them all out at the end, make shows out of them. I think it's the only way to work because you then have got the best stuff that you did in the series. For that reason I had to insist that they couldn't put the shows out until we finished them all. Not only because we want to throw away about a third of it, but because they're not necessarily balanced. One week you might do three wonderful sketches, or you might do two sketches that are rather similar, but both went well, and you don't want them in the same show. You shuffle them about. It was also about timing – you've got to get the show to a certain length and if you do three long sketches you can't have them all in. He didn't like the idea, because the BBC in those days seemed to think as soon as they've got something they should shove it out. They seemed to think it would go past its sell-by date, but it won't. We found it invaluable to be able to say, "That sketch didn't work as well did it? Let's throw it away." It was a wonderful luxury. We always had directors who were very accommodating. It was only the people further up who were saying they were perhaps paying a bit more than they should be for this stuff. But it's peanuts compared to the rest of the production cost. At the show's peak, I'd still only get £85 a minute. So it's really very cheap. But they knew what we did and they knew the shows were working so they left well alone. I always used to think of Dick Emery, who apparently was a charming man but he was so happy-go-lucky, he would turn up on Tuesday morning, say, "What are we doing this week?" They'd show him the sketches and he'd say "Fine." He had no concern about what kind of material he was doing. He was so funny in himself and all the characters he did were funny people and he just knew which characters to use in which sketch. Much like I did. When I started I wanted to do something new every week but you soon realize that you can't. By the time I did *Two Ronnies* it was very rare that I found a character that wasn't in the repertoire of twelve, or whatever it was I had, but sometimes you did. But Dick used to pick it up and do it. I could never do that. I would have to say, "I can't do that because I don't think it's funny. Whatever I do with that, it's not going to get many laughs." I would worry about that. And so would Ronnie C. So that was the difference and it certainly paid off that we could play around with the stuff and throw some away, and indeed get in on the editing, which I love doing anyway, because you can do almost anything with editing.'

•••

There was of course a visual aspect to *The Two Ronnies*. One was little, one was large (in fact, Ronnie used to tell the audience before each show, 'If you've enjoyed it, please tell your friends. If not, just remember that we're Little and Large'). This aspect however was one thing they never joked about. 'Ronnie C would always object to people mentioning his size, except for me. I could mention it because he was so close to me and respected me. But we never did those jokes because he is the man who makes jokes about his size par excellence, and it's exclusive to him, and he never stops in his monologues. He was always saying things like, "I was cleaning out the budgie cage and the door slammed shut on me." I would occasionally say something and I didn't mind him saying things about me. I know I'm fat and it doesn't worry me if someone says I'm fat because I am. So I'm never insulted. If someone said, "God that man looks like a great heap of blancmange," I would object to that because it's untrue. But we were the fat one and the little one.'

•••

With Ronnie B writing and helping edit the show, the balance of power between him and Ronnie C could easily have been thrown off balance, had both men not taken care to ensure the success of their relationship.

Corbett admits: 'I wasn't interested in that sort of power or jealous of it. Also I knew I was in very safe hands. And I suppose that I'm better at delegating than Ronnie. I can do that. I never felt he was pushing himself forward or making things easier for himself because he was making things bloody hard, working late, going to editing suites at night and so forth. But I guess there were maybe people at the BBC who would say that Ronnie was a bigger cornerstone in the show than me. Yes, he took a lot more of the load and it may well have been what tired him out more in the long run than it did me. But Ron never said, "I think you should wear this costume or put this wig on."

'On the other hand, away from *The Two Ronnies* he had the best writers of light entertainment that anyone could have – Roy Clarke (*Open All Hours, Last of the Summer Wine*) and Clement/LaFrenais (*Likely Lads, Porridge, Auf Wiedersehen Pet*). I was very blessed with writers Ian Davidson and Peter Tinniswood on *Sorry!*, but David Renwick has never rung me up and said, "Now I've done *One Foot in the Grave*, I'm going to write you a nice sitcom."'

One of the greatest strengths of *The Two Ronnies* was the fact that they were so different. Prior to being teamed up with Ronnie Barker, Ronnie Corbett had followed a tough apprenticeship in the most arduous of performance arts as a stand-up comedian. This was something for which Ronnie Barker paid Ronnie C all due respect, as

he had never attempted stand-up. It takes a lot of courage to stand on an empty stage, alone except for a microphone stand. There is no cast of players to provide support and there are no props to utilize, so as a stand-up Ronnie C did not have even the tatty furniture Ronnie B remembers from his rep days. Not even a sofa to fall back on, so to speak. The little Scotsman had a brave heart and learned the skills required in working an audience, developing an excellent sense of comic timing along the way. As well as working on stage in clubs, Ronnie Corbett had also appeared in a number of films long before he met Ronnie Barker and, indeed, long before Ronnie Barker's big screen debut.

Ronnie C's list of film credits is, nevertheless, quite substantial. His first movie was in 1937, when he was just seven years old. He played a schoolboy in a Will Hay schoolroom farce called *Good Morning Boys* (also sometimes known as *Where There's a Will There's a Way*). Ronnie also appeared in a comedy about a Scottish university (ironic since he never attended university) in 1952 called *You're Only Young Twice*. His next film role was in the remake of *Good Morning Boys* in 1953 when he played a student rather than a pupil, with Alfie Bass taking over Will Hay's headmaster role. Next came a St Trinian's-style movie called *Fun At St Fanny's* in 1956 followed by what was intended to be the sequel to *Whisky Galore*, *Rockets Galore* (1957). In 1962 Ronnie appeared in *Operation Snatch*, a war comedy starring Terry-Thomas, and in 1967 he was part of the glittering, star-studded cast of the James Bond spoof *Casino Royale*. Two years later came a movie called *Some Will, Some Won't*, a remake of a 1951 film called *Laughter in Paradise*, in which an eccentric millionaire leaves a will that requires the beneficiaries to perform outlandish tasks in order to receive their inheritance.

In 1970, Ronnie Corbett starred with, among others, John Cleese, Peter Cook and Arthur Lowe in *The Rise and Rise of Michael Rimmer*, a satirical comedy about an efficiency expert who takes over an advertising agency. Ronnie starred again with Arthur Lowe when the pair leapt from satire to farce in *No Sex Please We're British*. In 1997, Ronnie joined the team from *A Fish Called Wanda* – John Cleese,

Jamie Lee Curtis, Kevin Kline and Michael Palin – to play Reggie Sea Lions in a comedy set in a zoo that was titled *Fierce Creatures*.

'We were always very careful to be equal,' Ronnie B observes of *The Two Ronnies*. 'And the writers had a brief. When you did a sketch, obviously one character would feed the other. But in a show if I was being fed by Ronnie in one sketch, then I would be feeding Ronnie in another. When I was writing the serials and some of the musical items, I was always careful to share it out. I did a monologue and he did his chair bit. It was always very much in the forefront of my mind, and the director's mind, that it should be like that. We could never have worked that length of time if we hadn't got on. He just trusted me in terms of the editing, and knew that I had that feeling for things.

'Before Gerald Wiley was unmasked, it was easy. But after that he tried to be very honest with the sketches. He'd say, "It's very good Ronnie, but I don't think it's as good as that sketch." And there would be no hesitation about dumping anything that I'd written. Or changing anything. It was essential that we got on so well and were very aware of each other professionally. That was one of the secrets of our success I think.'

And successful *The Two Ronnies* were. The show ran for 12 series, a number of Christmas specials, two 'grumble and grunt' movies (*The Picnic* and *By the Sea*) and countless compilation shows that still regularly occupy prime time and Yuletide viewing, more than a decade after the last one was made. Twenty million people regularly watched *The Two Ronnies*. As Ronnie Barker once tried to visualize it, that's about two hundred Wembley Cup Final crowds a week.

•••

Over the years, there were many constants to the show, both on screen and off. The Ronnies always warmed up the crowds beforehand. 'We used to have Felix Boness on before to warm them up. He's a very funny man, and he used to introduce Ronnie C and Ronnie went out and used to do a few bits. Then I'd come out and just say a little warm-up routine that I had, which I gave to Felix afterwards and he's

still using it. I used to say, "Now, we want to test the reaction of the studio audience" – so I'd get them to applaud. Then I'd say, "I've got three questions here; I'll read out and then I say 3,2,1 and you all shout out the answer and we'll see how it goes. What are all men who mend shoes called? 3,2,1." "Cobblers," they would all shout. Then I would say, "If a door doesn't have a bell what have you got?" "Knockers," they'd shout. Then I'd say, "If a farmer has sheep, cows and bullocks on his farm and the sheep and cows die, what would he have left? 3,2,1" – "Bullocks" they'd all shout. And off we'd go.'

As ever, the two Ronnies' wives were on hand, offering support. 'The Two Wives were always there. You can hear them laughing away when no-one else was. Thank God for them. They've been the backbone to both our careers and they are the best of chums. They really love to meet and we love being a foursome.'

•••

As the years went on, they discussed playing around with the show's formula, but it seemed to work so well that there was no point in changing it. Occasionally they did impersonations – Ronnie B's Patrick Moore being a particular favourite. 'My best one was Patrick Moore, I thought that was quite good. I didn't consciously research them. I've always liked impersonations and impersonators and I've always thought I might be able to do impersonations and so I will watch them on television. I think it's a fascinating thing, I think Rory Bremner is the best there's ever been, he's so accurate. Because I've liked that so much I've done that with my characters. I think of someone in my mind that they're like, although it won't show to the audience that I'm doing that. For example, there was one sketch when we played two burglars and I played it like John Gielgud and Ronnie C played it like Noël Coward. No one noticed, but we knew. I did Barry Norman once and then I met him one day in the BBC car park and he said, "Oh that's what I do, is it?" I said, "Yes it is."'

•••

One of the things that come across strongly from the shows, particularly in Ronnie B's solo spots, is his love of language. From Spoonerisms to 'Pismonunciation', it's something that typifies his work, both in *The Two Ronnies* and beyond. It's worth noting how regionally specific all his sitcom characters have been. From the East End accent of Fletch to the Welsh lilt of *The Magnificent Evans* to the Yorkshire stutter of Arkwright, each characterization sees Barker playing not just simply with accents but with the specifics of his character's speech, each has their own perfectly observed language. 'It goes back to my love of language. David Nobbs sent in the "Pismonunciation" sketch. And I did about four of those eventually. He said he didn't know if he could write any more so I asked him if if he minded if I wrote one or two.'

The results were a true test of even Ronnie Barker's verbal acrobatics, as witnessed in this extract from a sketch entitled 'Pismonuncers Unanimous': 'Good Evening. I am the president for the loyal society for the relief of sufferers from pismonounciation; for people who cannot say their worms correctly. Or who use the wrong worms entirely, so that other people cannot underhand a bird they are spraying. It's just that you open your mouse, and the worms come turbling out in wuk a say that you dick knock what you're thugging a bing, and it's very distressing.'

'It was the same with the spoonerisms,' Ronnie recalls. 'Dick Vosburgh first sent those in and I said, "Can I write more?" and I did, and I love them!'

Two Ronnies fans love them, too. Here's a short piece where Dr Spooner, looking for a book of poetry, converses with an assistant in a bookshop:

Assistant: I'm afraid we're rather low on poetry at the moment, sir.

Spooner: Oh, pot a witty, pit a wotty. It was to be a gresent for my pud lady.

Assistant: Your pud lady, sir?

Spooner: My wife, the dear thing.

Assistant: Ah! If it is for a lady – perhaps something fairly easy to
             read – nothing too taxing for the female brain.

Spooner: On the contrary, nothing too simple. My wife is a right
             little bl... a bright little reader.

Assistant: A romantic novel, then? *The Vicar of Wakefield*?

Spooner: Possibly – providing it doesn't arouse her animal
             instincts. She likes red beading – beading in red, that is.
             Last month I bought *Wuthering Heights* for her and the
             following evening I found her needing it in the rude.

Assistant: I see.

Spooner: So I don't wish to encourage her to leap out of her
             vicars for the *Knicker of Wakefield* . . .

Ronnie enjoyed having fun with words, but there was another
reason why he chose to develop these ideas beyond the original
writers' submissions – he knew a good, funny theme when one
presented itself and loved the challenge of playing out that theme as
far as it could go. 'It was the same case with the "class" sketch in *The
Frost Report*, I wrote three of those afterwards. I've always said that
I'm a better script doctor than I am a writer. When I read a script by
someone else I know exactly what's wrong with it. I would rather
someone say, "Right there you are, sort that out." I'm very confident
that I can do that.'

•••

One of the few changes in the show occurred early on with the news
items. Originally, they were read in character as po-faced news
readers (as Barker says, a notion lifted from David Frost's deadpan

delivery.) But soon the two Ronnies started to laugh along, showing us the men behind the performers, indirectly endearing themselves even more to their already smitten audience. 'It was much more comfortable that way than when we started in episode one. We'd say something like, "The world's untidiest man died yesterday. He is now lying in a state." Then they'd cut to me and I'd be absolutely stone-faced. After a while I think I started it because I couldn't help but laugh at the jokes. I considered it very unprofessional to laugh, on the stage out of character; but this was different, they knew it was us, the two comics doing things like this. And I think I started it. I laughed at something Ronnie said and I knew it would be OK, and the audience liked it. We never faked the laughs because I used to enjoy it very much.'

In Barker's 2004 award/tribute show from the British Academy of Film and Television Arts (BAFTA), Corbett, the host, remarked that he felt those moments of laughter behind the news desk marked the only time that Ronnie Barker, the consummate character actor, ever revealed his real self on camera. Slightly reluctantly, Barker concurs.

'I suppose it was the real me, for an instant. But a joke has to be especially tickle-making. One of those news items was about a woman whose name was Teresa Quilp who was in a supermarket and a thief came in and she attacked him with a labelling gun, and Ronnie then said, "The police are looking for a man with a price on his head." That still makes me laugh. I liked the audience to see me laugh. I thought it was good to include me in the audience, as it were, when Ronnie was doing a joke. I laughed and they laughed, so I didn't try and stop it. We allowed that. We wanted to do that and Ronnie would do it to me.'

...

Among many memorable characters, the mock country duo Jehosaphat and Jones made several appearances, eventually cutting an album of their own in 1973.

'I love country and western anyway and it seemed to lend itself to us. We could do it easily. We did three appearances within the first

five series or so and someone came along and said they wanted to do an album with these chaps. I used to love writing the lyrics, getting internal rhymes into things. I found it such a great delight when I got something exactly right. If you've got seven syllables, say, and you've got to convey a thought or a joke, you can spend all day and you can't get it down to fewer than eight syllables and you throw it down and twist it round. And eventually you get it in, and it's a great satisfaction.'
Like C&W music, Ronnie has labelled the two Ronnies as being middle-of-the-road comedians, but he is quick to qualify that statement. 'We tried to be all over the road, cover a wide swathe. I think we offered the most acceptable form of general comedy, something to amuse most kinds of people without upsetting or insulting them.'

•••

Ironically, given how popular the two Ronnies were before a live studio audience (and how key a part of their show this was), the element of the show Ronnie enjoyed most was filming on location. 'I loved the filming best because it's a wonderful medium to play with comedy. I always think now, seeing the serials, that they were slow. We used to wait for laughs in places and sometimes you didn't get them, so I look at them now and I think they could be faster, they weren't tight enough.'

'I knew he enjoyed the filming,' says Ronnie C, 'because he conceived it all and was in there, calling the shots, helping the directors. And the directors too were very understanding, because they learned so much really. We all did. I'm surprised in a way that he has retired so completely. I thought he might have directed a commercial or two, or a short film, because I think that's what he enjoyed most.'

Ronnie was certainly able to do what he enjoyed most when the two Ronnies filmed the second of their two almost-silent movies, *By the Sea*. Not only was he able to work on what was effectively a self-contained short movie, but the location also allowed him to indulge his long-held love of British seaside postcard humour.

'My love of that came when I started collecting cards. It's not true that I have a preference for seaside humour and those cards, but I do think McGill especially was a wonderful artist and he did some wonderful stuff. He was so prolific, he did a card in the morning and a card in the afternoon for almost every day of his life, two cards a day. Very extraordinary.'

•••

Ronnie's passion for collecting and his devotion to his family meant that he had to work very hard to fit everything in. There was no question of cutting back, even though *The Two Ronnies* was tipped to be an ongoing success. Ronnie loved the diversity, he could enjoy playing different parts, and had reached a stage in his career where he was being offered some mouth-watering roles. In the very first of very few joint interviews to publicize *The Two Ronnies*, a *Radio Times* cover story from the week of 8 April 1971, Ronnie B was at pains to say, 'We like working together and we like doing our own things – separately.' From the moment *The Two Ronnies* became a huge success, he was quick to make sure that would remain the case.

CHAPTER 5

Porridge – Open All Hours

It don't mean that I don't love you,
When I punch you in the nose,
And go out with other women,
Never buy you any clothes.
How can we remain together,
With so many ifs and buts?
It don't mean that I don't love you –
But my wife – she hates your guts.

The song Ronnie wrote for Jehosaphat and Jones on *The Two Ronnies* was one of many that the Ronnies would sing together as those characters. In 1971 *The Two Ronnies* topped the TV ratings, becoming an instant success. The show took up around half the year for Barker when it was on air – from early writing to location filming (which often took up to six weeks alone) to studio recording, through to working with the show's directors on the editing and shaping of the shows. This, of course, left the actor with a further six months in which to pursue other projects. And there was always other work waiting for both men.

•••

Both Rons were much in demand, and it was Shakespeare that again tempted Ronnie Barker. He was very familiar with *A Midsummer Night's Dream*, but this time the role was Bottom and the production was for TV. Ronnie's co-stars included Edward Fox, two years away from the role of the assassin in *Day of the Jackal* that would bring him international renown; Eleanor Bron, who had been part of Peter Cook's Establishment and now had several movie roles to her credit; Robert Stephens, who was married to Maggie Smith and had starred alongside her in *The Prime of Miss Jean Brodie*, and (once again) Lynn Redgrave. The role of Titania was played by Eileen Atkins, whom Ronnie had known as an ASM at the Oxford Playhouse.

'We did that under extraordinary conditions. They had only two cameras. It was very early location work, I think it was video, that's why they had only two cameras. And it was done at night, everything was done at night. It was the most elaborate make-up I ever had and it took me about five hours to get made up and I had a great snout stuck on and strange teeth and hair all over the place and a great brow and it took for ever. I couldn't eat for 12 hours because I was actually in the make-up for seven hours. I was drinking through a straw I remember, much to the amusement of everyone else. They were all tucking into their evening meal, I was trying to drink soup through a straw.' The production was staged as an outside broadcast in the grounds of a stately home, and Barker was less than pleased with his own performance. As he has said, 'I find Shakespeare's clowns almost impossible to play. This could be why countless perfectly bright people find them almost impossible to follow. You can only get laughs with Shakespeare's comics by doing things that aren't in the play – physical business and gimmicks, in other words.'

•••

Back on the big screen, *The Magnificent Seven Deadly Sins* was another inauspicious British comedy movie that Ronnie appeared in, this one a series of sketches based around said sins. It featured a strong collection of British comic talents – old acquaintances Harry H. Corbett and June Whitfield, alongside the likes of Harry Secombe, Ian Carmichael, Alfie Bass and others – all of them generally badly served by weak scripting. Spike Milligan wrote and appeared in Ronnie's section, ensuring that the film was probably more fun to make than to watch.

'That was only a small role, I was just a man who kept saying he lost his walnuts at El Alamein. It obviously made Spike laugh. He kept ruining the takes by shouting out things. I was a bit concerned because my son Larry was in it as an extra and he was only 12 so I didn't want his delicate ears to hear anything obscene. I was doing my thing and Spike's voice came singing from the back, "I beg your pardon, I've done a pony in your rose garden." And I thought, "Shut up. Mad man, mad man."

'I told Larry he was going to be paid to do this, he stood in the queue and he thought he was going to get 6 shillings [30p] for the day and he got £6. He couldn't believe it. He said to me the other day, "You know you made me give £3 of it to my sister? I was very upset."'

•••

Despite his almost unprecedented success on the small screen, Ronnie Barker has never really found the fame he deserved in the cinema. It seems that the British film industry has always been singularly incapable of nurturing home-grown television talent, as if the two mediums were diametrically opposed to one another.

Despite universal acclaim and popularity on TV, his track record at the multiplex remains a series of dismal also-rans, as seems to be the case with much British comic talent, destined to live out their lives on the box in the corner rather than at the box office.

For Ronnie, it doesn't seem to have been a disappointment. 'I think I wasn't concerned with simply appearing in a film. It has crossed my mind that I would like to direct a film, but then again with a lot of things I say, "Now wait a minute, who says you're qualified for that?" That's why I haven't stepped in too deep on anything that I might have done. I have held back on a lot of things where I've thought, "No, you're not right for that." Even heavy things in the theatre. I'd say, "People think of you as a comedian. Those doors have closed behind you. You shouldn't be attempting that kind of stuff. You can't do everything, so don't." So no, I never really pursued film. And also, of course, I wasn't asked. Obviously, they did the film of *Porridge* and they asked me to play the part of Fletcher. And I'm glad they did because there weren't many people around who could do it. But no, I've never really hankered after film.'

Not that he was averse to helping the occasional film along. In 1967 he got to work with a hot young director whose previous films had included *A Hard Day's Night* and *Help!* with the Beatles, *The Knack... and how to get it* and *A Funny Thing Happened on the Way to the Forum* with Phil (Bilko) Silvers. 'I re-dubbed Jack Shepherd as the underwater vicar in Dick Lester's *How I Won the War* (which starred John Lennon without the Beatles). I also did some German dubbing for the same film for Dick Lester, the longest line I ever had to dub. I used to do voice-overs for commercials such as Walker's crisps. That was "BL" – "Before Lineker". The first voice-overs I did were for Watney's Ale and Watney's Pale.'

While he has no regrets about missed opportunities in his career, Ronnie does admit to one disappointment. Other actors regret having missed out on being cast as James Bond or yearn for the chance to play Hamlet, but Ronnie's fluffy little disappointment came in a small blue duffle coat. 'I failed to get the part of Paddington Bear. Michael Hordern played Paddington.'

•••

Radio was also something that Ronnie simply hadn't had time for in recent years, due to his hectic TV commitments. He redressed that in April 1971 with a new show for the BBC, *Lines from My Grandfather's Forehead*, a free-form sketch show, written in part by Barker.

'I wrote little bits of that. There was no gist at all. It was just out of the air, anything that came to mind. I got the name from a thing that Frank Muir once said, that he was thinking of writing something called "Leaves from My Dining Room Table". So I got "Lines from My Grandfather's Forehead". It was just a mishmash of stuff but it was good in that it was completely catholic in its taste. Everyone submitted things. Radio was so easy, with the script in your hand. You did the whole thing in about four hours. We had no audience for that, which made the thing a lot easier. Although I prefer to have an audience. I'm always more nervous if there isn't one. But it was fun to do because you could do anything, any snippets – four lines of doggerel could come in.

'That was the last time I did radio. Television is – dare I say it – much more important than radio, certainly to me. I'm afraid I hardly ever listen to the radio now at all.'

•••

Ronnie's first foray into sitcom since *Foreign Affairs* could have come in 1972. It was an area in which he would ultimately find his greatest personal successes – and indeed his only failures. Despite the success of *The Two Ronnies*, Barker was always eager to pursue the solo route, and was keen to find the right vehicle. Then producer, and by now long-time associate, Jimmy Gilbert, sent him a script for a new show called *Some Mothers Do 'Ave 'Em*. 'Immediately I read it I realized it was not me at all. Jimmy Gilbert had given it to me and my first thought was this was a knockabout, a physical comedian's part. I couldn't do half the things and I'm a lines man, I'm a dialogue chap. Thank God I did say that because Michael Crawford made such a wonderful success out of it. I was delighted I didn't do it.'

The series did, indeed, go on to be a huge success for the BBC and Michael Crawford. Crawford filmed 22 episodes over three series as the gormless Frank Spencer, performing stunts and hurling himself around the set in a way that is unimaginable for someone of Ronnie's build.

Over the years there were other examples of roles Ronnie was sought for, but never played, including the lead in what went on to become the classic sitcom, *The Fall and Rise of Reginald Perrin*.

'That was written by David Nobbs. Jimmy Gilbert said to him, "Who do you want to play this?" and he said, "Ronnie Barker." "Uh huh, Ronnie Barker, right, well then, Leonard Rossiter it is," he said. David didn't understand that at all but obviously Jimmy Gilbert had a reason for saying it. I don't know why. "Leonard Rossiter it is," as if he'd said Leonard Rossiter in the first place!'

•••

In truth, the two men were not so dissimilar. Rossiter, a comic actor with a string of character parts to his name, starred in 21 episodes of *Perrin* over three series (plus one Christmas special short) between 1976 and 1979. Astoundingly, while playing Perrin, a failed executive who fakes his suicide and begins a new life, Rossiter was at the same time starring in one of ITV's better sitcoms, *Rising Damp*. Exhibiting a similar approach to his work as Ronnie, Rossiter was concurrently playing a frustrated, miserly landlord and the ironic, world-weary Perrin.

While both men could turn their considerable talents to most parts, there are some that come out of the blue. Ronnie was offered one such – the lead role of the BBC's television adaptation, *I, Claudius*.

'I was offered *I, Claudius* very early on and Bill Cotton said, "No, I think you should stay in *The Two Ronnies*." If I'd taken it my career would have gone in a completely different direction. I wasn't allowed to tell anyone for a long time, until Derek Jacobi actually said it on television. He said, "Ronnie Barker was offered this before me." But I'm glad I didn't do it because I would have gone in the drama direction, and I'm so glad I didn't because *Two Ronnies, Porridge* and *Open All Hours* have been my life and my pension, I'm here to say.'

I, Claudius was a 13-episode serial produced by the BBC which proved to be highly controversial on both sides of the Atlantic, featuring as it did graphic and gory violence in its murders, assassinations and a notoriously bloody abortion. There were also objections to the scenes of nudity, decadent fornication, incest, prostitution, nymphomania, homosexuality, adultery and brutality both in the UK and the US. It certainly would have been a different direction for Ronnie, and one that would have required straight acting from him.

'A lot of comics want to prove that they're good straight actors. It's in the same pigeonhole as dancers wanting to be singers. They always want to be singers. I don't see the point of it, do what you want to do and do what you think best. You don't have to say, "I am a good straight actor as well," because straight acting, I think, is much easier than comic acting. I've had lots of praise from various people, Peter Hall, Jonathan Miller and various people like that, saying what a good actor I am, so that doesn't worry me. It never did.'

•••

Meanwhile Ronnie, as he would so many times in his career, had come back to a character he knew. Lord Rustless – in all his guises — remains a constant in Ronnie Barker's career, so naturally he turned to his Lordship in 1972 for his first starring role in a sitcom, *His Lordship Entertains*.

'This time I wanted to write. All these characters seemed so much fun to me and I loved being him. I thought I would go back to Rustless because I loved him so. I loved playing him, and he hadn't been done enough. Even in the silent films – what I call the silent films, the "grumble and grunt films" – he's still the same character. I just love him, the dotty old fool. He's like Fred Emney – that sort of man who lets the world go by and comments on it. He's stranded on the sidelines of life really, watching things happen.'

Barker decided to write the series himself. As with all his putting-pen-to-paper efforts, the modest actor took a pen name, this time

Jonathan Cobbold. The first episode opened with Rustless at the front desk of his hotel, taking a telephone booking from a potential guest.

Rustless: Yes, madam. I see. You'd like a double room with bath on the third. Preferably on the first floor. Double room, yes. Does the bath have to be double? No, single bath, overlooking the Downs. I see. That's the room, not the bath. No. Quite. Yes, it would. Well, I have a double room overlooking the Downs but no bath. Or I have a single room with a bath. Your husband? No. Not unless he slept in the bath. Overlooking the Downs, yes. Mind you, that's the second floor. Yes, I should think your best bet is to overlook the bath and have a first floor double room overlooking the car park.

'I think the challenge was part of it. It wasn't easy. You have to see the big canvas in front of you, so you're not fazed if a) it takes you longer and b) you have to find more scope to expand in many directions. You've got to flesh it out. So it didn't worry me but I thought, "It is different."

'It's a step forward, isn't it? I've never written a full-length play, I've often thought about doing that. I've toyed with the idea of writing a stage play for Rustless. Not that I would ever play it now, but I did toy with the idea. And obviously he'd be the squire of the village. I was going to call it "Raspberries from the Garden" because it's a very English thing; the curtain would go up and you'd hear – *(loud raspberry sound)* – that's gets rid of the title. But I never got round to that.'

The BBC apparently wiped the tapes of *His Lordship Entertains*, denying us the chance to witness a show that would now be of interest for many reasons. 'Fawlty Towers Mark 1, I call it,' Barker says nowadays. 'It was a daft hotel, run by a man who was quite incompetent at running a hotel. I suppose the two stories so far are identical. Mine was a dotty old fellow and the other one was a demented, opinionated man who suffered no fools.' For the first time, the aged gardener Dithers appeared on screen as a character, played with aplomb by a man who was now fast becoming a close friend of Barker's, David Jason.

By now, writing, which is something that Ronnie had originally begun out of necessity, was a fully-fledged second career, albeit one that was hidden from the majority of the viewing public. It would remain a dominant side of Ronnie's career right up to his retirement, his final series, *Clarence*, being penned under a pseudonym.

'I started writing sketches and the form of a sketch is fairly obvious if you've been doing it for a long time. You have to have two good characters, you have to be funny in the first minute, the situation has to be funny and the tag has to be funny at the end. There's not really much more about form you can attribute to a sketch. That's what you do. You get a funny idea – an optician who's as blind as his customer, for example, and they're both groping around (we did that one). You have to think of a tag and the tag in that case was they try each other's glasses on and they can see perfectly.

'When I came to write situation comedy, and I didn't write many, I wrote only two series – the other being *Clarence* – which was right at the end of my career, and I'd done so many sitcoms by then. The same sort of thing applies: you have to have a funny situation. The situation in a sitcom has to have more possibilities because a sketch only lasts three minutes and a sitcom lasts thirty. So you have to see the possibilities before you start writing it; where can we go in this series? By then I'd had so many good teachers – Frank Muir and Dennis Norden to start with, Dick Clement and Ian La Frenais, and Roy Clarke – that I wasn't really concerned if the format was OK because by the time I'd thought that this could make a series, I wasn't concerned that it wouldn't, based on my experience of the other sitcoms.

'You had to have good characters, you had to have idiosyncrasies about those characters and the scripts had to have a feel that they were developing. When you watch a good sitcom you grow to like the characters and you grow to learn what they do and what their failings are and what their good points are. So that has to develop within the series. As far as I'm concerned that is as far as form goes.

'Sometimes I used to write things, even in an actor's line, that made it imperative that he was in close-up, or that you couldn't see the other actor, or something like that. It was only suggested within the lines, but you never said that to a director...'

•••

No doubt hailing from his days back at Aylesbury, throughout his career Ronnie Barker has sought to create a veritable repertory company around himself. *His Lordship Entertains* was no different, featuring once again Josephine Tewson, the actress he had first spotted in *The Real Inspector Hound* and had recruited for *Frost on Sunday*. She would continue to work with Ronnie throughout his career, eventually recreating her role from 'The Removals Person' episode of *Six Dates...* in Ronnie's final series, *Clarence*.

Perhaps more importantly, however, was the opportunity *His Lordship Entertains* gave Ronnie to work with, and cement his relationship with, David Jason. When they first met, Jason still had his day job as an electrician. Working on *The Odd Job* together (in 1971), they both knew they were onto something special. Ronnie's first sitcom allowed them to develop things further, establishing a relationship that would come to full fruition in *Open All Hours*.

'He and I just happened, we fused as people. We love to be with each other and communicate and work with each other. He always called me "governor", I was the governor, meaning his main man. When I retired and he'd done so well, with *Only Fools and Horses* and things, I said, "Now you're the governor, I'm the ex-governor. I'm going to resign the governorship and give it to you." I wrote a long poem which I read out at some party we had, and handed over the governorship to him. It was written as a sort of stand-up monologue.

'I did that three or four times. We used to have some wonderful dinners after filming for *Open All Hours*, up in the wilds of Yorkshire. The producer, Sydney Lotterby, would never eat with us. I asked him, "What do you do for dinner?" And he said, "Whisky and peanuts." But occasionally you could cajole him to come to dinner if it was a special occasion. On David's birthday I got Sydney to come for dinner. David was always going on in a jocular way saying to me, "Why is it that whatever I do you come up and top it?" In life this is, socially, but he's a great comedy grumbler. He used to call himself the "Little Feed" and I remember writing a long poem, in Shakespearean metre or something, about the Little Feed and how one day he won't be the Little Feed any more. I love writing lyrics and rhyming couplets. You can't call it poetry. Poetry, I think, is superior rhyming to what I do. It's like art, I think there's no such thing as art, there's only craft. That's sorted it out for me. But with David – I'm sure we were terribly good for each other. As indeed Ronnie C was. David and Ronnie – those are the two really.'

•••

Things were going well for Ronnie Barker. His family life was secure – a loving wife, three healthy children and a spacious home in the quiet outer London suburb of Pinner. His career was going from strength to strength, the continued success of *The Two Ronnies* affording him just about every opportunity he wanted to pursue. Something had to go wrong. That something cropped up the night he lost his voice while appearing in a pre-West End run of *Good Time Johnny*, a Jimmy Gilbert musical based on *The Merry Wives of Windsor*. Set just after the First World War, Ronnie was playing the Falstaff role, the part that would later presage his retirement.

'It was set just after the war, about 1918, and it was great fun, with Joan Sims. We did it at Birmingham, until I lost my voice, and one of the chaps who was in it said, "My brother's a doctor, an ear, nose and throat chap, you must see him." So on Sunday I went to see him and he looked down my throat and said to his nurse, "Come and have a look at this, this is interesting." Immediately I thought, "God, what's that?" They saw a growth on my vocal cords and said they had to operate on it. So I had to come out of the show.

'The night before the operation, he told me I had to give up smoking and took my cigarettes and lighter and threw them out of the window. This surgeon, extraordinary behaviour.

'He said, "I'm operating at seven in the morning." The first time I'd been to see him, I'd asked about the show. He said, "Come and see me in another week." So I went to see him again and he said he had to do it tomorrow, which was worrying. I remember that night, sitting in the bath in the hospital and singing all my favourite songs because I thought I may never sing them again. He said, "There's a possibility it may impair your voice, it's a very delicate operation, cutting a bit off your vocal cords. I hope it won't because I know how important it is for you." The growth was a pre-cancerous growth which he had removed in time.'

The operation proved a complete success, with no damage to Ronnie's vocal cords; he was instructed to say nothing for the first three weeks, writing everything down on a notepad, but a full and speedy recovery followed. By comparison, *Good Time Johnny*, metaphorically speaking, died on the table.

Being forced to give up smoking, however, did take its toll on Ronnie. 'I found it terribly difficult to give up smoking. It took me a year really. I couldn't write. We'd just started *The Two Ronnies* and I went absolutely blank with the writing. I used to smoke like mad when I was writing. Ronnie Corbett used to say I always had a pack of two hundred cigarettes in my briefcase, Peter Stuyvesant was my brand. Giving up knocked me back for about a year. But it was pretty agonizing because I had been smoking at least 45 a day, since I was about 19 and I was 41 by then, so that was 22 years I'd been doing it. But I never went back on them. Not once. It had to be. An actor's instrument is his vocal cords. You just cannot dice with death.'

•••

Eager to find another TV vehicle, Ronnie went back to the tried, true and tested method of the Playhouse format, embarking on a series of six potential pilots. The idea was to call the show *Six of One*, but some high-up at the BBC decided they wanted seven shows, effectively knocking the potential follow up series – *Half a Dozen of the Other* – firmly on the head.

With *Seven of One*, Ronnie was looking for a new sitcom. What he found were two of the most enduring comedies in the history of British television, and, in the stuttering shopkeeper Arkwright and the experienced recidivist Fletcher, his two most popular creations.

•••

The first episode of *Seven of One* was called 'Open All Hours'. Written by Roy Clarke, it featured the penny-pinching Yorkshire shopkeeper Arkwright, a man moved only by the sight of the buxom nurse Gladys Emmanuel. David Jason played Arkwright's put-upon nephew Granville. The second week's show was titled 'Prisoner and Escort', and was written by the team of Dick Clement and Ian La Frenais, whose previous credits included the seminal '60s hit *The Likely Lads* and its even better '70s sequel, *Whatever Happened to the Likely Lads?* It told the story of one Norman Stanley Fletcher, a prisoner being escorted to his new home away from home – at Her Majesty's pleasure, of course – by two prison guards – the soft touch Barrowclough (Brian Wilde) and the by-the-book Mackay (Fulton Mackay).

'We did it to find characters I wanted to play. We sat round and started thinking of characters or situations, things I wanted to do. A couple of years ago I found in an archive file of jottings and early bits of writing, a piece of paper with five things I wanted to do for the series, and the fifth one just said one word –"Prison". When I met with Dick Clement and Ian La Frenais and they said they wanted to write two of these things, we had a lunch and I suggested the prison idea. But I had a much more joky perception of it. They had also thought about prison. They wanted to do one about an open prison and I wanted to do one a bit like *Bilko* in prison, I think. They asked if I had any stories, and I said that in one of them they smuggle a woman in and she has to be dressed as a man, and I could see them thinking, "We thought of something a bit more realistic, really." But I knocked the open prison idea on the head because the thing about prison I think is the harshness of it. And they soon agreed with that, almost immediately. So it became a security prison. I had no input on the script, though. We'd all agreed that we would do a prison series;

that they would write it and that was it. Then the script turned up. I had no idea that it was going to start outside, I had no idea at all what it was going to be like.

'Their original idea became a thing called *Thick as Thieves* which eventually starred John Thaw and Bob Hoskins. That was written for me. It was the series that they'd talked about, the characters had just come out of prison. They sent me the pilot and I said, "This is not prison, they're out of prison."

'"Oh, yeah, but we had an idea of these old lags," and I said, "I don't want to do that, I want to do prison."

'Then they said, "We'd like to write that as well." So they'd written a John Thaw thing, the whole six episodes, before they'd sent me one. I suppose they were a bit knocked back by that. But Jimmy Gilbert and Duncan Wood, who was the head of light entertainment at the time, were able to say "Ronnie doesn't want to do that, he wants to do a series in prison." So they went away and wrote it. Thank God.'

•••

It was an auspicious beginning; not that the rest of the *Seven of One* series didn't have plenty to offer as well.

'My Old Man' was about a pensioner trying to save his home from the demolition crew. Roy Clarke provided another, called 'Spanner's Eleven', the tale of a low-down-the-league football team. When one script proved to be below par, Ronnie himself penned 'One Man's Meat'. Reunited with his former co-star from the *Today* programme, Prunella Scales, Ronnie played a man forced to go on a crash diet when his wife stops him leaving the house by stealing his pants.

One of the undoubted highlights of the run was 'Another Fine Mess'. Written by Hugh Leonard, Ronnie and Roy Castle played Laurel and Hardy impersonators, who slowly become their characters as events escalate around them. It was an inventive idea, made memorable by two excellent performances from Castle and Barker, who both perfectly captured the detail of Stan and Ollie.

The lost gem of the series, however, was the final instalment. Written by Clement/La Frenais, 'I'll Fly You For a Quid' was the everyday story of a Welsh family that will bet on absolutely anything and everything. (The title comes from a line in the piece where Ronnie, as the dying grandfather, asks the vicar if he'll have wings in heaven. The vicar says yes, he will. He then asks the vicar will he also have wings when he gets there. Once again the vicar says yes. 'Right. I'll fly you for a quid,' the old man says and promptly dies.)

'I said to the boys I wanted to play a Welsh character and they said they'd got a thing about Geordies. I said "I can't do Geordie, can it be Welsh?" And when they explained it was about a gambling family that'll gamble on anything, we decided it could be Welsh. It was a very funny piece. I played both the father and the grandfather. I'd always loved the Welsh accent. I think it's a good comedic noise, a good comedic accent. Although very little has been done with it.'

•••

Ronnie was so taken with 'I'll Fly You For a Quid' that when the BBC asked him which one of the seven he wanted to develop into a series, he opted for the Welsh one. While the thought of any sitcom from the team of Clement/La Frenais being lost is a sad one, Ronnie, and indeed we, should be glad.

The BBC didn't want the Welsh one; they wanted the prison one.

'Little victories. That's what it's all about.' That was Dick Clement and Ian La Frenais's credo behind the show that became *Porridge*, evolving from 'Prisoner and Escort'. *Porridge* remains, simply, one of the best television sitcoms ever. On a par in this country with the likes of *Fawlty Towers* and *Dad's Army*; more than able to hold its own alongside such American classics as *Cheers* and *MASH*. Along with all these shows, it shares the hallmark of note-perfect casting, eloquently funny scripts and excellent ensemble playing. But more than that, the one thing all these shows have in common is their ability to look beyond the laugh, to find the humour in all aspects of their characters' lives – the joy, the pain, the success, the suffering. Shows of this calibre display a level of truth rarely seen in even the finest TV dramas.

Norman Stanley Fletcher had spent most of his life inside before he went down yet again for the five-year stretch that lasted the three seasons (and two Christmas specials) that was the run of *Porridge*. He was the proverbial old lag – knew the rules, knew the ropes, looked out for young Lenny Godber (Richard Beckinsale), kept his distance from old Grouty (Peter Vaughan) and skirted round the ins and outs of the lives of a variety of other inmates. There's an old story about *Porridge* that is still recounted by television comedy executives up and down the land. Clement and La Frenais were writing the show, they had the characters, they had the setting, they had the plot. The only thing they didn't know was what it was *really* about. They went to visit a recently released inmate who set them straight: when you're inside you know you've never gonna beat the system, so you don't try. What you try and do – each and every day – is quietly win one little battle. Little victories. That's what it's all about.

'It's about survival,' Dick Clement told the *Radio Times* in 1974. 'Little day-to-day triumphs that people need to keep their dignity.'

Ronnie attributes a great deal of the success of *Porridge* to the realism of the world Clement and La Frenais created (even if the prison set was housed in a disused water tank out at Ealing Studios).

'You really felt you were in a prison with maybe a bit of latitude given by the people in charge to allow you to be a bit more free and less constricted and downtrodden than you would have been in that situation. In other words, it's dramatic licence, but when Mackay shouted at us you really believed he had that power over us. He was the authority figure.

'Fletcher's in such a believable atmosphere with such realistic performers. They are all what I call legit performers, straight actors, not comedy actors. Obviously all had a great facility for comedy. Fulton Mackay's timing was wonderful, natural. He was very much a straight actor and very conscientious about his rehearsing and never said one word different on Wednesday from what he'd said on Tuesday, which is wonderful. So you never felt that Fletcher had the upper hand, that he could do exactly what he wanted with these people. That's why my character seemed real – because everyone else felt real.' Or, as Ian La Frenais succinctly put it at the time: 'The casting – that's the key. If the actors are right, then all your troubles are over.'

'I always felt as if this was the only thing I'd ever done when I was doing it,' says Ronnie. 'I was always that person. Luckily, I've had the facility all my life for doing that. I am that person when I'm playing them, even in *The Two Ronnies* for two minutes. You don't think that in a minute you're going to be an Indian guru and there you are sitting in a pub drinking a pint. You don't think that. You're only that character. Nothing else crosses your mind. You don't come outside of it.'

•••

When the commission came through to turn 'Prisoner and Escort' into a series, Dick Clement and Ian La Frenais began their research by putting themselves through the admittance routine at Brixton prison. They had their medicals, handed over their clothing and possessions and spoke to many of the men they would be writing about. 'We came out wondering how we could be funny about this,' said Clement. 'But then we thought that they're surviving. Let's write about survival.'

For once, Ronnie didn't feel the need to be involved with the writing. 'You very rarely had to change anything, you just picked it up and did it. There was only one episode where I did quite a bit of writing. I think the boys weren't around and it wasn't working. But mainly it was there. We would suggest lines of course. I remember there was one – "No Peace for the Wicked" – the one where Fletch was just trying to have a quiet afternoon and people kept coming in one after the other. Bunny Warren (Sam Kelly) came in and he was telling me a long story and I remember my foot was starting to go to sleep. So I said, "Look Bunny could you hurry up, me foot's going to sleep and I'd very much like to join it, know what I mean?" I put that in and it got a good laugh. With those sort of character bits you've really got to know Fletcher. I got to know him and then suggested things that he would say and get away with. So lots of little bits like that went in. The boys were fine about it, they said, "This works because it is Fletcher talking."'

Ronnie did, however, initially have a hand in casting. For the role of innocent inmate Lenny Godber he suggested Paul Henry, with whom he had appeared in *Good Time Johnny*.

'Ronnie brought in Paul,' recalls producer Sydney Lotterby. 'And I had found Richard so I said let's read this guy and you know, Richard's so good, he just convinced us. He was supposed to have a Birmingham accent, but he quickly changed it after the first episode.' Paul Henry meanwhile kept his Brummy tones and went on to find fame as Benny in the TV soap *Crossroads*.

When the role of an aged lag named Blanco came up, Ronnie once again looked to David Jason to carry it off. With his customary generosity, Ronnie gave Fletch the back seat and let Jason take centre cell. Jason acknowledges his debt.

'I don't think I know of anybody who has that attitude of Ronnie's. I know one or two who are exactly the opposite. Ronnie always looked at the centre and that was something I learned from Ronnie very early on. Of course he was generous but he also knew that by having the best people to support him, it made the show funny and if the show was funny then it reflected on Ronnie Barker because people would be saying, "Did you see that Ronnie Barker show last night?" He was never worried about that because he could more than bloody well hold his own. I don't think there was anyone who could top him on a line. I learned from that and have carried on the tradition as it were.'

•••

From day one of filming *Porridge*, the cast and crew were aware they were working on something special. 'I did the title sequence,' says Lotterby, recalling the show's austere beginning – a judge intones Fletcher's sentence over stark images of his journey to Slade prison, the doors slamming shut behind him. 'It was very different then. You couldn't normally do titles without music and the like, but we had a little bit of drama with the prison doors closing, the keys rattling in the doors. That was the first time I'd ever done a sitcom without music to open it. The writing was so good of course, it was Dick and Ian at their best. And the performances were great. That's what made it so successful.'

The Scottish actor Fulton Mackay was brought on board as the crusty prison officer Mackay, and Brian Wilde rounded out the principal cast as the less assertive prison officer, Mr Barrowclough.

As the success of *Porridge* grew, Barker and Fulton Mackay were called upon to make numerous personal appearances. The first of these involved a circus-style charity performance, housed in a large marquee, with several members of the Royal Family in attendance. During the course of the show, an announcement was made that a certain Norman Stanley Fletcher had escaped from Slade prison. Enter Barker – as Fletch – on a pushbike, cycling round the stage, only to be followed and apprehended by a certain Officer Mackay. The crowd loved it, and for Mackay it was his first experience of just how popular the show – and he – had become.

During *Porridge*'s run, Ronnie Barker was named Personality of the Year by the show business fraternity, the Water Rats. Once again, he asked Mackay to accompany him. Their planned skit – involving Fletch and the screw to be held together by a gold-plated set of handcuffs that had been presented to Ronnie by the cast and crew at the end of the first season – almost backfired when Barker got the two of them chained to the headrest of one of their car seats, before they could even enter the building. Crisis averted, the two graciously accepted the award.

Porridge was an instant hit with audiences, but quickly Ronnie decided he didn't want to take the role of Fletcher any further. 'I did one series of *Porridge* and then I said, "I've done that, now I want to do the shopkeeper in *Open All Hours*, written by Roy Clarke who did *Last of the Summer Wine*." So they said, "OK, fine, but we might come back to *Porridge*." I said, "Yes, we might," but I didn't want to get stuck. Even after one series. I didn't want to get trapped there, having the choice of two, which I was lucky to have. So we did *Open All Hours*, which, in their infinite wisdom, they decided to put on BBC2. And I said, "Why have they done that?" And they replied, "We think it's a bit more gentle" – and that's always a dangerous word because that means they don't think it's as funny.'

Open All Hours was in good company though. The BBC had also chosen to debut John Cleese's *Fawlty Towers* on the 'second channel' and it too struggled to find the huge audiences it would later draw. 'It got reasonable figures,' Barker recalls. 'But at that time, people wouldn't watch 2, they'd watch BBC1. So they said it was all right but let's go back to *Porridge*. So we did.'

'Ronnie just didn't want to be stuck in the one character,' Syd Lotterby, who also handled producing/directing chores on *Open All Hours*, explains. 'He didn't want people saying, "Oh Ronnie Barker, he's that prisoner."'

•••

Ronnie had other options of course. His postcard collection had swelled to such proportions that it had turned into a veritable cottage industry, with Ronnie releasing two collections of the cards in book form – the *Book of Bathing Beauties* and the *Book of Boudoir Beauties* in 1974 and 1975 respectively. Both went on to become bestsellers; several more would follow.

A series of well-remembered adverts for Sekonda watches was proving highly lucrative (ironically fellow *Frost* alumnus John Cleese could be seen on TV hawking Accurist watches around the same time), and a role in J. B. Priestley's *When We Are Married* had seen Ronnie reliving his theatre days, albeit in this television production of the classic play.

'It was the second play I ever did in rep and I remembered the part of the photographer very well. I had thought at the time, "One day when I'm older I'd love to play that." I was so pleased when I was asked to do it because it was fulfilling an ambition I'd almost forgotten about.

'Because there wasn't an audience I felt very nervous, trembling really. You get a little bit nervous obviously when you're doing a *Porridge* or an *Open All Hours* in the studio, but with this I was all over the place. I was scared of it but I knew I could only do it as well as I could do it. You will certainly not do worse. There's no point in saying, "Am I good enough for this?" Because you will find out if you're good enough if someone asks you to do it again. Or doesn't ask you.'

•••

Movies, too, were once again on the cards, when Ronnie was offered the plum role of Friar Tuck in Richard Lester's *Robin and Marian*. It was a promising idea, picking up as it did on the romance between Robin Hood (back from the Crusades after something of a delay) and Maid Marian in their later years, casting Sean Connery and Audrey Hepburn effectively in the title roles. *Robin and Marian* was shot on location in Spain during the summer of 1975. For Ronnie, it was not a happy experience.

'Awful. I'm afraid I didn't get on with Dick Lester really. He's a very clever man but our personalities didn't mesh. I remember him saying, "You're in the foreground of this scene, do something funny." And I said, "Well what do you want me to do? There's nothing in the script." He said, "Just think of something." That sort of thing never pleased me at all. If you want something funny there, say it to the writers. You don't say it just before a take.

'I had problems with him during the dubbing, too, because he continually wanted me to say things when my mouth wasn't moving. I'd be standing there on screen and he'd want me to say something like, "Look out someone's coming." And I'd explain, "But my lips don't move Dick." "No-one'll notice," he said. "Well I will, that's half of my performance, what I say." So he got annoyed with me and in the end he got someone else in to impersonate my voice. Guess who he got? David Jason! I listen to it now and I hear David. He did several people in the film, all saying things when their mouths don't open. So Dick and I parted, not on the best of terms.'

Ronnie's relationship with his fellow actors was more convivial when the situation allowed for it, on what was obviously what movie publicists term a 'troubled shoot'.

'Nicol Williamson and Denholm Elliot were at each other's throats often. And I was keeping them apart. I was in the middle for the whole ten weeks.'

Robert Shaw, who had recently finished filming *Jaws* and was cast here as the Sheriff of Nottingham, proved equally mercurial. 'I remember we were having a half day and it was lunchtime.

Everyone had had a few I think, and Robert Shaw was saying how he loved playing boulles. Now I've played it a bit. He was always challenging people to things to show he was best. He said, "I'll bet you a hundred pounds, I'll give you eight points and I'll beat you to 13 points." I said OK. And everyone came out to watch us. It was like a tournament. He started to catch me up. We got to the point where he had a ball right next to the jack and – they were all rooting for me, the other actors – I had one ball left and I thought, "I've got to bomb him out of there. I have to do this." I took aim and it flew right out and a great cheer went up. He was very angry, very upset about it. "Bastard," he said and threw his money down. I felt so elated. It was like David and Goliath. He was a nice man, but he was aggressive.'

Robin and Marian became somewhat surreal when Dick Lester, having realized that Sean Connery was playing Robin with his customary Scottish brogue, decided that the rest of the merry men should lose their north country accents and also play the whole thing as if they were Scottish. This was, after all, a mere half way into production.

This wasn't to be Ronnie's only problem on the movie. In the early stages he had made it clear to all and sundry that he would not be riding any horses. He went as far as to get this written into his contract so everyone knew the situation up front.

Upon his arrival in Spain he was taken out to the set to meet Dick Lester and was informed that his first scene involved him riding into shot – on a horse, no less!

At first, Lester couldn't believe this was a problem, but Friar Tuck had a copy of his contract tucked into the folds of his habit and promptly produced it. (Meanwhile, co-star Denholm Elliott was stashing his daily per diem – paid in pesetas – in his cod-piece, until at one point Ronnie had to point out it protruding a tad too much for a family film.)

•••

Between set-ups on *Robin and Marian*, Ronnie found the time to write another of his almost silent movies, as he calls them. *The Picnic* featured a similar ensemble to the country aristos of *Futtock's End*. Lord Rustless – though never mentioned by name – was back and Ronnie Corbett was along for the first time.

'They were, I suppose, a challenge. *Futtock's End* was much more exciting to me than either of the other two because I wanted that to capture that sort of far-off, childhood summer. The feeling you remember of slight weirdness. Although everything was funny in it, there was still a feeling of an unreal little encapsulated world. Which is the same with the others to a degree. In *The Picnic* it's an Edwardian picture. It's a situation that is unreal to most people, and that's what I liked about it. This man who rode over everyone and behaved how he wanted to and everyone else just fitted in. I loved that sort of thing hugely.'

Broadcast on New Year's Day, 1976, *The Picnic* was a highlight of the two Ronnies' career, a delightful collection of sight gags and comic moments, imbued with the Ronnies' usual level of sauce and double entendre. 'We used double entendre all the time. Not much single entendre went on. Occasionally I'd find myself holding myself back over some things. I'd say to Ronnie, "Oh we can't say that." So there was a censorship going on between us, yes, within the programme. You'd never leave an unfinished rhyme that started out with something like "duck", you would never do that. I remember we did a harvest festival thing, with jokes like, "he sits among the cabbages and peas". That's an ancient one, but we had to change it to, "he sits among the cabbages and leeks".'

•••

The Picnic proved so popular that the Ronnies returned to the format in 1982 with *By the Sea*. Both films were clearly influenced by the postcard humour that had become Ronnie B's other passion and, in many ways, it's easy to see *By the Sea* as the culmination of all that, itself something of a sentimental postcard to the seaside humour of bygone days.

'It is, absolutely. It's a harder film than *The Picnic* and *Futtock's End*. *Futtock's End*'s very moody. But this was a harder, glossier version of both of those earlier ones. *By the Sea* was much longer, it originally ran an hour and 25 minutes. There again, I crossed swords with Jimmy Gilbert. He cut it to 55 minutes and I said, "It's just about OK I suppose." Then he said, "I think I'm gonna cut it to 35." I said, "If you do I'm out of here. That's murder Jimmy, that's not cutting that's murdering it." He left it at 55.'

To emphasize its origins, the BBC produced a book of comic postcards to publicize the one-off special. 'It was fun to do because of that humour. We had the beach huts and those cut-outs you put your head through, they're all out-of-date things. The girls were dressed in a very modern way, but it was of days gone by. It wasn't modern. It could've been any date. It was sort of '30s in feel.'

Ironically, it was the old-fashioned jovial British humour of *By the Sea* that briefly incurred the wrath of self-appointed television watchdog/scourge, Mary Whitehouse, who accused the show of unnecessary violence, citing one scene where Ronnie Corbett's character was forcibly ejected from a revolving door.

Among the compromises Ronnie felt he made with *By the Sea* was the movie's final gag, which involved a small dog, which had been annoying everyone throughout the day, and was accidentally left tied to the back of the car as it drove off. 'It was obviously a toy dog – the car went round the corner and it swung right out. And then they stopped the car and the dog was perfectly all right. But the producer said we couldn't put that shot in. Now I've seen it many times in films. I was very annoyed about that because it was the last gag of the film, but he wouldn't let me. But that's what producers are there for I suppose. To put a spanner in your work.'

•••

Ronnie was lured back to a third and final series of *Porridge* in which the writing retained its high quality and, despite an 18-month gap, the cast was as fresh as ever.

Ronnie was all set to say goodbye to Fletcher when an interesting opportunity arose. Fletch's five-year stretch was almost up – how would he cope being back in the real world? The resulting series,

Ronnie B and Ronnie C plunder aged joke books as *The Two Ronnies'* Two Yokels.

A publicity shot for the Rons, with Ronnie B in customary striped blazer.

(clockwise from top left)
Ronnie drags it up again in a moment from *The Two Ronnies*
(although his wife didn't approve!).
Diana Dors rules the world in 'The Worm That Turned', one of *The Two Ronnies'*
most popular serials (except with feminists).
In serial mode once more, with bumbling detectives Piggy Malone and Charley Farley,
another hugely popular element of *The Two Ronnies.*

(from top)

His Lordship Entertains (1972) – Ronnie as Lord Rustless, with the ever reliable Josephine Tewson to hand, and an aged David Jason as Dithers the gardener.
Ronnie, as Fletch of course, with series co-stars Richard Beckinsale and Fulton Mackay, in the classic *Porridge*.

(from top)
A long-term professional and personal relationship – both Granville
and Arkwright, and Jason and Barker.
Just a song before I go – Ronnie and Jo Tewson in *Clarence* (1988).

(from top)
Another day, another awards ceremony – Ronnie and David Jason
share the limelight once more.
Out with the boys – Ronnie with sons Adam (*left*) and Laurence (*right*)
at the 1990 British Comedy Awards.
Barker and Corbett – old friends reunited.

(from top)
The movies once more – Ronnie returns as butler to Albert Finney's Winston Churchill in *The Gathering Storm* (2002).
Ronnie with wife Joy.

Back from retirement – Ronnie takes on the role of *The General* in 2003's
My House In Umbria.

Going Straight (complete with theme tune sung by one R. Barker), was once again penned by Clement/La Frenais and also featured Richard Beckinsale, as Fletch returns home to find that Godber has moved in with his daughter, Ingrid (Patricia Brake). The opening episode, 'Going Home', mirrored 'Prisoner and Escort', with Fletcher spending his return train journey to London with a departing Mackay. After that, it was life in the real world, five years on.

There's always a risk changing any successful formula and while *Going Straight* was undoubtedly a strong show, something was missing. Fletcher simply worked best when he had something tangible to react against. Put him in a small cell with an authority figure on every closely guarded landing and he knew what to do; put him back in the real world and everything simply became a lot more nebulous.

According to producer Sydney Lotterby, *Going Straight* was, in part, born out of Ronnie's desire to move on once again. 'Ronnie didn't want to do any more *Porridge*. But he wanted to extend it. Sadly that didn't work, probably because, despite it being the same characters, the public appreciation just wasn't quite the same, they wanted to see Ronnie in prison. It got a BAFTA, but after *Porridge* it was second-best.'

Ronnie agrees. 'Most people said it didn't work. I don't know why. It had Godber in it and that was perfectly legitimate because he had met him in prison; it just put Fletch in different situations. But it didn't seem to go well with the high-ups in the Beeb. Its fate is influenced a lot not just by the public but by the people who decide upstairs. I don't know who decided to pull it but they did. I get a lot of letters asking what happened to *Going Straight*. Sydney Lotterby wrote to someone very high up, "I've often wondered why you don't bring back *Going Straight*," he said and he explained all the plus points – the characters, opening up the situation, it was just as funny, got just as many laughs – "Why don't you bring it back? Signed, Sydney Lotterby." He got a letter back, "Dear Mr Lotterby, Thanks for your letter. It was interesting. It's always interesting to hear from a member of the public."'

•••

Norman Stanley Fletcher made just one more appearance, this time on the big screen in what was to be Ronnie Barker's only starring role in a movie. The British film industry in the 1970s consisted largely of increasingly dodgy Hammer horrors in the early part of the decade and TV sitcom spin-offs for the rest. The casts of *Dad's Army*, *Are You Being Served?*, *The Likely Lads* and *On the Buses* all made appearances at the local Odeon, most of them infinitely inferior to their televisual incarnation.

Porridge was something of an exception. It wasn't as good as the series – again something seems lost in the translation – but it wasn't that far off the mark. Unlike the series, the production was largely shot on location, which involved spending eight weeks in Chelmsford prison. 'I remember we were doing something involving cigarettes and matches and one of the extras said, "They don't do that. They roll 'em thinner than that." I thought, "Aha, he's been inside." One or two of the extras came up and said, "No, you're doing that wrong." While we were filming the movie, we were shooting a scene near a bit of garden and there was a little chap working away there and I was standing waiting and I asked him, "Are you in for a long time?" "Thirty years," he said. "I killed my wife." He was a little innocent-looking man, talking about how he put his wallflowers in. I did go round and meet some of the inmates and I remember most the deadness of their eyes, that look of submission, almost as if they were on some kind of tranquillizers. They weren't of course, but they had that look, as if they were really on downers. Doing *Porridge*, it felt as if it had a reality which *Open All Hours* certainly didn't have.'

A fire in the prison led to a few problems during filming. 'There was someone constantly drilling. You couldn't shoot. Every time they wanted to do a take they had to give this guy a fiver to stop. He made about £400 a day.'

•••

Several weeks after the movie finished filming Ronnie received a phone call from Sydney Lotterby, producer/director of the TV version of *Porridge*, informing him that his co-star, Richard Beckinsale, had died at the age of 31, from a heart attack.

'Richard was such a charming man and we were so close in that. It was a terrible shock when Syd rang me up and said that he'd died. He was in tears and I was streaming with tears. It was a terrible blow.

'I loved him, he was not as close to me as Glenn Melvyn because I didn't see him all day and all evening, but we were very, very similar in a way. He was just such a charming, sweet man that you could not dislike him. Everyone who met him liked him, and was fond of him. All the women were fond of him round the shows. They weren't fond of him in a sexual way, but they all thought he was so charming and sweet and nice and good, and he was. Tragedy, what a tragedy.

'A heart attack. It was cholesterol. He was up to here with cholesterol. And the funny thing is, we had the same physical examination by the same doctor for the film of *Porridge*; we'd just finished the film and we both had the same OK. The doctor signed us both off. They gave me a loading because of my weight, possible blood pressure and all that, so the insurers had to pay a bit more for me. But we came out of it both the same. Frightful, frightful. It happened about six weeks after we finished shooting the film. He never got to see it.'

•••

In February of 1978, Ronnies Barker and Corbett travelled to Buckingham Palace to receive their Order of the British Empire medals. In a break with protocol, the two Ronnies were presented to the Queen together, receiving her personal thanks for all the entertainment they had provided. 'She asked what we were doing now. I said, "We're at the Palladium Your Majesty – you ought to come and see us." She said, "I very well might." But she didn't.'

That entertainment was now about to be presented to the public theatrically, live for the very first time. The West End impresario Harold Fielding had for years been trying to persuade the boys to take their act onto the stage. Maybe it was the timing, maybe it was the money, 1978 was certainly the year. 'I'm very proud to say that I'm the only person who's ever started their variety career by topping the bill at the London Palladium,' Ronnie has said, although before they trod the boards in London they test-ran the show at the Hippodrome in Bristol. 'I probably initially enjoyed the stage show more than Ronnie because I was not so nervous,' Ronnie Corbett remembered. 'But Ronnie always said he never heard a noise like it. When we came on stage with the biggest show at the time, he said he'll never forget the noise of welcome when the doors opened and we stepped out.'

Terry Hughes, the director of the TV show was overseeing the production and Gerald Wiley was its chief writer. The set featured a large staircase, at the top of which were two doors, one large, one small. Needless to say, Ronnie C made his entrance through the large door and Ronnie B through the small. The show closely followed the structure of the TV series – news items to begin, the usual solo spots, a musical number, plus a selection of other variety acts in support.

Barker recalls: 'I was the most nervous I've ever been, I think. There were no retakes there. You couldn't stop and do a bit again. We had some very complicated stuff, like a piece I wrote as an old Chelsea pensioner talking about all the girls he ever knew; he starts a little dance as he sings and eventually he's kicking his legs up and then he collapses. It was called "Phyllis Hooter's Ball" and it was all very quick girls' names – "Clarissa you could kiss, you could meddle with Melissa and Vanessa you could press her and caress against the wall, you could have fun with Nicola but if you tried to tickle her, you'd end up with Virginia and she's no use at all . . ."'

•••

The opening of the show gave Ronnie his biggest worries, however. As a performer, he has always immersed himself in his characters. Starting with the make-up, building up through the costume, to the point where the man on stage was completely the character, never the actor. 'I never really thought of myself as a star, until very, very late on in my career, until the success of *Porridge*. With *The Two Ronnies* it was a team, we were a star team, but I think at the height of *Porridge* people wanted to see me in the street, they wanted to speak to me and I felt I had got there. But not much earlier on than that, certainly not during the early times of *The Two Ronnies*. It was just a show that seemed to be working and we were glad it was and we were a pair, a couple, a team.'

•••

But the opening of the show required Ronnie Barker to stand on stage as Ronnie Barker, a prospect he did not feel comfortable with, until Ronnie C made a suggestion – play Ronnie Barker as a character.

'I developed a sort of pseudo-me character. Rather like in the news items, but it had to be different. So I developed a smoother delivery, a more chummy, friendly thing, which worked. Ronnie thought it worked because he knew I was scared of being myself all through it. He was always himself on his chair, or that character that you think is him. So he knew I was worried about being myself and he said, "That's good, it's very avuncular, it's very smooth, it looks good, the costume's good and you look comfortable and affluent and all the things you're supposed to look in front of an audience." I got used to it and enjoyed it eventually, I'm talking about four weeks after we opened.'

'Once he found a way of doing it like an actor doing a role, he became comfortable,' Ronnie C concurs. 'It remained the same more or less each night. I would see him remembering to put his hand in his pocket at a certain time and so on, doing the performance, because he had to have it all in his mind I suppose. On his own admission, he can't go and open a fête or something because he doesn't know who to be. I was not so nervous, though I was nervous about forgetting my words.'

After all his experience performing, it might have come as a surprise to Ronnie to find that he was still capable of being nervous.

'No it didn't surprise me that much, because I was always nervous for *Porridge* and *Open All Hours*. Before *Porridge* I always used to lie down for half an hour with the light off, just lie there and get my brain going. That's about as much Stanislavsky as I ever did. Some people prepare for ages for a part, I think that's suspect sometimes.

Either they're not as good as they should be and they have to try very hard, or they're just deluding themselves into thinking they are researching something. Some people will say, "Oh I'm doing a country part so I have to go and live in the country for three weeks." I always tend to suspect it a bit. I think many actors pretend that things are a lot more difficult than they are because it makes them look clever. I've worked with actors like that but I've never done it.

'I remember Fulton Mackay during *Porridge* used to find it very difficult to do moves. He was fine on lines, but once we were doing a scene and he said, "It's no good Ronnie, I just can't do it. Can we do it again?" He was a great one for doing a scene again. He usually had about three and a half minutes in the show and he would take three-quarters of the rehearsal time, which I'm sure he wouldn't mind me saying, because he was meticulous at getting it absolutely right, and he succeeded. A lot of actors do have this about moves. I've never had it. If someone says, "You say, 'Gotcha!' and then you go over there," I say, "Gotcha!" and go over there.'

•••

When quizzed as to why they did the stage show Ronnie is blatantly honest.

'Money I think. Harold Fielding, who was a great impresario, wanted to do it, and he said we'd spend a lot of money on it. Lots of people loved it but it got criticized of course. A lot of the critics said it was just like watching television – they said they'd seen a lot of the material before. Nevertheless it was a great buzz and it was wonderful to do, and we did two seasons there. We came back and did it again.

'We were slightly worried that there was hardly any new material in the show but various people assured us that was what the public wanted to see, us in the flesh, on stage, and to see the things they knew. We did a news item bit at the beginning. It was very similar to the show.'

For the stage show, classic sketches were revived, Jehosaphat and Jones got to sing, even Fletcher got a look in. 'On the first stage show I did a *Porridge* sketch with Sam Kelly as "Bunny" Warren, written by

Dick Clement and Ian La Frenais, especially for the show. Ronnie C did some of his stand-up act to equal things out.'

•••

Whatever the critics had to say, the public voted with their money, with the run being extended from its initial seven and a half weeks to a full three months, and the duo performing seven days a week to keep up with demand. They then took the show to Coventry over the Christmas period in preparation for a 14-week run in Australia in May 1979. Ronnie B commuted to the performances in Coventry, using his time on the train to work on another of his books, *Gentleman's Relish*. His various collections of saucy postcards and long-forgotten magazine illustrations had proved to be a rather successful sideline for the actor. 'When I published my first one, the publisher said, "This will go extremely well. Your next book will go almost as well, and the book after that will go fairly well and the book after that will be sort of all right." He said, "I can say this from previous experience. It always happens. This sort of book starts off at its peak and goes gradually down." And he was right – the last one I did sold only about 20,000 and the first one I did sold 140,000.'

CHAPTER 6

Comedy Heroes

This evening, my friends, I want to talk about Sin. And I wish to speak only to those of you who are Sinners. All those who have never sinned should leave now. No one has moved. It's just as well. Because if anyone had dared to walk out, he would have been branded 'Liar'. This village – this village is overrun with Sin. It is rife! Rife! And I tell you, friends, that the Devil is everywhere, about his deadly work. He's at work in the village shop, watering the milk; he's in the public house, watering the beer; he is behind the public house, watering the daisies. He is at work upstairs behind the curtains of Oak Cottage, where old Mr Tomkins took a lodger as company for his young wife. His young wife is in the family way. And the lodger – she's in the family way as well.

The country church vicar for whom Ronnie wrote these lines and whom Ronnie portrayed on screen was one of what he describes as the 'dozen or so' basic characters he assembled in his head. They would sit there patiently in a pleasant little alcove of his mind, like patients in a plastic surgeon's waiting room, until he looked them over and called one in for a little remodelling. Then the character would be ready to step out in front of the cameras for a sketch, a serial, maybe even a whole movie, before returning to the purgatory of the waiting room once more. How long would they have to wait there, leafing through back issues of *National Geographic* or *Nip 'n' Tuck Monthly*? Not long, given Ronnie's workload. He needed all of his characters to be ready on call. How long had they been there? That is another question entirely. Where did they all come from? From whom did Ronnie draw inspiration for his repertoire of characters?

Throughout the years, Ronnie Barker has always acknowledged the performers who have influenced him, both those he watched and those he worked with. While he freely admits that in watching his favourite entertainers he was, first and foremost, enjoying the performances, unwittingly allowing the entertainers simply to do their jobs and entertain him, he also says that, whether he realized it at the time or not, he was also learning valuable lessons. And he makes it clear that he learned from them all. Of course, in terms of his own career, the first strong comedic influence was Glenn Melvyn.

'He was a wonderful, wonderful man. I met him in tatty weekly rep (but then all rep theatres have to be tatty, they haven't got time to be anything else really). Glenn was there as an actor at first and we just hit it off. He was so funny and I am drawn to people like that. Then he became director of the company, and I was there for another 18 months. We got very close and used to go the pub every night, as everyone did, and have a half pint of something and then sit in his car and sing. We used to love harmonizing, he was a great harmonizer, and I had church harmonies, from being in the choir. We used to sit and sing "The Way You Look Tonight" and those sort of ballads, standards, that were around at that time and we had a great time. Then he gave me my first television work.'

This of course included Ronnie's debut as a writer for TV. Melvyn did not credit him for the writing, but he did take three of Ronnie's scripts, paying him £50 for each. Not having a writing credit never seems to have bothered Ronnie, he was happy to be working with his old friend and even more happy to be gaining that all-important experience, especially when it came to scriptwriting, a discipline that was made all the more difficult for him by his fastidious nature and meticulous attention to detail.

'It's very draining, writing. It is hard work, brain work, but not painful. I never sat and tore my hair out and thought, "What can I do with this?" I always seemed to be able to write. Some of *The Two Ronnies* sketches I would write in a day. So I was quite prolific, I suppose. It's getting the ideas. I always wrote down on a bit of paper any scrap of an idea I had and stuck it in my pocket. I can't say I enjoyed the writing really but I enjoyed it immensely when it worked, when you performed it and it worked, you hear the laughs and you're very pleased that you've written it. But when you start, on the day, and you sit down and you write the first line, you're not pleased to be doing it, and if I wasn't completely pleased I tore it up and didn't use it. My way of writing was that I didn't write everything down and cross it out and write other little bits. I wrote it in my head in chunks of maybe five or six lines, I got those right in my head and then put them down, so therefore you got a fairly clean-looking page. Then my wife Joy would type it up. When you're writing lyrics you've got to write down the internal rhyme or the rhymes and you can't just remember those in your head. You write those on a scrap and when you've got the verse or the chorus or whatever you're doing, then you write that in.'

Nell of the Yukon (part one)

My tale is a weird one – 'twas found long ago,
In a book on my Grandpappy's shelf,
So hush while I tell it and don't make a sound,
'Cos I want to hear it myself.

It was writ in the days when the Yukon was rich,
And the miners got drunk every night.
It was writ all in red by my old Uncle Jed,
'Cos he was the one as could write.

Now the story begins with a quarrel one night,
Between Jed and his pretty wife Nell.
She'd lost all his dough at the gambling saloon,
And one of her garters as well.

Now Nell was a gal with a wonderful shape,
She could hit a spittoon at ten paces.
When she went on the town, she wore a tight gown,
And was seen in all the right places.

Ronnie's song 'Nell of the Yukon' gallops along for 23 verses and must have taken up a heap of scrap paper to note down the rhymes and keep the story flowing, but was ultimately produced as a clean script. Not everyone who submitted scripts to the boys was quite as meticulous, however.

'I remember on *The Two Ronnies*, people used to send in scripts they'd typed and then they x'd them out if they didn't like the line and it was just a mass of x's on these pieces of paper and I remember Ronnie C saying, "We can't read this! We can't read the stuff!" So we used to give it to the BBC secretary to make sense of it. To type out the lines that were left and then it was a script. But it was like an embroidery chart. I never did that. I'm still in two minds to say whether I enjoyed writing or I didn't enjoy writing. It's both. It was a means to an end.'

•••

Although he never harmonized in the car with them, Barker also learned his craft, in part at least, from a number of classic screen comics, many of whom he had watched in his childhood, among them W.C. Fields. William Claude Dukenfield (as he was christened) left home at the age of 11, worked in circuses and travelling shows and became one of America's most popular vaudeville attractions. By 1893, at the age of just 14, he was known as W.C. Fields and was making a fortune – up to $125 a week – while his slick-talking style was becoming legendary. Fields played at the Palace Theatre in London in 1901 where the show was watched by King Edward VII, who promptly invited the 22-year-old to play at the other palace – Buckingham Palace! Within 20 years Fields would become one of the highest-paid entertainers in the world, earning $1,000 a week and enjoying a film career that would ultimately span 33 movies. But his early years in travelling shows and his childhood spent on market stalls as the son of a fruit and vegetable pedlar gave Fields the air of a showman, the heart, in fact, of a barker. Whether he knew it at the time or not, Ronnie had at least that one small thing in common with W.C. Fields!

'I must have seen him first when I was a teenager. My friend's father had a projector and he used to show home movies, the old Super-8 stuff. That was also where I first saw Laurel and Hardy, whom I loved instantly.

'But W.C. Fields I thought was so droll and so clever with his physical business. That's what I liked about him, the things he did with his hat and his stick and there was one film where he kept getting caught up in some bead curtains in the house and he was having a row with his wife every time and he'd keep walking into these curtains, and he was wonderful at getting tangled up.'

•••

Something else that Ronnie shared with W.C. Fields was an innate comprehension of comedy. Ronnie has often described how he has surprised even himself by knowing instinctively what will work, what will be funny. Fields was the same. He had the instinct but was never quite sure why it worked. He once said, 'I know what makes people laugh but trying to get your hands on the why of it is like trying to pick an eel out of a tub of water.'

Nell of the Yukon (part two)

Well she'd come home that night, just a little bit tight,
And she threw off her clothes in disgust,
'What's the matter?' said Jed, and she drunkenly said,
As she undid her corsets, 'You're bust!'

Now Jed knew what she meant, all his gold she had spent,
And he sat there awhile making faces.
Then as she bent over to unlace her boots.
He gave her a belt, with his braces.

Nell gave a great jump, with her hand to her rump,
And a yell all Alaska could hear.
Then she made a quick run and she snatched up Jed's gun,
And she poked it inside of Jed's ear.

'That's the finish,' said Nell, 'I've had all I can take,
Do you hear me? Get out of my sight!'
Well old Jed he could hear and the gun in his ear,
Made him hear even better that night.

W.C. Fields not only had a sophisticated appreciation of dialogue –
an ear for a funny line – he was also marvellously funny when it came
to bumbling clumsiness or finely timed slapstick, which requires
enormous physical control. Physical comedians have always intrigued
Ronnie. American vaudeville comedian George Carl was another one
of those.

'I saw him first in the Crazy Horse in Paris. I thought he was
French at first. It was all mime, no talking at all, and he came onto
the stage which was incredibly small and you'd get eight girls with
nothing on but German helmets and they'd all cram onto this stage,
and the place was packed out at about £40 a seat. On he came, this
little man, and did his act, and I thought he was brilliant. I didn't see
him again until he appeared on the Royal Command Performance

and I found out he was an American. It's just the sheer dexterity of the man, I loved it and I find it very funny.'

Indeed, no-one who has ever seen the diminutive Carl go through his act, particularly the part which involves his taking off his jacket and turning it inside out without it ever leaving his body, could fail to find him very funny.

•••

Another act that Ronnie loved was an outfit called Wilson, Keppel and Betty. Jack Wilson was a Liverpudlian, Joe Keppel came from Cork in Ireland and they formed a tap-dancing duo when they met in America around 1919. It wasn't until they teamed up with the glamorous Betty, however, that they really started to make a name for themselves. Betty Knox had been comedian Jack Benny's vaudeville partner and had learned a lot of stagecraft from him. With Wilson and Keppel, she would perform a kind of dance of the seven veils as Jack and Joe grew ever more excited playing their flutes. It was their sand dance, however, for which the trio will always be remembered. Dressed in ridiculous mock-Egyptian attire, complete with fez, Jack and Joe would sprinkle sand on stage from a perforated coffee pot, then shuffle back and forth in time to the music, striking poses just like ancient Egyptian hieroglyphic drawings. They would sweep the stage after their act, pouring the sand back into the pot and telling everyone how special it was because it had come all the way from the Sahara. Although Betty was replaced several times (with each new dancer retaining her moniker), the sand never was and their act remained basically unchanged for over 30 years, including three Royal Variety Performance appearances. 'Yes,' says Ronnie, 'Wilson, Keppel and Betty were special. And Max Wall. I'm hysterical when they do those silly walks. It's something that tickles me, some people can take it or leave it but I can't. I think it's wonderful, absolutely wonderful. The only time I've ever fallen out of my seat with laughter was watching Max Wall.'

•••

Max Wall was a born entertainer. His parents, Jock and Stella, were great music hall stars and Max was paraded on stage in his father's arms in 1908 only days after he was born. Sadly, Max's parents split up but Max grew very close to the man who became his mother's new partner, Harry Wallace. He took the first part of Wallace's name to create his own stage name and his career as an entertainer would span 70 years. At first, Max performed on stage as a dancer. He was strong and athletic, even something of an acrobat, but he later turned to comedy and the poise of the dancer was obvious in the most famous of the characters he created, Professor Wallofski. Wearing the oversized boots of a clown, accentuated by black tights and a baggy black jacket, the whole ensemble was topped off with a wild mane of shaggy black hair. The poise of the dancer came through when Wallofski strutted around the stage to music with the most outrageous of rubber-legged silly walks. John Cleese later confessed that he had based his famous Monty Python silly walk on Max Wall's antics. Max's years as a dancer gave him the balance and the timing to make his walk look ridiculously clumsy, even impossible. But only an expert capable of doing something really well can do something really badly and make it look entertaining.

Nell of the Yukon (part three)

So he quitted the shack and he never looked back,
And he set out to search for more gold.
But his luck it was out and he wandered about,
Till at last he was dying of cold,

So he dragged himself into a nearby saloon,
Which was known as the Barrel of Glue.
It was one of those joints where the men are all men,
And most of the women are, too.

The place was a gambling hell it was clear,
Every man jack was betting and boozing.

Three miners were winning a strip poker game,
And a girl with no clothes on was losing.

Jed sat down at a table and bought himself in,
By producing his very last dollar.
And he started to deal with hope in his heart.
And three aces under his collar.

Tommy Cooper, another of Ronnie's favourites, was a master of the art of mishandling magic tricks. Cooper practised for hours to be able to do his tricks perfectly in order that he could then get them perfectly wrong. As an ex-guardsman, Cooper was able to use his build to great advantage, too. He was a physical comedian as well as a craftsman, blundering around clumsily with practised precision. So used were his fans to seeing him stumbling around during a performance that when he collapsed and died on stage at Her Majesty's Theatre in 1984, the audience thought it was part of his act.

•••

Another talented expert who created an art out of lousing things up was one of Ronnie's all-time favourites, Victor Borge. Born in Denmark in 1909, Borge was a musician through and through. His father had been a musician with the Royal Danish Chapel and Victor trained at the Royal Danish Academy of Music. He soon found that he could have fun poking fun at established musical traditions and at pretentious concert-goers. Comedy became an integral part of his performances and he was already an established star in Denmark before he had to flee the invading Nazis in 1940. Having been born Borge Rosenbaum his Jewish background made him an obvious target for the Nazis. Borge headed for America and there he became an even bigger star. It is estimated that during his lifetime he played over 6,000 concerts in front of more than 12 million people. Although he was a hugely respected conductor, composer and pianist, Borge loved to clown around. He would fall off the piano stool and play out of tune with the rest of his orchestra, or even just play the wrong notes, with such practised ease that he was always a delight to watch.

•••

'Les Dawson did that as well,' says Ronnie, referring to Dawson's legendarily awful piano playing, but he made Ronnie laugh in lots of different ways. Les had nurtured his act as a piano-playing comedian with a deadpan, mournful delivery through the working men's clubs of northern England before he won the TV talent show *Opportunity Knocks* in 1967. After that, he was seldom absent from UK TV screens either in his own show or as a compere of variety or game shows like *Blankety Blank*. Les was not just a gag man, however, he was also a wordsmith, concocting meandering shaggy dog stories that used the kind of flowery, poetic language that was so incongruous with his grumbling northern accent and flat, emotionless delivery. Les got through a lot of material in a single performance, writing much of it himself but also using a clutch of trusted comedy writers such as Barry Cryer. How other people have written their material, however, has never been of any great concern to Ronnie.

'I don't think I consider things from a writer's point of view,' he says, 'because the writer is one stage back. If I see someone who is very funny, says things very funnily, I laugh at them, and I love them for being a comedian. I laugh at them as a viewer watching this and listening to this guy who's got this wonderful material or point of view.

'Some people make you laugh as soon as they appear, like David Jason. Not for any reason often, like Jimmy Grout on *Inspector Morse*. As soon as he comes through a door I laugh, and Joy says, "What are you laughing at?" I say, "I'm laughing at Jimmy Grout, he just makes me laugh." A lot of people would say that of Tommy Cooper, and of Eric Morecambe too. There are other performers like Nat Jackley, the Chuckle Brothers – if they do a funny walk, I'm a sucker for them.'

•••

Nat Jackley was a music hall star who had had his own TV series as early as 1956. Like Max Wall, he had been a dancer, appearing at the beginning of his career with a clog-dancing group called the Lancashire Lads, with whom Charlie Chaplin had also danced. With the athleticism of a dancer, Jackley was able to move in the most discordant manner, a practised, rubber-limbed clumsiness that reduced his audiences, including Ronnie, to tears of laughter.

The Chuckle Brothers are a double act formed by brothers Barry and Paul Patton from Rotherham. They won the TV talent contest *New Faces* in 1974 and, while continuing to tour with their own summer shows and appearing in pantomime, they have been clowning on TV as incompetent odd job men since their first series, *The Chucklehounds*, in 1985. Since 1987 they have starred in 15 series of *Chucklevision*, which is broadcast as part of children's television on the BBC.

While the Chuckle Brothers are very much a traditional double act, sometimes Ronnie's sense of humour heads in a less obvious direction. After all, you wouldn't really expect a respected actor like Sir Alan Bates, CBE, to be on anyone's list of funniest performers. 'Alan Bates comes on and I'm gone. Joy knows now so she doesn't ask why am I laughing, she knows. I can't explain it, but I'm laughing at the man. His delivery, sometimes unintentionally, is very funny. A very good actor, I love to watch him. I remember him in a film called *The Shout*, with John Hurt, it was just this one line where someone said, "You could be here for weeks." And he replies, "It might be months." I always think of that line. It's not a funny line, it just makes me laugh.'

Nell of the Yukon (part four)

And he won thick and fast, when the evening was past,
He owned all the gold on the table.
As well as six mines and a three-quarter share,
In a Mexican showgirl called Mabel.

Then in walked Black Lou, with a sackful of gold,
And he challenged poor Jed with a leer:
'One cut and one call and the winner takes all,
And the loser must buy all the beer!'

What could Jed do? He hated Black Lou,
As everyone did in those parts.
So Jed shuffled the cards and both players cut,
And both players cut – Ace of Hearts!

Then up jumped Black Lou and his face went bright blue,
Which astonished a passing physician.
And he used a foul word which no-one had heard,
Since the time of the Great Exhibition.

Wonderful material, of course, need not necessarily be wonderfully sophisticated. Ronnie loved the quick-fire, abrasive delivery of stand-up comedian Frank Carson. Carson first drew attention to himself on a 1971 TV show called *The Comedians* where a string of stand-ups 'competed', one after another, grabbing the spotlight to fire off a few gags and steal a few laughs. With his strident Ulster accent and high-decibel delivery Carson never tried to do anything clever, he just belted out great gags and let people know why they were laughing with his catchphrase, again delivered at maximum volume, 'It's the way I tell 'em!' 'I like Carson because I just love gags,' says Ronnie. 'I love to hear a quick gag and he does them so well and manages to get such very good jokes.'

•••

Ronnie found a mutual admirer in another of his favourite funnymen, Alfred Hawthorne Hill, better known to all as Benny. Five years older than Ronnie, Benny Hill had started his career performing in clubs during the Second World War and made his first TV appearance in 1949 on a show called *Hi There*. By 1955 he had his own show on BBC television, sticking with the Beeb until 1969 when he moved to Thames TV to make the shows for which he became most famous. His style has often been described as a kind of saucy seaside postcard come to life, but he was also a master of slapstick and a marvellous writer of both gags and songs, even appearing on *Top of the Pops* when his hit single 'Ernie (The Fastest Milkman in the West)' topped the charts in 1971. Hill suffered hugely for what was perceived as sexism when political correctness set in during the eighties as his shows often featured scantily clad young women. Hill's reaction? 'I'm not against half-naked girls... not as often as I'd like to be!' Ronnie said, 'I only met Benny Hill once. He was a lovely man and he said, "How do you do all that clever stuff in *The Two Ronnies*?" I told him how much I liked his filming. I always thought his filming was brilliant. His gags were absolutely tremendous.'

•••

Some of television comedy's modern stars have elicited mixed reactions from Barker. Ben Elton, now a friend, was a taste that at first Ronnie wasn't too keen to acquire. It wasn't just that there was a generation gap between the two performers, although Elton was born in the same year as Ronnie's son Laurence, it was a question of style and, to a certain extent, taste. Ben Elton had emerged from the 'new wave' of comedians often referred to as 'alternative' comedians because they saw their acts as being so distinctly different from the more traditional comics like Les Dawson or Frank Carson. The 'alternative' crowd came from comedy clubs where the audiences, and the players, had experienced the mock revolution of Punk Rock, watched the Sex Pistols' shock tactics on TV and seen haute couture reduced to tattered tartan held together with safety pins. Ben Elton had the angry young man approach of punk and directed his vituperation against the establishment, the comfortable middle classes and the government, saving his most vitriolic outburst for the then Prime Minister, Margaret Thatcher.

'What I hated about his audiences was they never laughed. They only cheered and clapped and that means to me, you are not being funny if you are clapped and cheered. It used to annoy me because it's like mentioning the foreman's name. That used to be the cheapest trick on radio when they would go round to all the workers' factories during the war, on the radio show *Workers' Playtime*. They used to have comedians who would always say, "Well Mr Higgins wouldn't like that!" And the whole place would go up and you'd think, "What's that about?" That's the same sort of thing as shouting, "Mrs Thatcher". Cheap and easy. But then we somehow got to like him.'

Nell of the Yukon (part five)

'You cheated, you swine!' said Lou with a whine,
As he grabbed Uncle Jed by the neck.
And he started to squeeze till Jed dropped to his knees,
And with one final wheeze hit the deck.

The whole saloon froze as Black Lou drew his gun,
'Alright stranger!' said he. 'Have it your way!'
When in rushed a woman and as Lou turned round,
She spat straight in his eye from the doorway.

It was Nell! There she stood and she really looked good,
As she grabbed Jed and rushed him outside.
And they didn't stop running for seven long miles,
Till they found themselves somewhere to hide.

'Twas a room booked by Nell in a sleazy hotel,
A dollar a night double roomer.
It was built out of driftwood and named The Savoy,
By some guy with a quick sense of humour.

Of the newest crop of comedy talent, Ronnie admires a young man from Bolton called Peter Kay. Kay had had a number of dead-end jobs before deciding to have a stab at stand-up comedy. He discovered he had a talent for it, and was soon in great demand.

Before he knew it, he was appearing on TV, winning Channel 4's *So You Think You're Funny* talent competition in 1997 and going on to sell-out tours, his own TV show *That Peter Kay Thing* in 2000 and the following year the first series of a show called *Phoenix Nights*. Set in a northern club, the fictitious Phoenix in Bolton, the sit-com was highly praised. Kay is proud to admit that Ronnie Barker is his hero, and has been since childhood. He was delighted when he finally made contact with Barker himself.

'I think he's very, very funny. He's sort of whimsical, that's what I call it, he has a whimsical turn of phrase. And also you have to admit that if someone likes you very, very much, you tend to like them a bit. He wrote me a long fan letter and I didn't realize who it was from. Peter Kay didn't mean anything to me because it's a very ordinary-sounding name. And then it said, "I've just finished a tour, six months all round the place and I'm exhausted," and I thought, "just a minute, Peter Kay, this is the guy from *Phoenix Nights*." So I wrote back to him and he was delighted and wrote again.

'I had some *Porridge* notepaper, which had been printed for use on the set, and I sent him a letter from Fletcher on this notepaper and he really thought it was from a prison at first. He sent me a sort of squashed-down cake with a note, "This is for you to eat, but it's what's inside that counts," and he'd put a file inside it. Not a big file, just an emery board. At the BAFTA tribute he came round to where I was sitting at the back; suddenly this head came round the corner and it was him peering round. So we were able to meet at last.'

•••

Having been brought up in what is often described as the golden age of the cinema, the years before television decimated cinema audiences, the stars of the big screen were another big influence on Barker. Aside from W.C. Fields and Laurel and Hardy, Ronnie was obviously a big fan of Laurence Olivier, having named his son after his hero. One of his other favourite actors, however, was Alec Guinness. Born in 1914, Guinness had worked as a copywriter for an advertising agency after leaving school but yearned to tread the boards. He attended stage school for a while before John Gielgud took him under his wing and Guinness began to appear in classical roles. He had had 34 parts in 23 plays by the time he went into the navy during the Second World War. The first of his many film roles came in 1946 when he played Pocket in Dickens's *Great Expectations* but it was the 1949 movie *Kind Hearts and Coronets* that really made him a star. He played eight different characters in the film.

'He was one of my idols. I had idols in film. When I was in rep, before I was at the Oxford Playhouse, I remember going to see Alec Guinness in the film of *Oliver Twist* and adored him and thought he was wonderful. I was very pleased a while back when in his book he said I was his favourite actor. That's mind-boggling. When you think back, you wonder how he could say that. He actually introduced me when I got my lifetime achievement from the British Comedy Awards. I got it the first year and he did the intro.'

Nell of the Yukon (part six)

Well, they flopped on the bed, 'Thank the Lord,' said old Jed,
'My gambling days are behind me.
But I'm puzzled dear Nell and I want to hear tell,
How in hell's name you managed to find me?

'I've been wandering too, all around just like you,'
Said Nell, 'And the thought makes me wince.
And the reason, my dear was that whack on the rear,
I just ain't sat down ever since.'

And they lay there awhile, then Jed, with a smile,
Said 'I'll never more leave this old town –
We'll find peace you and I,' but he got no reply,
For young Nell was a-sleeping, face down.

•••

Music has always played a big part in influencing Barker, particularly in the way it allows a lyricist to play around with words. In that respect, the American entertainer Phil Harris was another significant influence. Perhaps best known as Baloo the Bear in Walt Disney's *The Jungle Book*, Harris had been a band leader in the 1930s, touring non-stop to play concert halls and small-town dances until he got his big break on Jack Benny's radio show in 1936. Harris's snappy one-liners and happy Southern good humour made him a regular on the show for 16 years. After the Second World War, when he and his entire 25-piece orchestra enlisted in the US Maritime Service, he had his own radio show with his wife, actress Alice Faye, called, naturally enough, *The Phil Harris–Alice Faye Show*. Harris also appeared in several movies, including a couple with Bing Crosby, *Here Comes the Groom* (1951) and *Anything Goes* (1956). Phil and Alice were married for 54 years until his death in 1995.

'Phil Harris goes back to when I was 17, and in the amateur company. My friend Mike Ford had all his records and I loved them, they were old 78s. We used to buy them in Oxford and I had a load of Phil Harris – "Woodman Spare That Tree", "The Darktown Poker Club", "That's What I Like About the South". I always remember that one because it was a list of things, and I love lists of things. I loved doing them in sketches. I don't know when I discovered it, but I love words and lists.'

•••

Lists, of course, often played a part in Ronnie's monologues. Just as his songs used a rhythm to give the rhymes a humorous touch, so in the prose of the monologues he could impart a rhythm to lists of words that made them funnier than they ever deserved to be. A lot of this comes from Ronnie's delivery – or as Frank Carson would say, 'It's the way I tell 'em!' – but the construction of his lists of words is a fascinating thing. Witness this excerpt from a *Two Ronnies* monologue:

Silence, please. I'd like to call this meeting to order and welcome everyone to the annual, or, in other words, twelve-monthly conference that we hold once a year for the Society for People Who Use a Lot of Words and Say Very Little. It is with tremendous pleasure, enjoyment, elation, glee, joy and delight and with very little pain, discomfort, embarrassment, melancholia and stroke-or-depression that I address you all verbally by speaking to all those of you who are listening with your ears to the vocal manifestations which are emanating from this hole in the middle of my face.

Now, not wishing to be brief, and in order more fully to beat about the bush, not to mention shilly-shallying and procrastination, although I have, in fact, just mentioned them – nevertheless, and notwithstanding, I don't propose to sit down without laying before you where I stand in relation to our policy of, or attitude to, and indeed our connection with, the attitude which our policy has always been concerned over.

For someone who maintains that he has never really been aware of being directly influenced by any other performer, Ronnie Barker actually has an impressive list of favourites who undoubtedly contributed to his development as performer, but not every comedian passes the Barker test.

'I don't like comedians who act out what they've just said: "He came up at me, he came at me, he came up like an ostrich or something," like Billy Connolly and Jasper Carrott. I wouldn't say I don't like Billy Connolly, I just think he could be twice as funny if he cut out all the wanderings.

'They can't leave it alone, they have to give impersonations and they have to act it when they've just said it. We don't want that. Anyone can do that. That's me talking as a viewer. It's nothing to do with writing, you can't write that. The thing that annoys me most about stand-up comedians today, is they say a gag and then they say, "My name is Charlie Farnsbarns, thank you very much, good night." Is that a get off? Would Max Miller have got off like that? Saying who you are and thanks very much? That's another thing that annoys me.

'I'd prefer if Eddie Izzard came on and was funny all the time without pretending to ad-lib. We know he's not, in every word, he knows what he's going to say, but he wanders and I don't take that on board, I don't believe that. So I don't want to see him wandering around and groping around for a gag which we could have had five minutes ago. Of course, you've got to do ten minutes, if you've got three gags, so you've to do all that or you could do one minute and then get off.'

•••

But what about the area in which Ronnie has truly excelled? Is there a TV comedy show that he rates above all others? Ronnie professes not to like much television comedy of recent years but he still has some favourites.

'I don't like many. I like the American sitcoms, I love *Frasier*. I like *Friends*. *MASH* was one of my favourites. Alan Alda was a hero of mine and I was delighted once when I met him. I think *Friends* is very cleverly written. Now, I look at that as a writer. But they have 20 people sitting round a table working on every line. America's such a big place, there's plenty to choose from. We couldn't find 20 people of any quality to sit round a table. I say that very nonchalantly. It would be very difficult to get the people together, but I often thought it should be done, because some of those people in *Friends* probably write one line or two lines, if they're lucky, and they rewrite after they record it twice on the one day, and they rewrite between those two recordings, and they take the best. They give them extra lines between, you could call it a matinee and an evening performance, two shows, two audiences and in between they rewrite. Frightening. For the actors apart from anything.'

•••

As far as British TV comedy is concerned, Ronnie's admiration of performers who can create vivid new characters has made him a great admirer of two stars in recent years who have shown great versatility in their work. Actor, writer and producer Paul Whitehouse had worked with Harry Enfield, Reeves and Mortimer and a host of other top names before he shot to fame himself in *The Fast Show* in 1994. Just as *The Fast Show* featured a multitude of disparate characters, so too did *The Catherine Tate Show*. One of the brightest young comedians in recent years, the multi-talented Catherine Tate was nominated for the prestigious Perrier Award prior to starring in her own TV show in 2004 where she appeared as the 'Death Row Wife', the 'Botox Babe', teenager 'Lauren' and 'Bernie the Irish Nurse'.

'I like Paul Whitehouse, and I really used to like *The Fast Show*. And I love Catherine Tate. It's her face that's so amazing. She plays a teenager one minute and then the next minute she's playing this ancient granny, with no make-up. She swears like mad, there's terrible f-ing language all the time. I don't like it in comedy really, but sometimes if someone does it so well, it is very funny.'

•••

Ronnie starred in two of the nation's favourite sitcoms of all time but, setting his own shows aside, what would his favourite sitcom be? When pressed to pick the one he enjoys the most, the answer involves an old friend. '*Only Fools and Horses* I think is probably my favourite sitcom of all time. I admire the writer John Sullivan so much. There are lovely performances in things like *One Foot in the Grave*, and David Renwick's a great writer; but for week-after-week funniness I think it's got to be *Only Fools and Horses*.'

CHAPTER 7

Two Ronnies Down Under

THE LAUGHING TAXMAN
I am a tax inspector,
A jolly chap that's me.
I deal with your assessments,
And drink a lot of tea.
You'll always find me laughing,
You'll never see me cry.
I find out what you're earning,
And then I bleed you dry.

Oh... A-ha-ha-ha... (*laughing chorus*)

I check the bills you send me,
I find out what you've bought.
I look through your expenses,
Then cut them down to nought.
I squeeze out every penny,
You all pay up like mice.
And if I catch you cheating,
I make you pay up twice!

Oh... A-ha-ha-ha... (*laughing chorus*)

I send you forms and pamphlets,
It's fun without a doubt.
To ask a lot of questions,
And try to catch you out.
There's only one man's tax forms,
I leave there on the shelf.
Oh yes, I make quite certain,
I don't pay tax myself.

Oh... A-ha-ha-ha... (*laughing chorus*)

Revolver shot. Ronnie groans, body falling.

Man: Got you, you swine!

Ronnie's 'Laughing Taxman' song pokes fun at the poor old tax inspector but, like so many entertainers before them, *The Two Ronnies* found themselves in a position where it made sense for them to spend some time out of the country in 1979 for tax reasons. The Rons decamped to Australia with their families in April, heading for sunnier climes while Britain foundered under a cloud of economic depression. The government had introduced a pay freeze, limiting wage rises to five per cent, and the result was widespread industrial action. The strikes meant that rubbish was no longer collected, with bags of rotting garbage piling up in the streets, many people were laid off work and even the dead suffered as bodies went unburied. That great British institution, *The Times* newspaper, was withdrawn, remaining unpublished for a year due to strike action.

•••

The Barkers and the Corbetts would be away from home for a whole year, and on the outward leg of their journey they had a brief stopover in Los Angeles, where the two Ronnies took part in an American TV programme called *The Big Show*. Masterminded by the extremely successful producer Lorne Michaels (the brain behind NBC's breeding ground of contemporary comedy culture, *Saturday Night Live*), *The Big Show* was a throw-back to the variety show days of the 1950s and '60s, albeit featuring contemporary acts. The two Ronnies appeared alongside a number of Barker's idols on the show – one of their few American appearances. Victor Borge was on the bill as was Loretta Swit, who played 'Hot Lips Houlihan' in one of Barker's all-time favourite TV shows, *MASH*.

As the 'Laughing Taxman' demonstrates, in many ways the Ronnies' shows, whether on stage or on TV, had their roots in old-time variety – itself derived from the days of British music hall.

'I think music hall has been an influence on me but I don't know where it came from. It must have been the variety shows I used to see at what was then the New Theatre in Oxford. We used to go and see variety bills; that was the only time I would see things like that because there was no amateur stuff going on at all, I never took part in any. I remember seeing people like Max Wall and I saw a young Dick Emery once when he was in panto, playing a Dame.

'My great thing, that I'm very proud of, is I do no research at all into anything. Even all the picture books that I've done, which are all Edwardian pictures and postcards, are all compiled using material I have at my home. I've never had to go and borrow anything, everything came from my collections.'

•••

One of the advantages of the year away was the manner in which it helped cement the friendship between the two Rons. Although they had worked closely together for many years, the two men rarely socialized, largely because of their differences in location. While both lived in London, Ronnie B was in the north-west (Pinner) and Ronnie C in the south east (Croydon).

'We went to each other's houses maybe twice a year. The friendship had been there beforehand. But at that time we lived diagonally opposite each other in London and it took nearly two hours to get to each other's houses, so we didn't visit very much. But now we were living in each other's pockets. Ronnie C was about a third of a mile away. We both had lovely places overlooking the harbour bridge and it was super. So the friendship really developed in a way. And our wives went to keep-fit classes and aerobics together and we met a lot, and we did become socially much closer. Of course, he and I were close, but as a foursome we weren't as close. We really cemented it all in Oz, it was a lovely time.'

Ronnie Corbett also enjoyed the consolidation of a 20-plus-year friendship. 'Ronnie B and I have never ever spent our days off together because I was on the golf course and he would be browsing round antique shops or galleries. He always feels he's not physically co-ordinated in that way, and he's very particular, so a golf course would drive him mad, putting and not getting the ball in the hole.'

•••

They performed an extremely successful version of the stage show in Australia – and they involved the family. Barker's son Larry became a bouncer at the theatre they played at, while his daughter Charlotte went to drama school there.

Away from the stage, the Ronnies soon found themselves back on familiar ground when they accepted an offer to move on to TV, down under. The show itself, aired on Kerry Packer's Channel 9, remained very like its British counterpart – with Barker insisting it couldn't be shown in Britain.

'In Australia we did six one-hour shows. They were quite happy that we did stuff we'd done before, here in England. They'd been showing those shows but they didn't mind that we did old material. We only took the stuff from the last two series and at the time they hadn't been shown there. We did some extra music numbers outside. We had a Jehosaphat and Jones number every week. Those were on strange locations that they found. There was a chain gang number and we went up into the Blue Mountains for that, on the railroad.'

> They said, 'Lay tracks for the railroad,
> Cos steam means speed and power.'
> So I'm doing my best and I'm travelling west,
> About 15 feet an hour,
> Oh, Lord, about 15 feet an hour.
>
> Oh I crouched all night laying track down,
> And the wind on my back made me choke.
> And I felt that the bottom had fell out o' my life,
> Till I found that my braces had broke,
> Oh, Lord, I found that my braces had broke.

'We were filming in the mountains and over dinner one night it started to snow, and all the dancers – 18-, 19-year-old girls – had never seen snow before. So they ran outside and started to play in it, while we old seasoned campaigners stayed inside with a bottle of red wine.'

There was also the high profile to contend with for the generally modest Barker. 'We were more popular there in Australia than we were here in Britain. You couldn't walk anywhere there, everyone seemed to know you.' It was also during this period that Barker would start to write his last-ever sitcom, *Clarence*.

However, before that happened, he had a shop to run.

•••

Given the self-imposed, tax-related banishment from the country, and as a result the absence of any new material from either of the Ronnies, the BBC had decided to dust down the 1976 series of *Open All Hours* – originally broadcast on BBC2 – and try it out on BBC1. The result was another instant ratings success, proving Ronnie's point that the Beeb had misjudged the show's original time slot, and broadcast channel plans were rapidly made for a new series on Ronnie's return, five years after the original had aired.

Writer Roy Clarke revived his crusty old shopkeeper, while producer/director Sydney Lotterby reassembled the team. Lynda Baron (Nurse Gladys Emanuel) had recently played the part of paramour to another eccentric shopkeeper, newsagent Harry H. Corbett, in *Grundy* and David Jason (Granville) was now to find himself almost constantly on the small screen as the latest series of *Open All Hours* was to be broadcast between the first and second series of *Only Fools and Horses*. Ronnie could not have had a better supporting cast for Arkwright as he dusted down his Glenn Melvyn-inspired stutter for the new series.

'Arkwright was in the writing. Roy Clarke made him a mean, money-grabbing man. There was no stutter at all. I just added it to the character and I asked Roy if he minded my stuttering because I said, "I think it's a very good timing device, it's an excellent thing, you can stutter along until you know the exact second to put the word in and finish the line." He said, "Fine, try it," and he was quite happy with the first episode. Then he started to write one or two in and I would add some and he would add some and so they did get written in, eventually, but not to start with. It's just a way of finding different disguises for each character. Originally for *Seven of One* I did this big, long drawing of six different characters, six heads and I added things to them to make the six different characters, their make-ups and I remember writing "stutter" against Arkwright.'

Arkwright had become one of the best-loved characters on British television and, perhaps because Roy Clarke and Ronnie had, between them, bestowed so many easily recognizable and endearingly familiar human frailties upon the character, the audience felt almost as if they knew him. Some, in fact, believed that they really did know him! 'We used to have a holiday house in Littlehampton, and there was a man round the corner who ran the local stores, and somebody wrote to me once and said, "Because you based your character Arkwright on this man can you please come and re-open our new premises?" I had to write back and say, "I'm afraid I didn't base it on him, it was based by Roy Clarke on his father, who, I think, had one of those sort of shops."'

•••

Despite the five-year lay-off, Arkwright still fitted Ronnie as comfortably as, well, an old brown shop coat. Certain members of the cast, however, needed a little extra help to get back into character. 'It was easy for us to go back. Although David Jason showed how much older he'd got. He had to wear a hairpiece when we came back because he'd lost his hair at the back. When we started he looked like a child.'

'Time was marching on,' agrees Jason, 'and I was having to dye my hair and trying to keep around the age we thought my character, Granville, might be, which was around thirty-ish. But as time moved on it was getting more and more difficult to try and maintain that innocence without becoming someone who isn't playing with a full deck. Granville wasn't simple, he was just overpowered by his uncle and couldn't break away from the situation. But he wasn't there because there was anything wrong with him mentally. He was just Granville.'

•••

Despite the years that had passed since Arkwright and Granville last opened for business in the corner shop, the Barker and Jason team was immediately back on the ball. The respect they have for each other and the ease with which he and David Jason interact made *Open All Hours* a joy for Ronnie to work on.

'It's the thing I enjoyed doing most,' recalls Ronnie. 'I think *Porridge* was the best thing I ever did, in many ways. It's a close-run thing between those two, but I think *Porridge* was most successful in terms of the public's appreciation. But I enjoyed *Open All Hours* more because of David. We had such a good time doing it, and it shows I think. You can see it on the screen.'

'I remember once when we were doing *Open All Hours*,' says Jason, 'we did something particularly silly in a rehearsal room and we really fell about laughing. Ronnie just stood there and said, "It's amazing isn't it?" I said, "What do you mean?" He said, "It's bloody marvellous, here we are getting paid very well for making each other laugh. Not a bad life is it?"'

The shooting of each episode of *Open All Hours* was always enjoyable, both for the audience and the cast, even if, occasionally, things did get out of hand. Seasoned professionals they may have been, but two funny men reading funny lines are hardly going to be able to resist having fun themselves. 'It's always the funniest thing when a joke that doesn't work makes you giggle,' says Barker. 'It's a wonderful moment but also a very dangerous moment. Both David Jason and I didn't mind doing a scene again because the audience never mind you re-shooting in sitcom. The danger is if you get it wrong twice. And sometimes we would purposely get it wrong. If you got a thing wrong twice by mistake, you'd stop and then David would deliberately get it wrong again. Then the third time you have to be very careful that they don't applaud if you get it right. You have to tell them, they can't do that.'

'I've always said that working with Ronnie, particularly on the last couple of series, it was like playing top tennis,' Jason continues. 'When you see people playing tennis, it's tennis. But when you see two top players, serving things that you think the other guy can't get and he does and he returns it. I've always likened that to Ronnie and me. There would be moments when I would do something unexpected and it would work – and likewise with Ronnie – and we would play games sometimes to see who could top each other. I'd invent a piece of business or a line and blow me, five minutes later when we did the scene again, he's invented something else even funnier than I've done. After one or two of those you give up and say all right, you win.'

•••

If Barker and Jason realized that they were producing some special TV moments with their performances in *Open All Hours*, the same observation didn't escape the rest of those involved. 'I think the strength of their performances came first of all from the admiration David had for Ronnie. David used to think, "This is the man I can learn from," and he did,' says Syd Lotterby.

Indeed it is a testament to Jason's respect for Ronnie that he remained playing what was essentially the second lead in a series, when he was finding full-blown stardom on his own in John Sullivan's *Only Fools and Horses*. On retiring Ronnie handed the 'governorship' over to Jason, who in many ways over the last decade and more, through such varied successes as *Only Fools and Horses*, *The Darling Buds of May* and *A Touch of Frost*, has filled the gap left by Ronnie's retirement. He has certainly matched his mentor in popularity with the public. 'I suppose in a way maybe that is true,' considers Jason. 'I'd like it to be true because I'm Ronnie's protégé, really. I served my apprenticeship with him, I learned a tremendous amount from him and I'm carrying his flag still.'

•••

Open All Hours ran for three series in the 1980s, with Ronnie once again opting to say goodbye to Arkwright at the height of his success, with a regular audience in the 20 million region. It is a good example of Ronnie's enduring perfectionism that his only disappointment with the show appears to be Arkwright's voice-overs which closed each episode, as the shopkeeper packed away his wares, reflecting on how his day had gone.

'I never felt it worked really. It was the one thing I didn't like much, mainly because it didn't sound like Arkwright. It was a director's thing, that it was very quiet, he was ruminating. And it felt strange after they'd been shouting all day in the shop. I think we just didn't do it right. My fault really. I remember in the second series thinking, "I mustn't drop this into my boots, I mustn't mumble this." But even so it's just the change in atmosphere. I think it could've been much better done.'

•••

As always Ronnie C (who by now was starring in his own successful sitcom, *Sorry!*) was gracious and grateful for his colleague's success. 'He was very good about it,' says Barker. 'He was always most encouraging about how well they were going. He was very generous, because it must be difficult if you're equal in a show but then someone else has got something that is getting very good and people are talking about that. But you never felt there was any envy or anything going on. He was just very generous.'

•••

The Two Ronnies was as popular as ever, with a 1983 return to the West End of the stage show breaking all their previous records there. Although it could be suggested that there was a very cynical financial incentive to revisit the stage show, Ronnie, his fastidious nature shining through, also enjoyed having the opportunity to work at the material to make it inch-perfect. 'We went back for money, I suppose,' admits Barker honestly. 'More money, and a percentage. We enjoyed it. It was very similar to the first show, we just did the sketches that we'd found since we did the first one, and it went really well. And it's very relaxing. Television was a first night every night; here you were doing what amounted to a television show but you had time to get into it.'

•••

Among the many highlights this time round was the classic 'Four Candles/Fork Handles' sketch, which was later named as the nation's favourite sketch of all time. It was written by Ronnie, although inspired by a member of the public.

'It's the one that everyone talks about. The idea for that was sent to me by a hardware shop in Middlesex. This man said, "We love your show and we always think there should be a sketch about our shop because someone came in the other day and asked for four candles and I gave them these four candles and they said, "No, fork handles".' I thought it was a good idea, so I wrote it and then we weren't sure when we read it. The director, Terry Hughes, who's very good, said, "It's clever, but I don't know if it's going to work." We decided to try it and we were delighted at its reception. It got twice as good during the Palladium shows because so much more went into it as we went on. Just little bits, but you knew you could relax into it.'

FORK HANDLES
(Or 'Annie Finkhouse?')

The scene is an old ironmongers shop. A shop that sells everything – garden equipment, ladies' tights, builders' supplies, mousetraps – everything. There is a long counter up and down the stage. A door to the back of the shop up left. The back wall also has a counter. Lots of deep drawers and cupboards up high, so that RC has to get a ladder to get some of the goods RB orders.

RC is serving a woman with a toilet roll. He is not too bright.

RC: There you are – mind how you go.

(Woman exits. RB enters – a workman. Not too bright either.)

RC: Yes, sir?

RB: Four candles?

RC: Four candles? Yes, sir. (He gets four candles from a drawer.) There you are.

RB: No – fork handles.

RC: Four candles. That's four candles.

RB: No – fork handles. Handles for forks.

RC: Oh, fork handles. (He gets a garden-fork handle from the back of the shop.) Anything else?

RB: (Looks at his list.) Got any plugs?

RC: What sort of plugs?

RB: Bathroom – rubber one.

(RC gets box of bath plugs, holds up two different sizes.)

RC: What size?

RB: Thirteen amp.

RC: Oh, electric plugs. (Gets electric plugs from drawer.) What else?

RB: Saw tips.

RC: Sore tips? What you want? Ointment?

RB: No. Tips to cover the saw.

RC: Oh. No, we ain't got any.

RB: Got any hoes?

RC: Hoes? Yeah. (He gets a garden hoe from the garden department.)

RB: No – hose.

RC: Oh, hose. I thought you meant hoes. (He gets a roll of garden hose.)

RB: No – hose.

RC: (Gives him a dirty look.) What hose? (He gets a packet of ladies' tights from a display stand.) Pantie-hose, you mean?

RB: No, 'O's – letter Os – letters for the gate. 'Mon Repose.'

RC: Why didn't you say so? (He gets ladder, climbs up to cupboard high up on wall, gets down box of letters.) Now, 'O's – here we are – two?

RB: Yeah.

RC: Right. (He takes box back up ladder and returns.) Next?

RB: Got any 'P's?

RC: Oh, my Gawd. Why didn't you bleedin' say while I'd got the box of letters down here? I'm working me guts out here climbing about all over the shop purring things back and then getting 'em out again. Now then (he is back with the box), how many? Two?

RB: No – peas – three tins of peas.

RC: You're having me on, ain't yer? Ain't yer! (He gets three tins of peas.)

RB: No I ain't. I meant tinned peas.

RC: Right. Now what?

RB: Pumps.

RC: Pumps? Hand pumps or foot pumps?

RB: Foot.

RC: Foot pumps. Right. (He goes off, returns with a small foot pump.) Right.

RB: No, pumps for your feet. Brown pumps, size nine.

RC: You are having me on. I've had enough of this. (He gets them from drawer.) Is that the lot?

RB: Washers?

RC: (Exasperated) Windscreen washers? Car washers? Dish-washers? Hair washers? Back scrubbers? Lavatory clean-ers? Floor washers?

RB: Half-inch washers.

RC: Tap washers! Here, give me that list. I'm fed up with this. (He reads list and reacts.) Right! That does it. That's the final insult. (Calls through door) Elsie! Come and serve this customer – I've had enough!

(RC stalks off. Elsie enters – a big, slovenly woman with a very large bosom. She takes the list. Reads it.)

Elsie: Right, sir – what sort of knockers are you looking for?

This was one of the few occasions where Ronnie took an item sent in by the public and adapted it for use in a show. One other example that springs to mind came during the making of *Open All Hours*. This time it wasn't an idea for some dialogue, or a few gags to write into the script, it was something far more intriguing. It was a photograph.

'What we did use in *Open All Hours* was a photograph somebody sent me. The lady who sent it said, "My grandfather used to have a shop like yours," and she sent me a copy of the photo. It was absolutely me. It looked like my grandfather, who was a plumber, a whitesmith as they were called in those days. He used to wear the flat cap and the big moustache and in the photograph there was a man standing outside his shop, looking just like him. I said to Syd, "We must use this somewhere," so we had it hanging in the kitchen and I remember I wrote a few lines about it so they could cut to it. It looked so authentic.'

•••

Ronnie Barker would be the first to admit that during these years, the landscape of British comedy had changed considerably. The advent of alternative comedy, arising initially from the opening of The Comedy Store nightclub in London, which quickly produced the off-shoot Comic Strip – featuring the likes of Rik Mayall, Adrian Edmondson, Dawn French, Jennifer Saunders, Peter Richardson and more – was radically redefining the boundaries of British humour. When Channel 4 opened for business in 1982, these performers found themselves with a television outlet, and there was some doubt over whether the more traditional form of *The Two Ronnies* could continue. Prior to this, the BBC's own attempt at harnessing this new movement, the satirical *Not the Nine O'Clock News*, had pilloried the Ronnies in a sketch, much to Barker's displeasure.

'I wasn't pleased with that because it was a bit inaccurate. It was saying that all we did was swear and say rude words, which was absolutely untrue. I think we only said "bloody' three times throughout the whole series. So I wrote to the papers because someone said Mel Smith and Griff Rhys-Jones were going to be *The Two Ronnies* of the '80s, and it was '83 then and we were still churning out shows. I wrote saying, "No, no, *The Two Ronnies* of the '80s will be *The Two Ronnies*, Smith and Jones may well be *The Two Ronnies* of the '90s."'

In an interview with the *Daily Telegraph* years later, Ronnie Corbett confirmed Barker's displeasure at this sketch. 'I think Ronnie was more upset than me. It was the most scathing affront because we were doing a big show on the Beeb at the time. The point I felt most strongly about was that until then we tended to revere what had gone before, Jack Benny or Bob Hope or Max Wall. Even if we didn't like it we would never have said so. We didn't want to bring it down.'

Nevertheless, in the guise of this new school of comedians, political correctness marched on. *The Black and White Minstrels* were no more (a good thing) and Benny Hill was dropped by ITV (a bad thing).

'I didn't personally agree with the political correctness movement in comedy. I thought it was overdone. The result seemed to be that comedy just got more scatological, because that seemed to be OK, to be rude, without being sexist or racist or ageist or fatist. I've never thought that anything has been as funny as the early shows we used to see. *The Fast Show* came near to being that, but you couldn't really call that alternative comedy. I've never been pleased with the sort of direction comedy has taken, because no-one finishes anything now. There's no tag, it's become a fashion because you can't think of anything to finish with.'

•••

Up to 1984, Ronnie Barker knew very little about failure on TV. A regular fixture in the top ten TV ratings, in not one but three series, it was almost impossible to imagine anything touched by this comedy

Midas not turning to TV gold. The BBC certainly thought so, priming him as one of their heavy hitters in the all-important autumn schedule. *The Magnificent Evans* proved them wrong.

It seemed like a guaranteed winner – Ronnie and Roy Clarke together again. With this tale of a small-town, determinedly individual photographer and his live-in girlfriend who insisted to all and sundry that she had her 'own apartment', surely lightning would strike at least twice. From Ronnie's point of view the pattern was familiar – just as he had first played Arkwright at the height of Fletcher's fame, here he was offering up Plantagenet Evans, possibly even intending him to take up the reins from where Arkwright had left them lying behind the closed shop door. It would be another example of how well the man avoided typecasting, always kept moving, always one step ahead but never failing to bring the audience along with him. Until now. As before, the producer/director was Sydney Lotterby. 'It didn't work,' Lotterby recalls. 'I think the character was perhaps a little bit too exaggerated. The truth of *Open All Hours* and the character, and of Fletcher, wasn't actually the same as Evans. He was too exaggerated. And, to be honest, I don't think it was written as well as it could've been. Roy Clarke's a very fine writer but this just didn't seem to fit Ronnie.'

•••

The Welsh setting of *The Magnificent Evans* had, of course, begun life back in Dick Clement and Ian La Frenais's 1973 *Seven of One* offering, 'I'll Fly You For A Quid'. Ever since then, Ronnie had wanted to do an entire series based around Welsh characters. Now, albeit in different form, his wish was being granted.

'I had told Roy Clarke I would like to do a Welsh character and he went away and thought about it. He came up with the idea of the photographer and the big car and all the character stuff. I enjoyed doing it but the audience didn't like it. I don't know if he was too soft a character. Sometimes he was ruminative. There was a bit of whimsy about it. But the audience preferred the harder stuff, that is, the sharper stuff.

'He was a terribly rude man, very chauvinist. But he was lovely to play, swanning about in a large cape and hat. It was lovely to do and I was sad that it didn't catch on. Maybe it was just too slow, especially in the filming. We did fall in love with the scenery a bit too much and allowed it to drift us into a slow ambling sort of pace. It was just too pretty and that made it slow. I must have been just as much to blame, I suppose, although I also blame Sydney Lotterby for the lack of pace, for leaving in too much stuff. Nevertheless, when he was setting up the shots, I used to say, "Can we get that river in the background there?" So I was just as guilty as he was really. Except he left it all where I would have probably said it had to go.

'Or maybe people just thought we don't believe this chap. I hope it wasn't that because I always thought that *Porridge* and *Open All Hours* were very different characters. I've never been an actor who looks the same. Some actors always look the same, some just prefer not to use make-up. But I would try and be as different as I could be in everything. And this was as different as anything I'd done.'

•••

The failure of *The Magnificent Evans* was certainly a disappointment to Ronnie, but putting things in context, his continued popularity in *The Two Ronnies* and *Open All Hours* meant that such a flop had little detrimental effect on his career. 'It certainly didn't faze me and it didn't happen until after we'd shot it. So we weren't there on location at eight o'clock in the morning saying, "What are we doing this for anyway? People hate it." They didn't hate it. But it wasn't as good as the others.'

In other people's eyes however, Ronnie Barker backing a loser came as something of a surprise. He had even bigger surprises in store for them. 'As of 1 January, I am retiring from public and professional life so I am unable to undertake any more commitments. To those people with whom I have worked, I would like to express my gratitude and good wishes. So it's a big thank you from me and it's goodbye from him. Goodbye.'

If you called the offices of Dean Miller Associates on or around New Year's Eve 1987, that was the message you would have unexpectedly heard. 'I put it on the answerphone. I said to Joy I'm going to do it now, New Year's Eve.' Who were Dean Miller Associates? 'They' were another phone line in Ronnie Barker's Cotswolds home. The line served as Ronnie's agent for the last few years of his career, with his wife Joy replying to the messages, generally with a 'No', given Ronnie's ongoing commitments. 'We set up an answerphone and called ourselves Dean Miller Associates, because Dean Mill is the name of the house, but Dean Miller Associates were never in, the machine would be on permanently. Joy would call them back and deal with things. When I was retiring I said that we had to give up "Dean Miller", so why didn't I just say it on the answerphone. Then of course the *Daily Mail* picked it up and everyone found out.'

•••

Ronnie had made the decision to retire in late 1985, shortly after Peter Hall had asked him to play Falstaff. 'He should have played all the great Shakespeare comic parts,' says Hall today. 'He would've been a wonderful Falstaff, a wonderful Toby Belch, there's about 15 parts in Shakespeare he could've done. And the parts that Molière wrote for himself – *School for Wives, Tartuffe, The Misanthrope* – he would've been wonderful in any of those. During my 15 years at the National I'd kept on asking him, offering him all these roles. But it never worked out because of the scheduling. I do think he's the great actor that we lost. I really do think that.'

Still, Ronnie Barker's retirement was meticulously planned. 'Peter Hall triggered it off but he wasn't the reason I retired,' Ronnie explains. 'The reason I retired was that the material was getting less good. It wasn't even a block, I'd run out of ideas, I was dry of ideas for sketches. Other writers had moved on and we only had David Renwick left. He was the only established writer. And I'd done everything I wanted to do, I had no ambition left.'

'I think we felt the loss of his quality,' says Ronnie Corbett, 'but I don't think he felt guilty over the fact that he couldn't come up with as much material as in the past. The fear he always had, and indeed I always had, was that eternal fear that on Monday you read material that is all rubbish and you've got to do it on Friday. That was the great fear.'

'The situation sort of pushed me,' says Barker, 'goaded me into asking, "Haven't you done enough?" And I had done enough. Peter Hall's thing showed me I shouldn't be doing this thing at all. You are much happier not doing it, you are much happier being in the Cotswolds. I had really got so used to it I didn't want to go back and do something. If I hadn't said it, in about a year and a half somebody high up in the BBC would've said, "We've had enough of these two." I'm sure they would and I didn't want that. Quit while you're ahead was my slogan. We may have learned a bit from Morecambe and Wise because as soon as they left to go to ITV people said their show wasn't as good. And it was fine, people just thought it wasn't because they expected it to be better.'

•••

The announcement was unexpected. Just days before, *The Two Ronnies* had once again dominated the TV ratings with their now traditional Christmas special. A new series, *Clarence*, was due to start a few days later. The press speculated that the relatively recent deaths of British comic legends Eric Morecambe and Tommy Cooper played a part in this decision.

'It's never worried me, you've got to die. It's very sad, awful. I hated the fact that we'd lost Eric Morecambe and Tommy Cooper. I got to know Eric in the last four or five years of his life and he was a very funny man. Off stage he was continually funny. He came to our house in Pinner once for dinner. He was very shy. He didn't like eating out so he used to be a bit reticent about going out. But he said he would come and a car brought him and his wife to the house and I went to the door and the driver was there and Eric said, "Hello Ronnie how are you?" Then he looked past me, looked around the hall and said back to his driver, "About an hour." He was a wonderfully funny man.'

•••

As Ronnie put it, the well had simply run dry. He had nothing left he wanted to do, no more ambitions to achieve, even though there was always talk of the Rons moving on to the big screen. 'Unfortunately, we were always so busy,' remembers Ronnie Corbett. 'We were always doing our own series as well as the Ronnies and we were asked to do something for film by Bernie Delfont. We always said, yes, we would love to but we wanted one thing – a good story – because Eric and Ernie and Cannon and Ball didn't make good films. So we said if we got a good story with good strong characters, we would do it. But it never ever transpired.'

•••

The shows in Australia had been a great success, but they signified the end for the partnership that had endured twenty years. 'I remember shaking hands with Ronnie at the end of the series and saying, "Well that's it." He was very good about me retiring. He was terribly good. I could foresee him being upset or disturbed by it, but he was fine. And he's done very well for himself since. I'm so glad about that because we're still very good friends.'

Corbett recalls: 'He told me 18 months in advance. We were down along the coast somewhere filming a Norseman sketch and we were having breakfast in the caravan and he said, "I have to tell you, I've decided to retire. The Christmas show after the next one is the last show I'm going to do." I was sort of surprised and gobsmacked. But because he'd given me so much notice and we were so independent as well, I was just so surprised and sad that he was going to have to do that and we would no longer do the show. But I wasn't absolutely shattered or mortally wounded in any way. Just sad. I think he probably did it at the right time. It was getting difficult to get the gear and we'd have had to rethink.

'I knew he meant it. I doubt he would have said it to me without having really thought it through before. I knew that he wasn't feeling very well, and that he was feeling the strain of the writing, so it was a natural time to break off.'

•••

The two Ronnies paid a second visit to Australia in 1986, this time staying for four months, during which time Ronnie B wrote his next and final sitcom, *Clarence*. It had been contracted, as had another Ronnies' Christmas special, so he worked his time out, convinced that these would be his final professional engagements.

•••

Clarence began life as 'Fred, The Removals Person' of Hugh Leonard's 1971 *Six Dates with Barker* episode. Like so many things in Ronnie's career, it was an idea that had stuck with him, something he returned to and developed.

'*Clarence* was carefully planned. I was scheduled to do another series and nobody knew what yet and I had always liked the Hugh Leonard script and I told them I wanted to have a go at this and they said that was fine. I had arranged that I would not retire until the end of '87 and if you're not retired you want to be working. I had planned to go to Australia, come back and film *Clarence* in the spring of '87, then I had a few weeks off and prepared for *The Two Ronnies* Christmas show. It was spaced out nicely, it wasn't a sudden thing, it was arranged.'

The first episode was a virtual remake of the original with both Josephine Tewson and Phyllida Law once again along for the ride. Ronnie once again played the short-sighted removals man who teams up with Jo Tewson's maid, setting up home in the country, sharing a bed and slowly working their way towards marriage. There was, inevitably, a poignancy in writing and filming *Clarence*, knowing full well that it would the last time he did either. This time Ronnie wrote the show under the name Bob Ferris. It wasn't an intentional reference, but one can't help but imagine that it was something of an unconscious homage to Clement/La Frenais, Bob Ferris being the name of Rodney Bewes's Likely Lad. 'Clarence was always a step lower in social class from Fletcher. Fletcher was upper working class really, you imagined him in a decent semi. But Clarence came really from much deeper, much lower parts. I insisted on that haircut, my God it was terrible. I tried to make him much more lower-class.'

•••

There's a lovely circularity to Ronnie Barker's career. Peter Hall brought him to London and Peter Hall's offer led him to retire. He grew up in Oxford and, for his final TV show, he ensured that the location filming was done in Oxfordshire, a place he had begun to find his way back to ever since he bought his mill house back in 1981. 'I was coming back to my roots, absolutely. When I was writing *Clarence*, I thought I'd write this and set it just around the corner. I also wanted the country thing and the fact that this cockney man didn't know anything about the country. I enjoyed that sort of peasant thing. He was very naive. I'd enjoyed it when I'd done the original, I thought this character has potential.'

•••

He may well have had potential, but the show's impact was inevitably affected by the previous week's bombshell. When *Clarence* began its run in January 1988, the message may well have been inadvertent, but it was nonetheless clear – don't get too attached to this man, he won't be coming back.

CHAPTER 8

And It's Goodnight From Him

A smartish hotel bar in Bournemouth. A pianist is tinkling away on and, who knows, when nobody is looking, possibly in, the piano. RC, in casual clothes, sits at the bar. A barman hovers. RB, seated a little way along the bar, is staring at RC.

RB: Excuse me.

RC: Yes?

RB: You're Robert Redford, aren't you?

RC: (Looks around to see who RB is talking to.) Sorry? You talking to me?

RB: Yes. You're Robert Redford, aren't you?

RC: No, sorry. You're mistaken. (He is flattered.)

RB: You must often get taken for him.

RC: Er – well, no, I can't say I do, not often, no.

(A pause. RC drinks, RB stares at him, then moves and sits beside him. RC only faintly embarrassed.)

RB: You're somebody.

RC: Ha ha! Well everybody's somebody, aren't they? Otherwise nobody would be anybody.

RB: No, you're somebody. I've seen you.

RC: Doubtful. I don't appear anywhere.

RB: You've appeared here, haven't you?

RC: No, I mean I don't perform.

RB: Oh, I'm sorry to hear that.

RC: I mean I don't entertain. I'm not an entertainer.

The lines come from a Ronnie Barker *Two Ronnies* sketch called 'You're Somebody'. Ronnie Corbett played the part of the man who had been 'recognized' in the bar and eventually becomes so irate that he performs a song-and-dance routine just to satisfy the annoying interrogator, played by Ronnie Barker. It's only when the Ronnie Corbett character storms out of the bar that Ronnie Barker suddenly remembers from where he recognizes the man. He works in the fish shop in the High Street.

•••

It was Ronnie Barker who was about to take on the real-life role of the man who says, 'I don't appear anywhere.' He was certainly 'somebody'. In fact, he was probably the most recognizable face on British television and, like the character in the sketch, he was about to go and work in a shop, albeit a Cotswolds antiques shop rather than a High Street fish shop. He knew he was going, and those closest to him knew he was going, but it was a struggle to keep it all under wraps until the time was right to make a public announcement.

The recording of the final *Two Ronnies* Christmas special was going to be the last time Ronnie Barker ever set foot in a television studio. Among the show's guests was an unexpected slice of movie glamour in the form of Charlton Heston. Then in his early sixties, Heston had been a major Hollywood star for 30 years, having won his Oscar for Best Actor in *Ben-Hur* in 1959 and gone on to play characters of great stature – Moses, John the Baptist, even God! He had recently been appearing on a number of (mainly American) TV shows but, while he was an instantly recognizable figure to everyone in Britain, including the two Ronnies, they were not quite so familiar to him.

'He'd never heard of us,' admits Barker, cheerfully, although he could have been forgiven for feeling that he and Ronnie C were being taken for granted, given the rather high-handed attitude of Mr Heston's entourage.

•••

'We were allowed half an hour for shooting. His manager said, "We will arrive at 10.30 and we will leave at 11 a.m." And poor old Mary Husband, who was our costume designer for most of *The Two Ronnies*, had failed to get part of his costume – his waistcoat hadn't arrived. But his manager had arrived and said, "Mr Heston's waiting in the car, I just came to see if you're ready for him." We said, "Unfortunately we've got a bit of a problem with the costume." "What?!" – she really went mad!'

But Ronnie soon found that the great star was not as hard to please as his underlings. 'I looked down at myself,' Ronnie recalls, 'and I was wearing a waistcoat and I said, "What about this one?" So he came in and he said, "Call me Chuck," straight away and Mary explained that the only waistcoat we had was Mr Barker's, and he was fine. It was all hype from his manager.'

•••

Ronnie almost changed it on the night. That famous line. He was sitting in front of his last studio audience, delivering his last news item, and he almost changed it. 'And it's goodnight from him,' very nearly became, 'And it's goodbye from me.' But he didn't. He knew people would notice, they'd ask too many questions. Ever the professional, Ronnie knew it would detract from the show. He knew that audiences looked forward to seeing shows like *The Two Ronnies*, especially the Christmas specials, and he didn't want to do anything to spoil anyone's fun. So he left quietly, following a celebratory drink with Ronnie C and their wives in a dressing room bearing the name 'Gerald Wiley' on the door.

There was also another old friend on hand for the final show. Ronnie's childhood pal Ivor Humphris had long since given up the dream of becoming an actor, and had instead made a life in teaching. But he still had his Equity union card so, as a symbolic gesture, Ronnie landed him a small role in the last-ever *Two Ronnies*. Ivor had been there all those years before in the beginning, and now he was present for what looked like the end. Ronnie recalls:

'I remember we had a big Disney-like set for the piece we were doing, "Pinocchio II: Killer Doll",' remembers Barker. 'I was at one end of it and I walked from one side to the other, through a glade and up over a little rustic bridge, and I was thinking then that this is the last time I was going to be on a set. I was very emotional. But all on my own. It was lovely, there was no-one about. So I just lingered about a bit and said goodbye to it.'

It was, of course, a poignant evening for Ronnie Corbett as well.

'I remember it being a rather sad evening in a way because nobody knew, apart from my wife Anne and me. I don't think he'd told anybody that it was going to be the last time he was in a BBC studio. I don't think he'd even told the technical crew. We were all ending the show and saying our goodbyes and Anne and I and Joy and Ronnie went off and had a curry in Westbourne Grove. That was the last time he was going to do anything like that, so it was a bit sad and lonely really because he hadn't made a thing of it. It was touching, though, that it was only the four of us. In a way for me it was quite moving that he'd done it so quietly.'

•••

Fifty-eight. It's a funny age to retire. Especially for an actor. They just go on, don't they? Nobody really thought he meant it. But, publicly, for Ronnie Barker, there appeared to be no regrets. He was going, leaving behind his life in the West End and the London TV studios of the BBC. Leaving behind London. The austere post-war capital city that Ronnie experienced when he first arrived in the mid-1950s; where wartime bomb damage lingered on as a reminder of the recent conflict; where the population was struggling towards a more prosperous era, teetering on the brink of the rock 'n' roll revolution; where the power of television was just beginning to assert itself, was now very much a thing of the past. Margaret Thatcher's Tory government was fresh from a third general election victory and proclaiming an economic nirvana in a new age of materialism. There were personal computers, mobile phones and miniature televisions in colour – all things that were the stuff of science fiction in Ronnie's early days as a Londoner. Sir Clive Sinclair declared that everyone would soon be commuting to work on electric tricycles... actually, that did turn out to be a bit of science fiction. The rock 'n' roll revolution was now a nostalgia industry and Elvis was dead, as was John Lennon. *Dixon of Dock Green* had been superseded by *The Bill* on television and London was about to become closer to Europe than ever before as an agreement was signed to establish a rail link between London and Paris, via a tunnel under the English Channel. Maybe everything was moving a bit too fast for Ronnie in the new London. Maybe there was a part of him which, like the northern shopkeeper Arkwright, really only now wanted a nice quiet life.

> Oh Mary Lou, I'm a-calling you
> Up on the telephone.
> To say thanks for coming to the dance with me,
> And letting me take you home.
> I'm sorry I seemed so nervous,
> And started to stammer and sweat.
> But it s-started as s-soon as I saw you,
> And I ain't got over it ya-yet.
>
> I stared at your great big bu-bu-bu-bu-
> Beautiful blue-green eyes.
> I wondered if you fu-fu-fu-fu-
> Flirted with all the guys.
> When you smiled I nearly sha-sha-sha-sha-
> Shot right out the door.
> Cos I'd never seen such pretty little ti-ti-ti-ti-
> Teeth before.

Ronnie's much-practised Arkwright-style stammering speech impediment came into play in the above Jehosaphat and Jones song 'Stuttering Bum', but his days behind the shopkeeper's counter were now a thing of the past. Not quite. He may no longer have had a use for Arkwright's old brown overall coat, but he had not yet pressed his last shop till key. Ronnie and Joy opened their antiques shop in the town of Chipping Norton in Oxfordshire, called The Emporium. The locals knew him and thought of him now as a shopkeeper, even though Ronnie and Joy worked in the shop themselves only on the occasional Saturday. It was a sideline.

At the time, even Ronnie Corbett was taken aback by his partner's decision to make his retirement a complete break from the profession he had so loved for 40 years. 'I'm surprised in a way that he retired so completely,' says Ronnie C. 'I thought he might have said he would direct a few commercials or maybe a short film, because I think that's what he enjoyed most. Of course it did finish, but I never saw it as being terminal or sad. He was still with us, he'd just decided to retire and was going to enjoy his retirement. Most people can't believe that he did it.'

•••

When news of Ronnie's retirement eventually did become public knowledge, as previously stated, there was much speculation in the press that it was health-related. Certainly, the tabloid press decided that for someone of Ronnie Barker's celebrity suddenly to turn his back on show business could mean only that his health was failing. Barker insisted at the time that this was not the case... but this was not strictly true. At least part of the reason was a heart condition, something Ronnie succeeded in keeping away from the press – after all, the work was the thing, his private life was always private.

'I can admit now that when I retired it was in part because of the heart thing. I told Ronnie Corbett that I'd got a problem. I hadn't had it seen to yet, but I said, "I've got this problem and I've got to slow down and take it easy. I think we've done *The Two Ronnies* enough." We both thought it was going slightly downhill at that point and Ronnie was wonderful about it. I stopped at the end of '87 but it was eight years before I had the operation.

'In between I had blood pressure checks and tests every six months. They did a thing called an angiogram where they open a vein in your groin and they put a probe in which goes right up in to your heart. They put various liquids in, looking at it as if on an X-ray.

'That was about two years before they did the operation. They simply said that the time was coming when I was going to have to have this operation.'

The operation occurred in June of 1996.

'I hadn't had a heart attack, but the doctor said it was getting very weak, the arteries were getting very narrow and it would be better to have the operation now rather than than waiting a year because, he said, "It's about 3 per cent fatality rate at the moment, but it'll be 30 per cent next year. So I strongly advise you to have it done," so I had it done.

'With the heart surgery they all said that I would be fine. You go and have it done and wake up, and when you wake up you think, "Who are these ghosts? What's happening?" Because everything's very dark. And it's the nurses. It's all the nurses in the night, silently walking about. You gradually come through and then it was all fine. You have to be still and be strapped up for some days and then you just get better and everything went fine with that.'

In a doctor's waiting room, the patients sit quietly, including Ronnie B. Ronnie C enters and is annoyed that no-one is talking or will even say good morning to him.

RC: Isn't it extraordinary how no-one ever talks to each other in a doctor's waiting room? (No response from RB.) Odd, isn't it? (No response.) No, of course, it's not odd. (Answering himself.) I thought it was. Well, it's not, so keep quiet. Sorry. Don't mention it.

(A pause. RC picks up a newspaper.)

RC: I see they are stopping all the tube trains tomorrow.

(There is a slight shuffling and a lowering of magazines from the patients.)

RC: To let people get on and off.

(He smiles, encouragingly. The patients, without a flicker, return to their maazines.)

RC: Simple Simon met a pie-man,
                Going to the fair.
                Said Simple Simon to the pie-man,
                'Pray, what have you there?'
                Said the pie-man to Simple Simon,
                'Pies, you fool.'

The 'Doctor's Waiting Room' sketch was written by Ronnie, or rather Gerald Wiley, for *Frost on Sunday*. In fact, this was the first piece ever submitted by Gerald Wiley. The Ronnie Corbett character turns out to be a rival doctor intent upon luring the private patients from the waiting room round the corner to his own surgery. It's not clear whether any of them were heart patients like Ronnie, and Ronnie, in fact, no longer considered himself a real heart patient either. He had had the operation, he had recovered and he was better. That was that. Unfortunately, his heart condition didn't agree with him.

'Nine months later, 1 April it was, ironically, I developed a pulmonary embolism, which is a blood clot. That was the worst bit, because I could have died then. The clot can either go to the lungs or to the brain. Mine went to the lungs. It just got increasingly difficult to breathe and move anywhere and it developed over about a week, I suppose. Eventually I was gasping for breath and the doctor was sent for. It wasn't my own doctor, it was a duty doctor, and I was immediately ambulanced to the nearest hospital, and put on a wonderful drug they've got called a "clot buster". They'd only just discovered it and they put me on it straight away and by the evening my own heart specialist, who'd done the operation, said, "I think you've turned the corner, I think you'll be all right."'

While Ronnie lay under the influence of said drug, he was unaware of the level of concern from his family.

'I hadn't realized that all my family was round my bed. My wife was there anyway, and my daughter had come to stay with my wife because she didn't like to be on her own. My wife stayed overnight at the hospital and my daughter Charlotte asked if Adam, my younger son, could come and stay at the house as well because she didn't like to be there on her own. My other son, Larry, happened to be coming from London, going through to Birmingham, so he popped in on his way. They all had wonderful excuses, and I didn't realize. Then I came round a bit. I was half conscious and half not, and they were all standing there and it didn't occur to me then that this was a gathering for someone who they thought was about to die! Although I must admit, I did think as I went in the ambulance that this could be it.'

Initially, following his operation, public appearances were few and far between. In 1996, he sat with Ronnie C, celebrating the BBC's anniversary, and unexpectedly picked up a Lifetime Achievement in Comedy award.

'We were in the studio where we used to do *The Two Ronnies*. It was an audience full of famous faces. So it was wonderful when Michael Parkinson said at the end, "There's one more award to come." I had no idea. "This is an actor who retired eight years ago," and I thought, "Who else? I retired eight years ago." And Ronnie looked at me and said, "It must be you." It was a wonderfully proud moment because they all stood up. I was proud but I was thinking on my feet because I thought, "No one's going to see them stand-up." So I said, "Thank you very much ladies and gentlemen, please sit down." That was a career thing really, something in me said make sure that people know that your peers stood up. It was a strange feeling, in the middle of all this surprise, but I managed to do that. Then I met Robert Lindsay at the party afterwards and he said, "Congratulations. I know why you said that." And he was absolutely right.'

•••

The following year, Barker appeared in the celebrity-packed audience of Ronnie C's TV special *An Audience with Ronnie Corbett*.

'I felt it was a bit of a lumber getting him to come along to *An Audience with. . .*' said Ronnie C, 'because he doesn't like those sorts of things. But it was very important for me to have him there. I thought it was lovely. And I was still asked silly questions by people I didn't really have any connection with.'

On shows that follow *An Audience with...* format it is common practice for the programme makers to 'seed' the audience with friendly faces primed to ask predetermined questions that will allow the performer to reel off a few anecdotes and keep the show bouncing along at an acceptable pace. 'It's very difficult to get the people that you really want in the audience,' says Ronnie C. 'Danny LaRue couldn't be there, neither could David Frost or John Cleese. These were key people who would've been asked under normal circumstances, so I was very pleased to have Ron there to ask me a sensible question. And it was a lovely last shot as the credits ran with him saying, "More, more." People loved to see him there, and they love to see me at his dos.'

Of course, Ronnie Barker didn't hold with the notion of a sensible question. 'I said I must ask you a silly question, Ron,' says Barker. 'So I said, "Who did you most enjoy working with?" He said, "What'll I say to that?" I said, "Say Basil Brush." He did and that went well. It was odd to sit there and not be doing anything. Quite strange.'

It meant a lot to everyone – not just Ronnie C – to have Ronnie Barker there, but still there was something odd about seeing the two of them together. How could they be there together, and yet not be together? How could Ronnie Barker bear to be sitting on the sidelines when he knew how much everyone so wanted to see him there on stage with Ronnie C again? Was this perhaps a little hint of a comeback? Sadly, it appeared not.

•••

Rumours of Ronnie 'retiring' from retirement and getting back to work were again sparked by a brief appearance at the 1997 Royal Command Performance. The two Ronnies, appearing on television for the first time in a decade, rode on in disguise as the TV chefs the

Two Fat Ladies. Clarissa Dickson Wright and Jennifer Paterson were two upper-class English ladies of significant stature who starred in their own hugely popular BBC TV cookery programme where they hurtled round the country on a motorcycle and sidecar combo cooking up meals fit for royalty. The fact that their outrageously shrill, tweedy accents made it sound as though they had just left Her Majesty's shooting party at Sandringham only served to make their banter all the more enjoyable. Had they been appearing on TV ten years earlier, they would have made prime material for a *Two Ronnies* skit. Now the two Ronnies were 'doing' the Two Fat Ladies anyway and it took the audience completely by surprise. Nobody knew about it beforehand and the ovation that greeted their appearance was a genuine outpouring from the audience, even though the Ronnies were only there to introduce another act. 'I was asked to do something in it and they said Ronnie C was going to be doing something,' shrugs Ronnie. 'I said, "I'm retired, I'm not going to do anything." But I'd had an idea that we could look exactly like the Two Fat Ladies and I'd said to my wife some months earlier that if Ronnie and I had still been working together we'd definitely be doing them. Ronnie's bit eventually fell through and he was just left with introducing someone.'

'He had the idea,' says Corbett. 'We always had one attitude to the Command and that is it's downhill all the way after you've said yes. It never gets well reviewed, it's never totally enjoyed, it's an evening full of luvvies, so it's always been a struggle. Then Ron rang up and said he'd had an idea for us for the Command. I was surprised. But he just couldn't resist the idea, and I was only too pleased to say yes because I knew it would work.'

'I explained the bit to him,' continues Barker, 'and he thought it was great. So I rang up the director and said that I would just introduce someone, providing I could get Ronnie to do it and I thought I could. I'd already got him to do it of course. They thought the idea was marvellous. We kept it a secret and it went wonderfully well. As we came off Jim Davidson was standing in the wings waiting to follow us and he said, "Oh, thanks very much."'

Afterwards, Prince Philip summed it up best when he greeted Ronnie in the post-show line-up. 'Ah, they've exhumed you, have they?' he said. But sadly at that time they hadn't. Anyone hoping that the roaring greasepaint and the smelling crowd would lure Ronnie back were once again disappointed.

'All it stirred in me was the feeling of how proud and pleased I was, and am, that I'd made all those people laugh during my career, because I think it's better to make people laugh than cry. I would rather have been an actor who was funny than be a great Shakespearean actor who had moved people. That's what came back to me then. The length of the applause just went beyond the pleasure of seeing us. They suddenly realized, I think, that they were saying thank you for the whole thing. And that's when the applause took off and it carried on for a long time. But it didn't make me feel that I wanted to get back. It was just marvellous how much they appreciated it all. We were lucky enough to provide that laughter for so many years.'

•••

The offers still came but they weren't considered. People respected what Ronnie did, but both within the industry and among the viewing public he was sorely missed. Millions of people had welcomed Ronnie Barker into their homes every weekly. Now he wasn't there, there was a hole. People felt they were being neglected by an old friend. What had they done to upset him? Why didn't he pop in any more? Repeats are like looking at old photographs, they're a nice memory but they're not as good as the real thing. What remains, however, is a comic legacy that endures and improves with age. Ronnie Barker did it all until there was nothing left to do, no ambitions left to fulfil. Except one. 'Someone once said, "In life, you must have some ambition left," and I said that my one ambition is to own a tree on which mistletoe is growing.' Somewhere in the Cotswolds, outside a picturesque mill house, a small tree grows. And on that tree, some mistletoe blooms. That's a full life.

•••

Then that full life simply began overflowing. Ronnie Barker had, technically, given it up. That was it. His job was done. He had recovered his health, closed down his antiques business and was all set to enjoy his later years with Joy, catered for by a pension that came – as he himself admits – courtesy of constant repeats of his numerous, successful shows on British cable TV networks and beyond.

But people started calling again. There was the occasional awards-show appearance – 'I never said I wasn't going to do awards shows, or tributes. I certainly wouldn't ignore the people I'd worked with, if they wanted me there.'

Then the sightings began. Ronnie published his writings, finally revealing to the general public the man behind Gerald Wiley, Bob Ferris and numerous other pseudonyms. The TV show *Heroes of Comedy* – generally a show that honoured dead comics – decided to pay tribute to him. It seemed that people just hadn't had enough of Ronnie Barker.

And he turned his hand to writing once more. His play *Mum* was performed at the King's Head theatre in London and was a very personal piece for Ronnie, designed to highlight the talents of his actor daughter, Charlotte.

'It really was a showcase for her. It showed her comedy thing and it showed her tragic thing. She's very good and she's often made me cry; I've seen her in plays and she's very touching and so that was a strong element in my writing it. I had to think of something where she was on her own and talking all the time and I thought, "If there's no-one there, who's she talking to? She can only be talking to her dead mother or someone who's dead or someone who she thinks is in heaven." I decided that the mother would be in the armchair on stage, which you couldn't see into, and she would just talk to the chair all the time and you realized about ten minutes in that there was no-one in the chair.'

Unfortunately, it did not prove to be one of his biggest successes. Barker admits, 'It bombed. The critics didn't like the play at all. They liked her, but I think they were dying for it to fail because I'd been so successful. They all love saying, "It's all very well writing sketches for *The Two Ronnies* but this is a different matter." But it's not a different matter at all. It's just a longer version, more writing. I think they were very pleased to knock it because they didn't knock her. They were just getting at me there.

'It was good for Charlotte, but she didn't get any work from it. It's very sad really. The casting director has a lot to answer for nowadays. For instance, they say, "We need a 40-year-old man," and they go into the book of actors that they've got and they know and they don't move out of the office half the time. They're not casting directors, they're "sorter-outers" really. They send you a bunch of names they think can play the part and new people just don't get a look in. They're not seen. My daughter said recently, "If you look at the *Radio Times* tonight, apart from the soaps, which are all actors, there's not a single performance tonight on any channel. No actor is performing on any channel, they're all reality people or sports people or gardeners or make-overs," and she was right. The soaps, of course, always have a generous supply of actors and that, I think, really is the only way you're going to get anything at all. You've got to go into a soap, if you can.

'I was disappointed with the reaction to the play because I thought she played it so well and I thought it worked as a script, but I was mainly disappointed that they decided to take that attitude. It strengthened my opinion that critics in the main would rather report something bad than something good. If there were two stories in the news, and one was the tragic death of someone and the other was someone being made a knight, they would certainly go for the tragic story, because it's like watching an accident. They think people want that. They think people want to have all the nastiness they can get.'

•••

Not having written anything for the best part of a decade, one would expect Barker to find some difficulty in assuming the role shouldered for so many years by his old friend Gerald Wiley. In an attempt to boost the play's profile, he allowed his real name to be used, which was something that would have been anathema to the man a few years before.

'I wasn't intimidated by starting again so many years later, it didn't worry me at all. I just sketched out a shape, not a plot, then added in all the various ingredients that I wanted Charlotte to have to do, to play, to perform. Then I started to write it and wrote through. Took me about a fortnight, I think.

'I had a very strong reason to do it then. I thought she must somehow be shown to the public, but I don't have that about anything else now. There's nothing else I want to show to the public. I don't care. I think it's that. You've got to have a very strong incentive. I had a very strong incentive at that point and haven't had it since. I've had no desire at all to ruin anyone else's career!'

•••

After the failure of the play, Ronnie insisted he was still retired... then the movies came calling. The first was a production by the leading American cable network, Home Box Office – and the cast was pretty good, it has to be said.

The 2002 film, *A Gathering Storm*, was a strong drama, and also starred Albert Finney, Vanessa Redgrave, Jim Broadbent, Tom Wilkinson and Celia Imrie.

Finney played Winston Churchill in the days leading to the inevitability of the Second World War. Redgrave played his wife Clementine, and Barker played Churchill's butler, David Inches. Ronnie found the role immediately attractive. If nothing else, it meant that he could chalk another Redgrave on the list. Having previously worked with Lynn and Corin, he was now being offered the chance to appear with Vanessa. How could he turn it down?

At the time, the film's PR spun the fact that Ronnie was dragged out of retirement at the request of Finney, but that wasn't actually the case. 'The press release says my old friend Albert Finney persuaded me to do this. I'd never met him before!' says Barker. 'But he's lovely, very nice, very professional, very easy. He knew his lines, did it well, didn't do many takes and was very nice to me. He seemed to respect me as a performer. It was very easy and enjoyable and I acted with him and Celia Imrie, who was very good. I only had one tiny little scene with Vanessa Redgrave, but it went very well. It's taken as read that you don't discuss each other's performances because we know each other's work. It's much easier than someone coming in who nobody knows and who has to fit in with people that everyone knows.'

•••

Delighted with Barker's performance – and with the fact that he had, essentially, dragged him out of retirement – *A Gathering Storm*'s director, Richard Loncraine, recruited Ronnie once more for his next movie for HBO, another period piece entitled *My House in Umbria*. This time, he was given an even more substantial part, alongside an old colleague from his Oxford Playhouse days – Maggie Smith.

'Maggie Smith and I were in several things together at the Oxford Playhouse. There was a play called *The Housemaster* where I was playing a 14-year-old boy and she was playing a 15-year-old girl. And then there was Ben Travers's *The Old Rookery Nook*. I had met her in between, just a few years back, and I said, "I thought I told you to give up this business, you're still at it, aren't you?" She was already a Dame by then. But she greeted me with such joy when we met in Italy. So much had happened to both of us in between times.

'There was a great to-do about the billing on *My House in Umbria* because they'd already decided it was going to be Maggie Smith at the top and then alphabetical order, so I was first after her, which at the trade show created a great murmur that went round the audience. The slight row about it was concerning Chris Cooper, because he had to take billing below me and his part is much bigger. But that had been decided and they didn't want to shift it, so his agent said OK. This was before he'd won his Academy Award. I don't think they'd allow it now.'

•••

It's easy to speculate, as some inevitably did, that Ronnie decided to take on the film roles in *A Gathering Storm* and *My House in Umbria* because they were serious parts – he was not being expected to play the clown. That, however, had nothing whatsoever to do with his decision to take a peek out of the shelter of retirement.

'If they'd been comedic roles I'd have been just as happy. It wouldn't have worried me. I certainly wouldn't have turned them down on the grounds that they weren't comedic. I quite like not doing comedy roles, but it's rare. I used to love it in rep when you got a straight part or less of a comic part, but it's not like a dancer wanting to be a singer, trying to get away from comedy because you want to do something higher or better. I don't think straight roles are better than comedy roles in any way. There was no conscious choice. The point about those two was they were offered to me and I read them and I liked them. That's why I said I'd do them. There was no great decision made about whether this was "the right way to go" or not.'

•••

A large part of the decision to accept the role in *A Gathering Storm* was influenced by Ronnie's desire to work on film again. Once he had re-acquired his taste for movie acting and had the reassurance of feeling confident in director Richard Loncraine, agreeing to make *My House in Umbria* became a much easier decision to make.

'I've never been strong on films at all, there are very few films that I've been in and these just interested me, and with *A Gathering Storm* I thought it would be nice to do a film again. Then the next one came because it was the same director, Richard Loncraine. He said, "Could you play a general?" I said, "Yeah, I can do a general. I can do anything you like." He said, "I'm going to get in touch with the head of casting at Warner Brothers." The head of casting at Warner Brothers, when I was suggested, said, "How can he play a general? He's a butler, he can't play the general." The naivety of the woman! How can you get to become the head of casting if that is how you think? It seemed that she thought I was a butler, not an actor playing the butler. She's now seen the film and she's delighted with it. "Oh he can, he's a general, he's not a butler!" I did those two films, and I would do it again if Richard asked me. He keeps saying he wants me to play a heavy in something. I would be happy to do that as long as it wasn't in Iceland or somewhere outlandish.'

•••

For a man who once juggled two roles in West End productions, sprinting between theatres and costume changes, it might be difficult to accept that an accumulation of years have made the rigours of outdoor location filming in certain locations too much of a challenge. Ronnie's health scares, however, and his strong sense of self-preservation, leave him in no doubt that he needs to be sensible about the work he agrees to take on. At this stage in his career, after all, he is not necessarily looking for a great new challenge. 'I was asked to play Father Christmas,' he recalls. 'I said "Where are they shooting?" They said, "Alaska" and I said, "How long?" They said, "Ten weeks." I said, "Forget it!" I said, "That would kill me if I just went there, never mind doing it!"'

•••

As a young actor, Ronnie harboured grand dreams of a great career in the movies. His career, of course, took a different direction and, while he has no illusions about fulfilling those early dreams now, he will never be averse to considering the occasional film role.

'That was in my dreams once, wanting to play a big part in a big film, but that wasn't to be and it still isn't to be I don't think. It would still be wonderful if I was asked to play a role like Ben Kingsley or Ray Winstone. If they wanted some old heavy with a big part, that might be good. I still would be happy with that. But I don't hold any ambition in that direction really. I don't expect it to happen, that's why I was pleased with the part of the General in *Umbria*, that was a nice part, a good part.'

•••

Ronnie also made other brief forays out of retirement, one to revisit an old friend. Norman Stanley Fletcher featured in a BBC mock documentary showing certain characters' *Life Beyond the Box*.

Fletcher, the great schemer and ultimate survivor in Slade Prison was finally seen to have made good. He ended up with two hundred and fifty grand and a pub in his native Muswell Hill. 'It was strange to do,' says Barker. 'I felt the same, of course, although I looked vastly different. But the lines sounded like Fletcher and I did them and that was Fletcher. The notion of him finishing up in a pub was a good idea. That's where he would finish up, I think. And he sang his favourite song, 'You Belong To Me'. It's funny how that song got stuck in *Porridge*. It was in the script and I used to sing it whenever I had to sing anything.'

•••

In 2004, the British Academy of Film and Television Arts (BAFTA) decided to honour Ronnie with a special award show, complete with television broadcast. As fastidious as always; as concerned as always that the 'show' should be as entertaining as possible for the audience, Ronnie, naturally, had his own ideas about how the presentation should be staged.

'They said, "We've got a nice place for you in the audience." I said, "No, no, I'm not going to be in the audience." "What?" they said. "Everyone is always in the audience so we can see how they appreciate their tributes." I had to explain that that was just what I didn't want, I didn't want to sit there and be cut to every two minutes, because the audience would be fed up with me before I came on. I always hate that, and I said, "Trust me, when I come on at the end, it will be a much better reception than if I'd been sitting in the audience all the time." Afterwards they said, "Yes, you were absolutely right, it was a terrific reception." I watched it all from the back on a large monitor. They'd made almost a little dressing room, just behind the set.'

Joy was in the audience. In fact, the whole family was there – Joy, Larry, Charlotte and Adam were all sitting proudly out front, listening to the sparkling and truly sincere tributes being paid to Ronnie.

'I cried at the end. It is very moving when people say such wonderful things about you. It was lovely when I had my two best friends, Ronnie C and David, either side of me on stage at the end. It worked so well. And there was a wonderful party afterwards in the next studio which was all dressed: they had complete black drapes over everything with tiny pinpoints of light so it looked like a starry sky. They said, "What sort of food do you want? Do you want the trays?" I said, "No, no, no. Buffet. Hot buffet." They seemed to have money to throw around, so we had a wonderful hot buffet. Everyone was so pleased – "Oh, the food's so good" – because those dos usually offer tiny little things that you pop into your mouth and you see the waiter about every 20 minutes and they walk by and that's it, that's your food for the night.'

•••

Attention to detail always pays off. Whether keeping your audience happy when creating a show or keeping your guests happy with a hot buffet, Ronnie never likes knowingly to put a foot wrong. And the hot buffet may well have paid dividends for, after many years of being relegated to the relative obscurity of cable or satellite TV, the BBC, in all its wisdom, decided that *The Two Ronnies*, so long a staple of their weekend evening schedule, should be so once again. The new shows would not be entirely new, however, more a recollection of their career, rather than a recreation.

'We're sitting at the desks, like we did, and discussing, in short duration, the best of the old sketches, and then showing them. So it's 95 per cent showing the old sketches, and the rest will simply be discussion. There's no new sketch material at all.' These new introductory links are designed to be scripted, however, so Barker will not only be performing, but putting pen to paper once again. 'It will be scripted, but it will be us talking to each other and to the audience and hopefully finding little bits of story that we remember, little bits of memoirs of that particular sketch. Some we won't have any memories of, but some we will, so it's a kind of informed repeat with us guiding them through it, with me and, of course, Ronnie Corbett choosing the final stuff.'

•••

The return of the two Ronnies was due in no small part to the BAFTA tribute show and the fact that TV controllers perhaps missed what they had grown up with. Perhaps it was even an acknowledgement that they hadn't found anything worthy enough to replace it in between.

'It was because of the BAFTA tribute to me, that I met Beatrice Ballard, who's very high up in the BBC. During the discussions about that night I mentioned the idea of bringing back the Ronnies and it caught her ear or caught her eye or whatever it caught, and she said, "I must mention that to the head of BBC1." The response came back positive, so it's a go, providing we survive it. It'll be an easy week, just one day a week. I go up there and arrive at 11 o'clock on the morning, and we work through until 6 o'clock, but it will all be already in the drawer – we just go and rehearse it and do it and finish it and come home the same night, because, as I said to them, Ronnie's now 74, one year younger than me, and the energy isn't there with us now. I said, "We must take it easy when we're doing this. We don't need to rehearse too much because we're only doing about 10–12 minutes of material between us and that can be rehearsed in 10–12 minutes. So it'll be a comfortable thing to do." I said, "It needs to be comfortable simply because of age."'

•••

More than anything, Barker (a man who himself has cribbed from old joke books, rightly insisting that if a joke is funny, it stays funny) wants his work to be seen once again. 'They deserve to be seen again, because the stuff doesn't date. I just thought it's a waste to consign it to the bin now when it hasn't been repeated for a long time. The idea was to highlight the old material. There isn't any new material. I haven't written a sketch since I retired in 1987. But it's a shame to throw it away because the laughs are there and that's what it's about – making people laugh. I think these will make not only the younger generation laugh, but it will make the older people laugh all over again.'

As if the process of selecting sketches to be included in the original shows wasn't exacting enough, Ronnie went through the stock of old material all over again, applying a new standard and viewing each one with the benefit of hindsight.

'Some you think, "No that wasn't so good," and strike that out, and that's the point. I've got 74 sketches and you need 24, four per show, so with 74 that's plenty of choice.

'I looked at each sketch and I gave each sketch two ticks or one tick or a question mark, that's the way I graded it, but there was a lot of stuff I didn't remember doing. I saw myself there doing this thing, walking around the sofa or taking a drink or something, and I thought, "I can't remember any of that at all." Very strange.'

•••

Ronnie Corbett also embraced the idea of taking the two of them back to a prime time Saturday night spot.

'It came about as a result of the fact that Ronnie had the appetite to get into the studio and do something again. It's largely old material but it will not look like repeats because we are presenting it there in the studio, doing bits and pieces and recalling a few memories before saying, "Here you are, another sketch."

'I think once the BBC saw the atmosphere that greeted us at BAFTA, and the figures that it got as well, compared to quite trendy shows that were around at the time, they decided to go with it.'

From the way he talks about the show, you can tell that Ronnie C has been enjoying this trip down memory lane, especially since reviewing his past performances hasn't been as painful as he perhaps expected it might.

'You forget some of them. The early ones I watched were reassuring because I was laughing, myself, at things that I was in. Somebody who was putting these tapes together for us to watch said, "Where is this sort of work now? This standard of words and characters and sets and productions costs – you don't see that now."

'Obviously I think it has dated because I did it so many years ago, but I see sketches on *Little Britain* that we would have done. I think the sketch style hasn't changed much, it's other things that have changed. We are older and we are looking different now, but I think people will enjoy seeing the sketches again.'

•••

Having performed two different roles in the making of so many of *The Two Ronnies* sketches – those of writer and performer – Ronnie B wears neither hat when revisiting the material. If anything, he takes on a third job – that of a critic.

'I just watch them as an entity, the whole thing, it doesn't matter about the performance. If I thought I was terrible in something I would secretly cross it out anyway, without telling anyone, but there are only one or two like that which I've taken out. Mainly it's just looking at the thing as a whole. Mostly, you know it's going to work because you've seen it work before. You know it works and the one thing I can say to the audience is that the great advantage about showing all these sketches again is you don't have to worry whether they're going to get any laughs or not, because you know the laughs are there and any laughs they add is just extra.'

•••

Despite having recently reneged on his promise to retire, Ronnie still feels like a man who is taking life at his own pace.

'I really don't do much and I don't have to go and do anything at all, but I do do oddments. But fundamentally, there's no itch there. There's no itch at all. Certainly no itch to get onto television, though I have no doubts about bringing *The Two Ronnies* back. Except we'll be much older. I thought actually the first thing we should say when we're on should be, "Good evening, ladies and gentlemen, we used to be 'The Two Ronnies'." I should say that. Just to get a loyal hooray. We are much older, but that's the beauty of it, it's just us sitting there saying, "This is a sketch we used to love, we loved doing this," and then show it. It's the work that's important to see, not us two old fogeys talking about it.'

•••

Ronnie Barker is now 75, in a year that sadly saw the death of his older sister Vera, the lady who all those years ago passed on to him her job at the bank. It was the job at the bank, of course, that led to his becoming involved in amateur dramatics and set him on the path his life was to follow. It's been a life and career that Ronnie now has time to look back on with some fondness.

'Being 75 – well, it's not as good as it used to be,' he reflects. 'Certainly not as good as it used to be at 35. It's harder work. Just moving about is harder work. You realize that age inevitably invites decrepitude. You're tireder, so I have a nap every afternoon and I just do less. But I'm happy. I love being in the country, I just love everything about it. I'm quite happy to drift around during the day and just potter.'

•••

Ronnie Barker sees his career as a mixture of chance and ability. Both have served him well. At the BAFTA tribute to him, he summed it all up in a speech he had written.

Good evening. I am speaking to you once again as chairman of the Loyal Society for the Prevention of Pismonunciation. A society formed to help people who can't say their worms correctly. I myself often use the wrong worms, and that is why I was erected charming of the society. Firstly, let me try and put you in the puncture regarding our mumblers. Peach and every plum of them have dickyfelty in conversing with the people they meet in everyday loaf – their murkvates at the figtree or the orifice; even in their own holes, min and woof, sather and fun, bruzzer and thistle, unable to comainicute. This can be an enormous bandy-chap to our tremblers at all times, but especially at Bismuth time; because Bismuth is a season of grease on earth and pigswill to all men when the family get together to ear, drunk and be messy – to gather round the fireside, cracking nits, smelling tories and singing old pongs and barrels. Many of our rumblers lose out on these skinful pastimes – a very close fringe of mine, for instance, once went carol slinging with the local church queer, but instead of slinging, 'Good King Wenceslas stuck out, And his feet were steaming,' he sang, 'Go rest your belly gentlemen, Let nothing rude display,' which, of course, caused havoc among the queer and deeply upended the knickers wife. This is just one instance of what my tremblers have to stiffer with a lipped upper stuff.

Actually, that's another speech entirely, but one that the BAFTA audience would no doubt have loved. On the evening in question, Ronnie's speech really was about how he considered himself a very lucky man...

'All through my 50 years in the business, two words have always been in my thoughts – these two words are 'What Luck.' What luck to have met in the far-off days of weekly rep a marvellous comedian called Glenn Melvyn who gave me my first TV job, and taught me how to stutter. What luck to have been in Oxford Rep when a young Peter Hall arrived as director and brought me to London's West End. What luck that James Gilbert saw me do a radio show and put me in *The Frost Report*. What luck that the star of that show, David Frost, put me under contract, that resulted in *Porridge* and *Open All Hours* and who paired me with the wonderful Ronnie Corbett. What luck to have had a wife for forty-five years who, throughout my television career, sat in the audience of every show and laughed louder than anyone else... what luck, what wonderful luck.'

Ever the professional, he wasn't going to leave this crowd on anything but a laugh. 'I might cry now,' he said. 'Gwyneth Paltrow watch out.'

Afterword

When I was first asked to write a book about Ronnie Barker, I have to say I was delighted. I pondered the idea for hardly any time at all before accepting. The one thing I wanted to work out for myself was why I was so keen to do it. At the time this was originally posited, Ronnie had been in retirement for many years and was, in essence, unreachable. While I was quite prepared to write *about* the man, I was more eager to write *with* him. Or at least with his blessing.

The reason for my desire to do this book, I came to understand, was that I couldn't remember a single time when Ronnie Barker wasn't there, when he wasn't a part of my life, even if it was an abstract part. I grew up watching him, relying on him to deliver the goods and make me laugh. I watched him with my parents, and I watched him on my own. I still do. I now at times watch him with my children (although, admittedly, trying to explain the phrase 'Naff off' to a five-year-old sometimes gets difficult). And he never fails to make me laugh.

But there was more to it than that. First and foremost, I really wanted to write about Ronnie B because of *Porridge*. You see, when I watch *Porridge* I don't see Ronnie Barker at all. I see Norman Stanley Fletcher, or 'Fletch'. I don't see the man I watched on an endless Saturday night of *The Two Ronnies*; I don't see Arkwright – I just see Fletch. I've long been of the belief that those who are skilled in comedy can make great actors, because they're fearless. They've already had it as bad as it gets – that moment they deliver a line on a stage and it doesn't get that expected laugh. Barker comes at it from the other side – he's an actor first, a comedian second. And that to me, at a young age, was a revelation. Fletch was as real as any character any British sitcom has ever created. We who were watching knew he lived that life 24/7; we were graced by being allowed half an hour a week just to look in on him.

•••

So how could I say no? Well, there was one reason. As I looked into the rest of Ronnie's career, and reviewed his considerable achievements, I began to get cold feet. What I really wanted was to write a book that allowed me access to this most reclusive of men. To write about him – without his contribution – seemed to hold the potential of doing him a disservice.

So I did a desperately unprofessional thing. Knowing that he no longer had an agent through which to contact him (he and his wife Joy having taken care of that side of things for the last few years of what can now be termed his 'first career'), I looked up the antiques store he was apparently now running somewhere in the Cotswolds. I got the number from Directory Inquiries (back when it had nothing to do with those infuriating '118's) and spoke to someone who gave me the address. When I rang, I didn't realize that the lady I was speaking to was Ronnie's younger sister, Eileen, who ran the shop on Ronnie's behalf with her husband.

To cut a short story long, I wrote to Ronnie, explaining to him that I had been commissioned to write a book about him, and would be deeply grateful if he would at least peruse the text on a purely fact-checking basis, just to reassure me I wasn't messing up.

Much to my surprise, he called me back. It was an inauspicious moment. Ten to nine on a Monday morning, if I'm not mistaken. My wife took the call and told him I was 'occupied at the moment' to which Ronnie quickly replied, 'Oh, he's in the toilet, I see. I'll call him back in ten minutes.'

Sure enough I was, and sure enough he did.

Why Ronnie agreed to talk to me, having remained silent and in repose for over a decade, I have no idea. I think part of it may have been that he was flattered, part of it a genuine desire to have his work acknowledged and appreciated, and recorded in some way. Either way, he agreed to meet me in a hotel in Chipping Norton. The fact that he showed up in a mac only added to the espionage-like feel of the whole encounter. I think we were both grateful that some British tabloid wasn't there with a telephoto lens, ready to write a headline, 'RETIRED COMIC MEETS ODD BEARDED MAN IN HOTEL ROOM LIAISON.'

These meetings – at Chipping Norton's Crown and Cushion (plug! – although, they never gave me a discount) – went on over several months, and what I found was a delightful contradiction. While Ronnie was remarkably relaxed and was willing to talk about his career in the most candid of terms, he was fiercely protective of his private life and did not want to discuss his wife and children on the record. And while I have met his wife Joy now on numerous occasions, Ronnie was keen that this book respect the privacy he has managed to afford his family, despite his profile as one of the country's biggest entertainers. (And no, that's not a size joke – the man's practically svelte these days.) This book was intended as a biography of his career. Obviously his family does impinge on that, and Ronnie has shared those moments.

Our assignations in Oxfordshire hotels rooms continued apace, and as we progressed Ronnie revealed details of his heart problems – now thankfully in hand, but published here for the first time. We would work in the morning and the afternoon, with a break in the hotel bar for an hour's lunch. I was pleased to discover that Ronnie has a taste for chilli con carne – as do I – and theirs wasn't bad. It was fascinating, though, watching him interact with the locals in the bar. He felt obliged to say something funny, and I'm sure I noticed him timing it by the moment he chose to put his hand in the pocket of one of those striped blazers he favours. It reminded me of *The Two Ronnies*' run at the London Palladium, when Ronnie Corbett recalls an incident where Barker invented a stage version of himself for fear of revealing his true self. My feeling is that Ronnie B is both the man behind the mask and the mask itself – he knows how to play the character, and he knows that his audience expect to see him as well.

In our time together, I think I did get to see the real Ronnie Barker. In our initial conversations he seemed almost pleased to be able to talk about the things we talked about, as if it were a chance to unload.

•••

Our paths crossed again over the years before this book was finally published, and in many ways I want to take credit for single-handedly dragging him out of retirement. Before I showed up he was a closed shop (and his shop closed)! Initially, the idea was to collate all his writings. Under various pseudonyms, Ronnie has written his own material for the best part of his career, something of which the public was, for the most part, completely unaware. I spent many a month compiling *All I Ever Wrote*, a collection of those writings, and despite countless hours of inputting very old typed pieces of paper, I never failed to find something – often as midnight approached – that made me laugh.

> She drew in a deep breath, followed by another. 'I think I am being followed by another,' she said. They were standing in the sitting room, by the big window that overlooked the lawn. She could see that distant figure of the gardener, who had also overlooked the lawn for several weeks now. She stared out, running her hands over her body nervously. It was in a terrible shape. All lumps and bumps, with little tufts of moss growing in the more inaccessible places.
>
> 'Followed? By a man?' He felt something stir in his breast. It was the teaspoon in his waistcoat pocket, stolen from the Tea Shoppe that very afternoon. 'I think you're imagining things, darling.'
>
> 'No, I'm not.'
>
> He felt her quiver. 'I asked you not to feel my quiver,' she said. Her eyes swept the ground. Then they dusted the mantelpiece and cleaned out the grate.

See what I mean? That was an extract from a little unexpected nonsense short story called 'Born to Riches' written by Ronnie, but the more familiar sketches always made me laugh, too. I laughed partly through nostalgia (having seen the piece years before) and partly because it was just so damn funny, and well written. The rest of the nation also agreed – albeit not at midnight – when they voted 'Four Candles/Fork Handles', a perfect example of the way Barker the writer plays with words, the Nation's Favourite Sketch.

The exemplary Channel 4 series *Heroes of Comedy* also chose to honour Ronnie, and I interviewed him off camera for the show. Ever the perfectionist, he drafted in his make-up lady from the *Ronnies* days for the shoot. He's earned his comforts.

A couple of years later I met with Ronnie again at a lunch at a posh London restaurant. He had by then lost a lot of weight, and I was dining with Terry Gilliam (it's another book – don't worry about it), who had once shown me two sketches he'd drawn of Ronnie way back in 1968. Ronnie informed me that he had just made a film for HBO in the States opposite Albert Finney. He credited me with dragging him out of retirement and I said something along the lines of, 'Not a moment too soon.' He countered that by revealing that he was off to Italy to do another one. All of this was good news.

•••

The next time I met Ronnie was not to be in a hotel, but at his house, a delightful converted mill house, Oxfordshire-way. Given my complete inability to drive and being dependent on public transport, he very graciously agreed to pick me up at the train station. I have to admit that it's a very strange moment when you leave the train in the morning among a throng of business commuters and they all notice Ronnie Barker waving at you from the car park.

I've spent a few occasions at his house, mulling over his old times, looking at his family photos and browsing through his various collections, postcards, cigarette cards and so on. It's a lovely home – and Joy is a lovely hostess.

Ronnie has always juggled his career and his home life and, commendably, he has always known that the latter is really where his heart lies. I have enjoyed his company and I admire him both as a performer and as a man. And I hope I didn't pismonounciate that.

Bob McCabe

FILMOGRAPHY

WONDERFUL THINGS! (1958)
Director: Herbert Wilcox. *Starring:* Frankie Vaughan, Wilfrid Hyde White.

Ronnie made his film debut (unbilled) as a stuffy Head Waiter in this vehicle for Vaughan, a singing Portuguese waiter.

KILL OR CURE (1962)
Director: George Pollock. *Starring:* Terry-Thomas, Eric Sykes, Dennis Price, Lionel Jeffries, Ronnie Barker.

Ronnie has a small part alongside Terry-Thomas who is a clumsy detective investigating events at a health club.

THE CRACKSMAN (1963)
Director: Peter Graham Scott. *Starring:* Charlie Drake, Nyree Dawn Porter, George Sanders, Dennis Price, Ronnie Barker.

Ronnie co-starred as a small-time con with TV favourite Drake working under the duress of crime boss Sanders.

DOCTOR IN DISTRESS (1963)
Director: Ralph Thomas. *Starring:* Dirk Bogarde, James Robertson Justice, Samantha Eggar, Dennis Price.

Bogarde's last appearance in a Doctor film sees Robertson Justice hogging the camera. Ronnie appeared unbilled as 'Man At Railway Station'.

FATHER CAME TOO (1963)
Director: Peter Graham Scott. *Starring:* James Robertson Justice, Leslie Phillips, Sally Smith, Stanley Baxter, Ronnie Barker.

Ronnie in one of his more substantial roles on film as a builder disrupting the life of newly-weds Baxter and Smith. Robertson Justice is the father of the title.

THE BARGEE (1964)
Director: Duncan Wood. *Starring:* Harry H. Corbett, Hugh Griffith, Eric Sykes, Julia Foster, Ronnie Barker, Derek Nimmo.

Galton and Simpson scripted slice of comic life on the canals of England. Ronnie played Corbett's cousin.

A HOME OF YOUR OWN (1964)
Director: Bob Kellett. *Starring:* Ronnie Barker, Bernard Cribbins, Richard Briers.

Ronnie's first nearly silent comedy, set on a building site.

RUNAWAY RAILWAY (1965)
Director: Jan Darnley-Smith. *Starring:* Ronnie Barker, Graham Stark.

Another silent film, this time set around a railway station.

THE MAN OUTSIDE (1967)
Director: Samuel Gallu. *Starring:* Van Heflin, Heidelinde Weis, Peter Vaughan, Charles Gray, Ronnie Barker.

A serious spy movie with an American star, Heflin, as an ex-CIA man still in Europe.

A GHOST OF A CHANCE (1967)
Director: Jan Darnley-Smith. *Starring:* Ronnie Barker, Bernard Cribbins, Patricia Hayes, Jimmy Edwards, Terry Scott.

Grown-up ghosts help three children save their home.

FUTTOCK'S END (1970)
Director: Bob Kellett. *Starring:* Ronnie Barker, Michael Hordern, Roger Livesey.

The first outing for prototype Lord Rustless (Barker) in a silent, or grunt and grumble, film starring the eminent Hordern as butler.

THE MAGNIFICENT SEVEN DEADLY SINS (1971)

Director: Graham Stark. *Starring*: Ronnie Barker, Bruce Forsyth, Bernard Bresslaw, Joan Sims, Leslie Phillips, Harry H. Corbett.

Python Graham Chapman and Barry Cryer-scripted romp through the deadly sins.

ROBIN AND MARIAN (1976)

Director: Richard Lester. *Starring*: Sean Connery, Audrey Hepburn, Robert Shaw, Richard Harris, Ronnie Barker.

Ronnie plays Friar Tuck as a middle-aged Robin (Connery) returns to Sherwood looking for Marian (Hepburn).

PORRIDGE (1979)

Director: Dick Clement. *Starring*: Ronnie Barker, Richard Beckinsale, Fulton Mackay, Brian Wilde, Peter Vaughan.

Co-writer Clement (with La Frenais) directs film version of the TV series.

THE GATHERING STORM (2002)

Director: Richard Loncraine. *Starring*: Albert Finney, Vanessa Redgrave, Jim Broadbent, Derek Jacobi, Ronnie Barker.

Unexpectedly out of retirement, Ronnie plays butler to Finney's excellent Churchill in the run up to WWII in this HBO film.

MY HOUSE IN UMBRIA (2003)

Director: Richard Loncraine. *Starring*: Maggie Smith, Ronnie Barker, Timothy Spall, Chris Cooper.

Following a terrorist bombing of a train, an ageing English author offers solace and a place to stay to a disparate group of survivors of the attack (including Ronnie's General) at her house in Umbria.

TV PROGRAMMES

SAILOR OF FORTUNE (1955–6)

(26 × 30 mins episode)
Ronnie got his first screen work on this British filmed series starring Canadian Lorne Greene (later the 'Pa' figure on the Ponderosa in *Bonanza*).

I'M NOT BOTHERED (1959)

(26 × 30 mins episode)
Ronnie's mentor Glenn Melvyn created, wrote and starred as the stuttering Wally Binns in this single-series sitcom. He also gave Ronnie parts in two of the six episodes.

IT'S A SQUARE WORLD (1960)

(56 × 30 mins)
Ronnie guest starred briefly on Michael Bentine's classic comedy series.

THE KEYS OF THE CAFE (1960)

(TV Play)

THE HOLLY ROAD RIG (1960)

(TV Play)

SEVEN FACES OF JIM (1961)

(7 × 30 mins)
Ronnie appeared in some episodes of this seven-part run of Jimmy Edwards's playhouse-style series.

SIX MORE FACES OF JIM (1962)

(6 × 30 mins)
Ronnie elevated to regular co-star.

TONIGHT (1962)

Ronnie starred in the human comic strip Evelyn during this daily news show.

MORE FACES OF JIM (1963)

(6 × 30 mins)
Another series alongside Jimmy Edwards.

SYKES AND A... (1964)
(24 × 30mins)
Ronnie starred in one episode titled 'Sykes and the Log Cabin'.

CHARLEY'S AUNT (1965)
(1 × 90 mins)
Ronnie appeared as Spettigue in this TV version of the much-loved farce. Also starred Coral Browne and Danny La Rue.

BEFORE THE FRINGE (1965)
(14 × 30 mins)
Ronnie appeared in six of these old-fashioned variety and sketch shows.

NOT ONLY... BUT ALSO... (1965)
(7 × 45 mins)
Ronnie made a gunk-dipping appearance in Peter Cook and Dudley Moore's 'Poets Cornered' strand of their sketch show.

A TALE OF TWO CITIES (1965)
(1 × 60 mins)
Ronnie appeared as Jerry Cruncher in this Sunday afternoon adaptation of Dickens's classic tale.

GASLIGHT THEATRE (1965)
(6 × 60 mins)
Ronnie took a variety of roles in a series of Victorian melodramas, each presented 'live' on stage. No tapes remain of the show.

FOREIGN AFFAIRS (1966)
(6 × 30 mins)
Ronnie starred as a Russian aide alongside Leslie Phillips (a Brit civil servant) in this short-lived sitcom set in the Foreign Office.

THE FROST REPORT (1966)
(13 × 30 mins)
Ronnie was a regular in this, the first series.

THE FROST REPORT (1967)
(13 × 30 mins)
As well as appearing in the 2nd series, Ronnie also contributed written pieces.

FROST OVER CHRISTMAS (1967)
(40 mins)
A Christmas special of the regular series.

THE SAINT (1966)
Ronnie guest-starred as a bumbling French detective in one episode, 'The Better Mousetrap'.

CRACKERJACK (1967)
A one-off appearance in this popular Friday tea-time children's series alongside his old friend, Leslie Crowther.

THE AVENGERS: (1967)
Ronnie appeared as a cat-loving baddie (Cheshire) in 'The Hidden Tiger' episode.

THE RONNIE BARKER PLAYHOUSE (1968)
(6 × 30 mins)
Ronnie's first headlining series, each a different sitcom-style 'pilot'.
'Tennyson': Ronnie as a loud-mouth Welsh poet barred from a recitation contest.
'Ah, There You Are': Lord Rustless deals with a film crew in his country abode. (Acted as pilot for *Hark at Barker*.)
'The Fastest Gun In Finchley': Ronnie and Glenn Melvyn fight a duel to become chairman of the Hendon Cowpokes' Assoc.
'The Incredible Mr Tanner': Ronnie the escapologist wants to be the new Houdini.
'Talk Of Angels': Ronnie as a silent monk caught between a married couple.
'Alexander': Ronnie as a shy Scotsman forced to deal with a group of possessive women and his overbearing mother.

FROST ON SUNDAY (1969)

(23 × 50 mins)

Ronnie was a series regular on series 1 of the weekly news-based show.

FROST ON SUNDAY (1970)

(12 × 50 mins)

Ronnie made regular appearances in series 2 of Frost's weekly news show

HARK AT BARKER (1969, 1970)

(Series one 8 × 25 mins, series two 27 × 25 mins)

Ronnie as Lord Rustless co-starring with Josephine Tewson and David Jason. He also wrote some episodes (as Gerald Wiley).

SIX DATES WITH BARKER (1971)

(6 × 30 mins)

In a similar vein as *The RB Playhouse*, each episode involved new characters and situations, each set during a different era.

'1937: The Removals Person': Ronnie as a short-sighted removals man named Fred (later rewritten as *Clarence*) helps an upper-class household to move house on Coronation day.

'1899: The Phantom Raspberry Blower Of Old London Town': London is being haunted by a man who makes a great farting noise. (Later developed as a serial for *The Two Ronnies*.)

'1970: The Odd Job': A suicidal husband (Ronnie) hires an odd job man (David Jason) to become a hit man and then has second thoughts. But the odd job man takes every job seriously. Jason and Graham Chapman starred in the film version (1978).

'1915: Lola': Ronnie plays two females in sitcom set during World War I.

'1971: Come In And Lie Down': John Cleese script has Ronnie as a shrink whose patient pretends to be a gas man, not a patient.

'2774: All the World's A Stooge': Ronnie has seen the future and humour has become the new religion.

THE RONNIE BARKER YEARBOOK (1971)

(1 × 45 mins)

A one-off designed to establish Ronnie as a solo performer just before *The Two Ronnies* began. Also starred Ronnie Corbett.

RONNIE CORBETT IN BED (1971)

(1 × 45mins)

Ronnie Corbett's solo show designed to establish his solo credentials before the beginning of *The Two Ronnies*. Also starred Ronnie Barker.

THE TWO RONNIES (1971–1986)

(72 × 45 mins, 20 × 50 mins, 2 × 60 mins, 1 × 30 mins, 1 × 55 mins)

One of Britain's longest-running and best-loved comedy shows ever. Over the space of 12 series and 98 episodes in 15 years, Messrs Barker and Corbett entertained millions of Britons with sketches, one-liners, shows and serials. There were also Christmas Specials.

A MIDSUMMER NIGHT'S DREAM (1972)

(1 × 60 mins)

Ronnie starred as Bottom alongside Edward Fox, Lynn Redgrave, Robert Stephens and Eleanor Bron in Shakespeare's comedy.

HIS LORDSHIP ENTERTAINS (1972)

(7 × 30 mins)

Ronnie as Lord Rustless, again with Josephine Tewson and David Jason. For this series, however, the family home (Chrome Hall) has become a hotel in what Ronnie fondly calls 'a kind of Fawlty Towers Mk I'.

SEVEN OF ONE (1973)
(7 × 30 mins)
Another series of one-off sitcom 'pilots'. Proved to be the breeding ground for both *Porridge* and *Open All Hours*.
'Open All Hours': Penny-pinching A-a-a-a-a-r—kwright makes his corner shop debut.
'Prisoner and Escort': Recidivist Norman Stanley Fletcher takes the train to Slade Prison, accompanied by prison officers Mackay and Barrowclough.
'My Old Man': Ronnie as an old man who refuses to leave his soon-to-be-demolished house.
'Spanner's Eleven': Ronnie's Albert Spanner struggles to bring his local football team up to scratch.
'Another Fine Mess': Ronnie and Roy Castle become Laurel and Hardy.
'One Man's Meat': Another script penned by Ronnie. He plays a man forced to go on a crash diet when his wife hides his clothes so he can't leave the house to get food.
'I'll Fly You For A Quid': Gambling confusion and hi-jinks amongst a family of Welsh compulsive gamblers.

PORRIDGE (1974–1977)
(18 × 30 mins over three series)
Arguably the finest British sitcom of the 1970s. Written by Clement/La Frenais, Ronnie is brilliant as Norman Stanley Fletcher, Fulton Mackay completely believable as Warden Mackay, Richard Beckinsale a suitably gullible Godber. There were two Xmas Specials (*No Way Out*, 1975, and *The Desperate Hours*, 1976. Both 1 × 45 mins).

WHEN WE ARE MARRIED (1975)
(1 × 60 mins)
Ronnie as the photographer in J.B. Priestley's classic play.

THE PICNIC (1976)
(1 × 30 mins)
The first of *The Two Ronnies'* almost silent specials features a bunch of old English aristocrats. Also starred Ronnie Corbett.

OPEN ALL HOURS (1976)
(6 × 30 mins)
The first series of the now classic sitcom starring Ronnie as Arkwright and David Jason as his nephew Granville was aired on BBC2 at 9 pm.

THE BEST OF THE TWO RONNIES (1977)
(1 × 45 mins)
A compilation special, featuring the best sketches and songs from the series so far.

OPEN ALL HOURS (1981–1985)
(19 × 30 mins over three series)
Five years after the first series Arkwright was back in business. This time on Sunday nights at 7.15 pm. It proved a huge success.

BY THE SEA (1982)
(1 × 50 mins)
The second almost silent special spun off from *The Two Ronnies*. Shot on film it's a veritable moving saucy seaside postcard.

THE MAGNIFICENT EVANS (1984)
(6 × 30 mins)
Writer Roy Clarke created a sharp character for Ronnie as a photographer in Wales whose eye roves far more than his camera.

THE TWO RONNIES (1986)
(7 × 30 mins)
The series made for the Nine Network of Australia while the two Ronnies were spending a year down under.

CLARENCE (1988)

(6 × 30 mins)

Writing as Bob Ferris, Ronnie expanded on a character first introduced in *Six Dates With Barker* (1971, by Hugh Leonard) to create his short-sighted removals man.

AN AUDIENCE WITH RONNIE CORBETT (1996)

(1 × 50 mins)

Ronnie was seated in the audience for this tribute, in the form of a performance, to Ronnie C.

THE ROYAL VARIETY PERFORMANCE (1997)

(1 × 60 mins)

Careering on stage on a motorbike and sidecar, the two Ronnies appeared as the *Two Fat Ladies* (TV chefs Clarissa Dickson Wright and Jennifer Paterson) to introduce an act. They received a standing ovation.

HEROES OF COMEDY (2000)

(1 × 60 mins)

Part of Channel 4's series celebrating the life and work of Britain's comedy greats. Ronnie was the first to appear on his own show.

LIFE BEYOND THE BOX — NORMAN STANLEY FLETCHER (2003)

Ronnie as Porridge's Fletcher, twenty-five years on. Running a pub he's fairly happy. He even sings 'You Belong To Me'.

A BAFTA TRIBUTE TO RONNIE BARKER (2004)

(1 × 60 mins)

A star-studded tribute show honouring Ronnie, who made his appearance at the very end to tumultuous standing applause.

THE TWO RONNIES SKETCHBOOK (2005)

Ronnies B and C introduce their favourite sketches and songs from the original series.

RADIO PROGRAMMES

THE FLOGGITS (1958)

With: Elsie Waters, Doris Waters, Anthony Newley, Ronnie Barker

THE NAVY LARK (1959—1967)

With: Dennis Price, Leslie Phillips, Jon Pertwee, Stephan Murray, Ronnie Barker

VARIETY PLAYHOUSE (1961-1963)

With: Ted Ray, Leslie Crowther, Ronnie Barker, June Whitfield

ROUND THE BEND (1961)

With: Michael Bentine

CROWTHER S CROWD (1963)

With: Leslie Crowther, Ronnie Barker, June Whitfield

NOT TO WORRY (1964)

With: Cyril Fletcher, Ronnie Barker

LET S FACE IT (1965)

With: Ronnie Barker

LINES FROM MY GRANDFATHER S FOREHEAD (1971)

With: Ronnie Barker

LINES FROM MY GRANDFATHER S CHRISTMAS FOREHEAD (1972)

With: Ronnie Barker.

DISCOGRAPHY

IRMA LA DOUCE (1958)
LP cast recording, Phillips BBL 7274

ON THE BRIGHTER SIDE (1961)
LP cast recording, Decca LK 4395/SKL 4134

THE FROST REPORT ON EVERYTHING (1968)
LP TV compilation, Pye NPL 18199

A PINT OF OLD AND FILTHY (1969)
LP, MGM C 8107

VINTAGE VARIETY (1973)
LP compilation includes *Crowther's Crowd* extract, BBC Records TEC 134M

FIFTY YEARS OF RADIO COMEDY (1973)
LP compilation includes *Navy Lark* extract, BBC Records REC 138M

JEHOSAPHAT AND JONES (1973)
LP, Phillips 6308

THE BEST OF THE TWO RONNIES (1976)
LP, Transatlantic TRA 328

THE TWO RONNIES (1976)
LP, BBC Records REB 257

COMEDY SPECTACULAR (1976)
LP compilation includes *Two Ronnies* extract, BBC Records REB 249

THE TWO RONNIES VOLUME 2 (1977)
LP, BBC Records REB 300

PORRIDGE (1977)
LP, BBC Records REB 270

COMEDY SPECIAL (1977)
LP compilation includes *Porridge* and *Two Ronnies* extracts, BBC Records REH 294

THE TWO RONNIES VOLUME 3 (1978)
LP, BBC Records REB 331

RONNIE BARKER'S UNBROKEN BRITISH RECORD (1978)
LP, K-tel NE 1029

GOING STRAIGHT/STRING BEAN QUEEN (1978)
Single, EMI 2768

FUN AT ONE (1979)
LP compilation includes *Two Ronnies* extract, BBC Records REB 371

THE TWO RONNIES VOLUME 4 (1980)
LP, BBC Records REB 393

MORE FUN AT ONE (1980)
LP compilation includes *Two Ronnies* extract, BBC Records REB 399

THE LAUGHING STOCK OF THE BBC (1982)
LP compilation includes *Two Ronnies* extract, BBC Records LAF 1

WE ARE MOST AMUSED (1982)
2 LP compilation includes *Two Ronnies* extract, Ronco RTD 2067

THE VERY BEST OF ME AND THE VERY BEST OF HIM (1984)
LP, BBC Records REC 514

BOOKS BY RONNIE

RONNIE BARKER'S BOOK OF BATHING BEAUTIES (1974, Coronet)

RONNIE BARKER'S BOOK OF BOUDOIR BEAUTIES (1975, Coronet)

IT'S GOODNIGHT FROM HIM (1976, Hodder and Stoughton)

SAUCE (1977, Hodder and Stoughton)

GENTLEMAN'S RELISH (1979, Hodder and Stoughton)

FLETCHER'S BOOK OF RHYMING SLANG (1979, Macmillan)

SUGAR AND SPICE (1981, Hodder and Stoughton)

OOH-LA-LA! THE LADIES OF PARIS (1983, Hodder and Stoughton)

PEBBLES ON THE BEACH (1985, Hodder and Stoughton)

A PENNYWORTH OF ART – RED ALBUM (1986, Herbert Pess)

A PENNYWORTH OF ART – GREEN ALBUM (1986, Magi)

IT'S HELLO – FROM HIM (1988, New English Library)

DANCING IN THE MOONLIGHT (1993, Coronet)

RONNIE BARKER – ALL I EVER WROTE – THE COMPLETE WORKS (1999, Essential, *HB*)

RONNIE BARKER – ALL I EVER WROTE – THE COMPLETE WORKS (2001, Macmillan, *PB*)

BIBLIOGRAPHY

IT'S HELLO – FROM HIM
by Ronnie Barker (New English Library 1988)

THE RELUCTANT JESTER
by Michael Bentine (Transworld 1992)

DANCING IN THE MOONLIGHT
by Ronnie Barker (Coronet 1994)

RADIO COMEDY 1938–1968
by Andy Foster and Steve Furst (Virgin 1996)

THE GUINNESS BOOK OF CLASSIC BRITISH TV 2ND EDITION
by Paul Cornell, Martin Day and Keith Topping (Guinness 1996)

JUST KEEP TALKING
by Steve Wright with Peter Compton (Simon & Schuster 1997)

RADIO TIMES GUIDE TO TV COMEDY
by Mark Lewisohn with a foreword by Ronnie Barker (BBC 1998)

OTHER SOURCES

LAUGH MAGAZINE, THE RADIO TIMES, THE DAILY MAIL, THE GUARDIAN, THE DAILY MIRROR, THE TIMES, THE DAILY EXPRESS, THE DAILY TELEGRAPH, THE DAILY STAR, TODAY, EVENING NEWS, EVENING STANDARD... NOT THE SUN!

INDEX